Known for his somewhat dry and juridical appeals to a kind of permanent Kantian Law, Jürgen Habermas—the central intellectual of the EU's German center—arises here in a very different light. This timely study reveals instead an urgently popular thinker concerned with simple dignity and fellow-feeling, berating his troubled homeland as a "self-absorbed colossus" as Europe teeters on the brink. This book gives cosmopolitanism a new life at the very moment of its threatened extinction.

Timothy A. Brennan, *University of Minnesota*

Jürgen Habermas and the European Economic Crisis

The European Union entered into an economic crisis in late 2009 that was sparked by bank bailouts and led to large, unsustainable, sovereign debt. The crisis was European in scale, but hit some countries in the eurozone harder than others. Despite the plethora of writings devoted to the economic crisis in Europe, present understandings of how the political decisions will influence the integration project continue to remain vague. What does it actually mean to be European? Is Europe still a collection of peoples that rally together during good times and then retreat to nationalism when challenges appear? Or has Europe adopted a common identity that would foster solidarity during hard times?

This book provides its reader with a fresh perspective on the importance identity has on the functioning of the European Union as exemplified in Jürgen Habermas' seminal text, 'The Crisis of the European Union: A Response'. Rather than exploring the causes of the crisis, the contributors examine the current state of European identity to determine the likelihood of implementing Habermas' suggestions. The contributors' interdisciplinary approach is organized into four parts and examines the following key areas of concern:

- Habermas' arguments, placing them into their historical context.
- To which degree do Europeans share the ideals Habermas describes as crucial to his program of reform.
- Influence of Habermas' cosmopolitanism through religious and literary lenses.
- Impact of Habermas' notions in the arenas of education, national economies, austerity, and human rights.

Jürgen Habermas and the European Economic Crisis will be read by scholars in the fields of Political Theory and Philosophy, European Politics, and Cultural Studies.

Gaspare M. Genna is Associate Professor of Political Science at the University of Texas at El Paso.

Thomas O. Haakenson is Associate Provost at the California College of Arts.

Ian W. Wilson is Associate Professor of German and Humanities at Centre College, Kentucky.

Routledge Studies in Social and Political Thought

101 The History of Compulsory Voting in Europe
Democracy's Duty?
Anthoula Malkopoulou

102 The New Materialism
Althusser, Badiou, and Žižek
Geoff Pfeifer

103 Authenticity, Autonomy and Multiculturalism
Geoffrey Brahm Levey

104 Marxism, Religion and Ideology
Themes from David McLellan
Edited by David Bates, Iain MacKenzie and Sean Sayers

105 Distributive Justice Debates in Political and Social Thought
Perspectives on Finding a Fair Share
Edited by Camilla Boisen and Matthew C. Murray

106 Re-Grounding Cosmopolitanism
Towards a Post-Foundational Cosmopolitanism
Edited by Tamara Caraus and Elena Paris

107 Panarchy
Political Theories of Non-Territorial States
Edited by Aviezer Tucker and Gian Piero de Bellis

108 Gramsci's Critique of Civil Society
Towards a New Concept of Hegemony
Marco Fonseca

109 Deconstructing Happiness
Critical Sociology and the Good Life
Jordan McKenzie

110 Novels and the Sociology of the Contemporary
Arpad Szakolczai

111 Liberty, Toleration and Equality
John Locke, Jonas Proast and the *Letters Concerning Toleration*
John William Tate

112 Jürgen Habermas and the European Economic Crisis
Cosmopolitanism Reconsidered
Edited by Gaspare M. Genna, Thomas O. Haakenson, and Ian W. Wilson

Jürgen Habermas and the European Economic Crisis
Cosmopolitanism Reconsidered

Edited by Gaspare M. Genna,
Thomas O. Haakenson, and
Ian W. Wilson

NEW YORK AND LONDON

First published 2016
by Routledge
711 Third Avenue, New York, NY 10017

and by Routledge
2 Park Square, Milton Park, Abingdon, Oxon, OX14 4RN

First issued in paperback 2018

Routledge is an imprint of the Taylor & Francis Group, an informa business

© 2016 Taylor & Francis

The right of the editors to be identified as the author[s] of the editorial matter, and of the authors for their individual chapters, has been asserted in accordance with sections 77 and 78 of the Copyright, Designs and Patents Act 1988.

All rights reserved. No part of this book may be reprinted or reproduced or utilized in any form or by any electronic, mechanical, or other means, now known or hereafter invented, including photocopying and recording, or in any information storage or retrieval system, without permission in writing from the publishers.

Trademark notice: Product or corporate names may be trademarks or registered trademarks, and are used only for identification and explanation without intent to infringe.

Library of Congress Cataloging in Publication Data
Names: Genna, Gaspare M., editor | Haakenson, Thomas O., 1972– editor. | Wilson, Ian Waller, editor.
Title: Jèurgen Habermas and the European economic crisis : cosmopolitanism reconsidered / edited by Gaspare M. Genna, Thomas O. Haakenson, and Ian W. Wilson.
Description: New York, NY : Routledge, 2016. | Series: Routledge studies in social and political thought ; 112 | Includes bibliographical references and index.
Identifiers: LCCN 2015047623 | ISBN 9781138185838 (hbk)
Subjects: LCSH: Habermas, Jèurgen. | European Union. | Cosmopolitanism–Europe. | European federation. | Democracy–Europe. | Europe–Politics and government–21st century.
Classification: LCC JN30 .J873 2016 | DDC 330.94/05611–dc23
LC record available at http://lccn.loc.gov/2015047623

ISBN 13: 978-1-138-54348-5 (pbk)
ISBN 13: 978-1-138-18583-8 (hbk)

Typeset in Sabon
by Wearset Ltd, Boldon, Tyne and Wear

This book is dedicated to Michael DeVoe Waite (1970–2015), whose compassion and understanding for others, at home and abroad, made the world a much better place.

Contents

List of Figures xi
List of Tables xii
Acknowledgments xiii
List of Contributors xiv

Introduction 1
GASPARE M. GENNA AND IAN W. WILSON

PART I
Foundations 11

1 Democracy as Ideal and Practice: Historicizing *The Crisis of the European Union* 13
CHRISTIAN BAILEY

2 Habermas on Human Dignity as the Origin of Human Rights and Egalitarian, Utopian Thinking 37
JENNIFER FREDETTE

PART II
Values 55

3 Cosmopolitanism, Trust, and Support for European Integration 57
GASPARE M. GENNA

4 European Reform from the Bottom Up? The Presence and Effects of Cosmopolitan Values in Germany 77
AUBREY WESTFALL

PART III
Tools   103

5 Reason, Faith, and Europe: Two German Perspectives on
   What is Europe?   105
   JAMES M. SKIDMORE

6 Cosmopolitan Reflections: Jürgen Habermas and W. G.
   Sebald   121
   IAN W. WILSON

PART IV
Institutions   139

7 Educating the European Union: Internationalization
   through Integration   141
   THOMAS O. HAAKENSON

8 European Integration and Economic Interests   157
   MARCELLA MYERS

9 Does German Austerity Travel? The Baltic States'
   Reactions to the Euro Crisis   175
   DAVID O. ROSSBACH

10 On the *Pouvoir Constituent* of the European Union   192
   ERIK O. ERIKSEN

   Conclusion: European Identity, Crises, and Integration   215
   GASPARE M. GENNA AND IAN W. WILSON

   Index   221

Figures

1.1	Distribution of Seats in the European Parliament by Transnational Party Groups	19
3.1	Percentage Point Change in European Integration Support by Political Trust Category for Germans	69
4.1	German Responses to Cosmopolitan Descriptions	81
4.2	Support for Cosmopolitan Values in Germany Over Time	82
4.3	Average Scores in Cosmopolitan Index by EU Country, 2012	82
4.4	German Responses to The Question "To What Extent Do You Think Germany Should Allow People of this Group to Come and Live Here?" As A Percent of the Total Responses	84
4.5	German Responses to the Question "To What Extent Do You Think Germany Should Allow People of This Group to Come and Live Here?" As A Percent of the Total Responses Over Time	85
4.6	Percentage of Respondents Who Distinguish Between Desirability of Immigrants	86

Tables

3.1	Principle Component Factor Analysis for Trust in EU Nationalities (Varimax Rotation)	67
3.2	Ordered Logit Model: Support for European Unification on Trust for Europeans	68
4.1	Descriptions of Cosmopolitanism	80
4.2	The Effect of Cosmopolitan Values on Support for European Unification	90
4.A.1	Descriptive Statistics of Dependent and Independent Variables for Years 2004, 2006, 2008, 2012	96
4.A.2	Pearson's R Correlation Coefficients the Independent Variables in Table 4.2, Pooled	98

Acknowledgments

This volume has its origins in a German Studies Summer Seminar on the topic of Germany and the European Union that was organized and sponsored by the German Fulbright Commission in the summer of 2012. Seven of the authors, including all three editors, took part in this lively intellectual experience. We therefore owe a debt of gratitude to the German Fulbright Commission—including our seminar's two organizers, Charlotte Securius-Carr and Carolin Weingart—and to the broader Fulbright Program of the United States Department of State. Such an extraordinary experience has led to this interdisciplinary volume; its program of international exchange plays a vital role in maintaining a cosmopolitan intellectual community in the United States and abroad.

Following the seminar, many of the authors contributed to a forum edited by Thomas O. Haakenson in the *German Studies Review* (2013). We thank Prof. Sabine Hake, editor of the *German Studies Review*, for her support of this forum. Building on that success, many members of the group—eight of the authors—took part in the inaugural round of three-day seminars at the German Studies Association Annual Convention in Denver in 2013. We are thankful to have had the opportunity to gather scholars from diverse fields and present early versions of these papers on Germany, the European Union, and Jürgen Habermas. We would like to thank Prof. Suzanne Marchand, who coordinated our seminar, and the rest of the seminar committee: Prof. Lutz Koepnick and Prof. Irene Kacandes.

The volume would not have been possible without the support and guidance of the Routledge staff. We would particularly like to thank Natalja Mortensen for her enthusiastic support of the project from its early beginnings and up through its completion. We also thank Lillian Rand for her attention to detail and for answering our never-ending set of questions.

Finally, we would like to acknowledge the important role that the works of Jürgen Habermas have played in helping guide our discussions of these matters.

Contributors

Christian Bailey, Assistant Professor, School of Humanities, Purchase College, State University of New York, USA.

Erik O. Eriksen, Professor, ARENA Centre for European Studies, University of Oslo, Norway.

Jennifer Fredette, Assistant Professor, Department of Political Science, Ohio University, USA.

Gaspare M. Genna, Associate Professor, Department of Political Science, The University of Texas at El Paso, USA.

Thomas O. Haakenson, Associate Provost, California College of the Arts, USA.

Marcella Myers, Associate Professor, Department of History and Political Science, Andrews University, USA.

David O. Rossbach, Assistant Professor, Department of Political Science, Chatham University, USA.

James M. Skidmore, Associate Professor, Department of Germanic and Slavic Studies, University of Waterloo, Canada.

Aubrey Westfall, Assistant Professor, Department of Political Science, Wheaton College, MA, USA.

Ian W. Wilson, Associate Professor, German, Chinese and Japanese Program, Centre College, USA.

Introduction
Europe at the Crossroads

Gaspare M. Genna and Ian W. Wilson

Bank bailouts sparked the European Union's economic crisis in late 2009 and led to large, unsustainable sovereign debt. The crisis was European in scale, but hit some countries in the eurozone harder than others. The question before the European Commission and the EU member states was how best to deal with the crisis. Suggestions ranged the entire spectrum: from calls for greater integration, solidarity, and aid, to jettisoning the more problematic countries (like Greece) from the common currency, to scrapping the common currency altogether. Given that this was the first major crisis since the adoption of the euro, many pondered how the political decisions would impact the integration project. Preserving the EU is important due to its role in the longest sustained period of peace and prosperity in European history. At the heart of the suggestions to remedy the crisis was the answer to one fundamental question: what did it mean to be European? Was Europe still a collection of peoples that rally together during good times and then retreat back to nationalism when challenges appear? Or had Europe adopted a common identity that would foster solidarity during hard times?

Jürgen Habermas believes that solidarity, through a common identity, is the solution. He explores the concept of cosmopolitism in his book, *The Crisis of the European Union: A Response*, which is critical to understanding one of the essential foci of European integration, specifically, how the goals of economic and political integration require a transformation of trust and solidarity for Europe and its peoples. In this edited volume, we seek to elaborate on his views by addressing the importance identity has on the functioning of the EU, especially in times of economic crisis. Some of the authors find support for his ideas, while others challenge them. We do not go into a deep exploration of the causes of the crisis. Instead we acknowledge the severity of the crisis as we examine the current state of European identity and attempt to determine the likelihood of implementing Habermas' suggestions.

Each of the chapters of Habermas' book includes a basic assumption: democratically elected politicians need to be decisive during hard economic times if they wish to remain in power. A plan of action acceptable to the electorate is also important. An acceptable policy is difficult to achieve when the main solution to the crisis involves curtailing government debt. Who gets cut out of the budget and the realignment of spending priorities are difficult waters to navigate. To help solve these economic woes in a manner acceptable to most Europeans, Habermas suggests the application of one model of cosmopolitism and the associated concepts of human rights and dignity. Using a cosmopolitan approach that considers the absolute need for basic social and political rights, the EU can craft non-zero-sum solutions for the member states.

Habermas is critical of current actions regarding the EU economic crisis. He argues that national leaders, including the more pro-EU ones, are not practicing enough solidarity envisioned under the integration project. For example, instead of leading the charge for "more Europe," he states that Germany is acting as a catalyst in the erosion of solidarity. He also states that current trends in fragmenting Europe politically are not consistent with the integrating efforts in the development of a "multicultural world society" (2012: 7). He challenges the claim made by Euroskeptics that solving the crisis at the continental level requires a level of legitimacy that the EU does not have. His normative claim is that the EU can have sufficient legitimacy when decisions are embedded in the constitutional makeup of the political community. In fact, he claims that the unique character of democratic state sovereignty is the basis of solving the crisis at the European level. Since the states are sovereign democratic countries, which are legally empowered by their citizens to act on their behalf, any joint decision made by them at the EU level is legitimate if democratic principles are also applied at the supranational level.

The EU's evolution is a result of decisions made by democratically accountable leaders. Also, more and more decisions to advance integration are up to the will of the people through referendum. The defeat of the treaty establishing a constitution for Europe by voters is a clear example of how democratic state sovereignty is very much in charge of the process. Throughout the process of integration, as Moravcsik (1998) notes, the member states were clear that the creation of EU citizenship would rest on the continuing existence of European states. As a result, Habermas agrees, currently only the member states can guarantee basic democratic rights (Habermas 2012: 13) due to their "socio-cultural and regional distinctiveness" (ibid.: 42).

Habermas also points out that member states, individually, are not capable of solving the crisis because "financial markets have developed beyond the control of even the most powerful nation states" (ibid.: 53). Financial markets are indeed global in scope. Member states' debts are held by individuals far and wide, given the ease of lending due to liberal regulations and advances in technology. These same forces have made it easier for states to borrow. The problem arises when the communal feeding at the financial trough becomes unsustainable. In order to maintain market stability in an integrated environment, the EU member states will need to work jointly. Indeed, Habermas has argued for years that new, democratic "postnational constellations" are necessary to "meet the challenges of globalization" (Habermas 2001a: 88).

Joint decisions made by the EU member states will have a democratic quality because Europe has built a supranational political community by both EU citizens and European peoples (Habermas 2012: 28). Institutions that represent the collective citizenship, like the European Parliament, usually examine proposals through ideological lenses instead of national ones. Recent exceptions to this are the Euroskeptic members of parliament who do have nationalist agendas. However, for now, their numbers are small. Other institutions, like the Council of the European Union, focus on the member states' interests and therefore represent the European peoples. The bicameral nature of these institutions allows for debate based on European and national interests. In this way, there is a reduced chance that one member state will "win" over others and that some member states will be "losers."

Member state joint decisions are credible because they are based on a firm legal foundation, which is based on two innovations (Habermas 2012: 54). First is the subordination of the sovereign member states to EU law. The member states are both subordinate and sovereign[1] because the strength of EU law is based on the member states' recognition of the law. In other words, EU law has supremacy because member states adopt EU law as their own national law. If they do not apply the EU law, then they are in fact in violation of a portion of national law. For this to work effectively, the member states adopt these laws collectively and therefore create a web that joins them into a common entity. In addition, the Court of Justice of the European Union ruled in the *Van Gend en Loos* case (1963) that European law has a direct effect on individuals, even if the member state has not adopted a European act into its legal system.

The second innovation is the shared sovereignty between the member states. The growing number of policy areas that require joint decision-making prevents unilateral action by the member states. The evolutionary development of pooling sovereignty is different than the Euroskeptic claim of surrendering sovereignty. As already noted, the bicameral nature of decision-making requires the inclusion of member state representatives. As also noted, the member states are the constitutional source of EU law. Finally, the source of practical enforcement comes from the member states. None of the central EU institutions have independent enforcement power. In the end, the legal foundation of the EU rests exclusively with the member states.

For this formula to be successful, Habermas notes there needs to be "mutual trust among the European peoples [that] will give rise to a transnational, though attenuated, form of civic solidarity among the citizens of the Union" (2012: 29). The decision-making structure requires the belief that the member states are interested in mutual success and that no one member state or subgroup of members are attempting to take advantage of the others. As Habermas has argued for years (see Habermas 2001b), the democratic nature of the EU also requires that the European peoples, and not just their leaders, have a transnational trust. A lack of this trust can prevent support for joint decisions made under the legal structure.

Trust comes about when Europeans adopt a more cosmopolitan view of the world. This view sees an injustice done on one person as an offense against everyone's moral sensibility (Habermas 2012: 64). The nationalist view of injustice rests on subdividing humanity into exclusive groups, whereas a cosmopolitan view—often cast by Habermas in terms of cosmopolitan Europe—encourages seeing "citizens of another nation as fundamentally 'one of us'" (Habermas and Derrida 2003: 293). The injustice found outside of the group can be sympathized with under nationalism, while cosmopolitanism motivates taking rectifying action because the injustice is against another human being. Cosmopolitanism recognizes that all persons have universal human rights and that human dignity is the moral source of these rights (Habermas 2012: 75). Therefore, if Europeans viewed the material outcomes of the economic crisis through the lens of cosmopolitanism, they would see the violation of human dignity as individuals are humiliated due to lack of basic rights. Trusting fellow Europeans would come easy if individuals believed that others cared about human dignity and, as a result, sought out remedies that are mutually beneficial.

Human dignity is the idea that humans, all humans, have inherent worth and need to be respected. Habermas demonstrates that the scope of dignity correlates with the scope of basic human rights as the latter evolved over time (2012: 79). Each category of rights—freedoms, civil rights, social, and cultural—has as a justification the degree of respect and sense of worth we extend to each other. Freedom requires that we respect each other as equals. In order to fully express our freedoms, we need to be able to participate equally in a democratic society (civil rights), and therefore respect the worth of everyone's voice. Full expression of rights requires that all categories of rights are met; otherwise individuals cannot participate fully in the democratic process. This requires that individuals live in dignity, in the material sense. Finally, individuals' cultures need to be respected so that we place each person's freedoms, civil, and social rights in equal standing. Habermas' earlier calls for the development of a European public sphere and a shared political culture (Habermas 2001b: 17–21) can be seen as precursors to his argument in *The Crisis of the European Union*. The result is that each person can have a full guarantee of their human rights.

Understanding cosmopolitanism in light of human rights and dignity brings us full circle to democratic lawmaking and the cosmopolitan approach to solving the European sovereign debt crisis. If human rights form the basis of decision-making in a democracy, then the morality of equal respect guides the legal process. This guideline, however, underlines the "human" aspect and not national concerns. Human dignity, and the correlations with the evolution of human rights, requires a solution that would be good for Germans and the other peoples of the EU. Therefore, the democratic decision-making process outlined at the start of this introduction would need to use a cosmopolitan approach if human rights are respected and human dignity upheld. Habermas has argued similar points for many years, including in *The Postnational Constellation*, where he argues that democratic institutions allow states to "close the holes of social integration through the political participation of its citizens" (Habermas 2001a: 76). Habermas maintains his emphasis on the public sphere in *The Crisis of the European Union*. He describes "the 'people' as the functional requirement for the democratic process ... the political-cultural conditions for appropriate communication processes in the political public sphere" (Habermas 2012: 22), which he insists is the "medium of integration of civic solidarity," one of "three building blocks ... in every democratic political community" (ibid.: 21). This emphasis continues later in the volume, in discussions of the limitations of administrative decrees and the need for a European public sphere (ibid.: 46–48) and his discussion of the unfeasibility of developing effective global public opinion, while at the same time recognizing the possibility of a "shared political culture" in a "territorially restricted union of citizens and states shaped by common historical experiences" (ibid.: 62), such as Europe.

The eurozone taxpayers understand that they will need to bear the joint liability for the budgetary risks of member states. How to manage that liability becomes the fundamental question. According to Habermas, Europe is at the crossroads where it can turn towards greater integration or proceed towards a focus on national concerns. The former requires that the citizens and peoples of Europe adopt the cosmopolitan approach, one not simply of an enlargement of national models but rather one of mutual opening up and interpenetration (Habermas 2001b: 18). Otherwise, in his view, a social injustice would be perpetrated on the most vulnerable social groups when they bear "the brunt of the socialized costs for the market failure" (Habermas 2012: 102). These social groups are not necessarily concentrated in any one member state, but those members that must cut back social spending the most will have to inflict the harshest pain on these vulnerable groups. Their dignity would be harmed because they were not the winning recipients of globalization; they are not at fault for economic crisis, but must bear the brunt of the costs. If Europe recognizes the moral basis of their rights, the cosmopolitan approach would hold their dignity in esteem and preserve the required social benefits. Elsewhere, Habermas suggests that converting the eurozone into a strong political entity would go a long way to achieving these ends (Habermas 2013 and 2014).

There is deep concern that the approach to solving the crisis of the EU is not taking the cosmopolitan road and that German leadership is part of the nation-centered approach. Habermas views Germany as a "self-absorbed colossus in the middle of Europe" that is not incorporating the perspectives of others and is instead "withdrawing into an egocentric blend of aestheticization and utility maximization" that "can no longer even guarantee that the EU will survive in its unstable status quo" (Habermas 2012: 124–125). The authors of this volume tackle the importance of German leadership in solving the EU crisis by taking a position on the cosmopolitan approach and the German role.

The contributions found in this volume are organized into the following four parts: in "Foundations," we examine the basis of Habermas' arguments, placing them into their historical context. In "Values" we question the degree to which Europeans share the ideals Habermas describes as crucial to his program of reform. In "Tools" we examine the influence of Habermas' cosmopolitanism in religious and literary fields. Finally, in "Institutions" we describe the influence of Habermas' notions in the arenas of education, national economies, austerity, and human rights. A concluding essay brings the various strands of our discussion together.

Christian Bailey's essay, "Democracy as Ideal and Practice: Historicizing *The Crisis of the European Union*," establishes the foundations for our discussion of Habermas, cosmopolitanism, Germany, and the European Union. Seeking to situate the argument in the history and implementation of European attempts at integration since the end of World War II, Bailey traces developments in attitudes, approaches, and philosophies regarding democracy over this period. Bailey then turns to Habermas' cosmopolitan ideas specifically. He begins his discussion presuming that the first stage—the formulation of a governing treaty or constitution—has already taken place and that tasks then turn to political and cultural efforts to develop a new sense of European solidarity. Bailey's emphasis on this "distinctively German approach" to European integration focuses on political parties in the European Parliament (EP) and on institutions that could serve to create a European public sphere. In the political parties, Bailey finds enduring issues preventing transnational political movements, with troubling consensus sometimes forming around more negative, Euroskeptic perspectives. Nor has the limited cohesion in the EP led to increased senses of European political membership in EU citizens. Bailey argues that Habermas is overly optimistic in his belief that the existence of a public sphere necessarily means support for the space that enables such a public sphere. Indeed, here, too, he locates transnational cooperation that seeks to ultimately undermine EU programs. Finally, regarding the role of EU-wide mass media, Bailey remains skeptical of the reach of such media, largely for either the focus on high-brow, elite programming, tied to stories focused on national interests, or simply ineffective even when united on European issues (as was the case with the French media recommending a "yes" vote on the European constitution in 2005).

Jennifer Fredette's essay, "Habermas on Human Dignity as the Origin of Human Rights and Egalitarian, Utopian Thinking," emphasizes Habermas' vital discussion of human dignity. This focus on a cosmopolitan approach to a fundamental feature of human rights leads Fredette to German, French, and European case studies; she outlines how different jurisprudential traditions define the notion of "human dignity" and points to ways states can even use the notion to undermine individual rights. What Habermas argues is essential to his ideas of cosmopolitanism because it is so transnational and transcultural, Fredette explores in a more cautious and detailed way in order ultimately to direct us to ways Habermas' argument can be reformulated and saved.

Beginning our discussion of values related to European cosmopolitanism, Gaspare M. Genna's chapter, "Cosmopolitanism, Trust, and Support for European Integration," discusses the vital issue of trust among Europeans, which he describes as a precondition for cosmopolitanism. His essay describes the challenge faced by cosmopolitanism: accepting others from outside one's own national group into a political community. Genna develops a political cohesion model based on social identity theory and finds that difference in trust relates closely to the level of support for European integration. He describes the closest relationship between trust in out-groups and support for European integration coming when trust in those in eastern member nations increases, followed by trust in those from southern member states and finally that in those from northern member states. Though Genna qualifies our ability to generalize from his data, he states that the relationship between trust in others and support for integration is strong, supporting this element of Habermas' discussion of cosmopolitanism.

Aubrey Westfall, in her essay, "European Reform from the Bottom Up? The Presence and Effects of Cosmopolitan Values in Germany," continues the discussion of European values but turns to the opinions of the Germans themselves. If—as Habermas argues—the future of the European Union rests in the ability of its members to expand notions of sacrifice and solidarity beyond national borders and to view all members of the union as having equal claims to the rights and privileges conventionally granted to national citizens, then the actual existence of cosmopolitan attitudes among citizens of the EU would be necessary elements in any such increased integration. Due both to practical, economic reasons (such as Germany's increasingly leading role in the EU following the economic crisis) and to internal German historical and philosophical reasons mentioned by Habermas himself (see Habermas 2013), Westfall sees the German case as central. Her chapter's examination of aggregate levels of public opinion in Germany as a test case for the existence of individual cosmopolitanism and solidarity provides empirical support for Habermas' assertion that cosmopolitan values exist and are empirically associated with support for European integration.

Describing the first tool to assess the importance of cosmopolitanism, James M. Skidmore's essay "Reason, Faith, and Europe: Two German Perspectives on What is Europe?" uses religion as a lens for examining Habermas' ideas. Centering his discussion around an encounter between Habermas and Benedict XVI (then Joseph Ratzinger) in 2004, when the two met face to face in Munich for a public discussion of the topic "Vorpolitische moralische Grundlagen eines freiheitlichen Staates" (Pre-political Moral Foundations of a Free State), Skidmore explores the role of religion and secularism in debates around integration and cosmopolitanism. Though the EU's Charter of Fundamental Rights (2000) mentions the "spiritual and moral heritage" of Europe (Charter 2010), neither it nor drafts of the EU constitution make direct mention of any specific religion or deity. In Skidmore's reading, Habermas' (2004) presentation centered on the idea that states do not require a moral foundation and find their ideal expression in democratic institutions, while Ratzinger's contribution questioned European's tolerance for continued extreme rationalism. Ultimately, Skidmore finds points of connection between the two thinkers' emphasis on dignity, though he does not determine which may ultimately prove the most helpful for the European project.

The volume's second essay focusing on tools, "Cosmopolitan Reflections: Jürgen Habermas and W. G. Sebald" by Ian W. Wilson, examines the cultural and aesthetic sides of Habermas' theories of cosmopolitanism through a literary lens, suggesting that W. G. Sebald's final book, *Austerlitz* (2001) provides a model for a cosmopolitan subjectivity. In its focus on Habermas' arguments in *The Crisis of the European Union* and other texts that call for the development of a European, i.e., not exclusively national, identity, Wilson argues that the unnamed narrator and the eponymous protagonist represent two possible models for such European identity. Brief moments that suggest a fusing of the narrator and the protagonist complicate the matter further, providing aesthetic illustrations of Habermas' philosophical-political argument. Furthermore, given these cosmopolitan elements, its polyglot nature, and its broad European setting and focus, Sebald's novel serves as a typical example of a new "literature of the European Union."

Turning now to institutions, Thomas O. Haakenson's essay, "Educating the European Union: Internationalization through Integration," discusses the "symbolic crystallization" of constitutional law Habermas describes as necessary to found a European political identity (2011: 6) as well as his emphasis on the development of a European public sphere (2012: 7). Education, Haakenson argues, is integral to ensure that such institutions develop. Most would recognize an educational system dedicated to the creation of democratic citizens as crucial to the creation of a successful public sphere, but Haakenson highlights the European overemphasis on educational outcomes vs. access to education as a barrier to achieving the success Habermas envisions. Ultimately Haakenson maintains that the member states of the EU must refocus their attentions on access to education as a form of individual self-determination—crucial to most conceptions of cosmopolitanism—rather than maintain its current focus on the standardization of transfer credit and degree requirements as vehicles to general European educational quality if they wish to create the kind of European public sphere Habermas envisions.

Marcella Myers' essay, "European Integration and Economic Interests," draws our focus to the institutional aspects of national economies, especially as they relate to globalization. Myers' argument moves from a discussion of the general perception of a "democratic deficit" in the EU and the economic crisis to the contention that EU national economies are willing participants, not helpless victims, of globalization. The deregulation and privatization that have typified the era of increasing European integration thus far, Myers argues, draw our attention to an important change: though economic concerns have driven integration in Europe thus far, a pivot must now be made to the development of common European identities for more profound political cooperation.

David O. Rossbach's essay, "Does German Austerity Travel? The Baltic States' Reactions to the Euro Crisis," examines the successes German-style austerity has had in other countries, specifically the Baltic States. Latvia, in particular, makes an interesting test case, as its economy contracted quite significantly after late 2007 and it became one of the first European recipients of IMF aid. On the other hand, however, the Baltics seem to have rebounded better than some other European states. Rossbach questions, then, why the German insistence on short-term austerity and structural reforms has worked well in some states, while it has failed or been met with protest in others. He argues that accession processes in the Baltic States reflected precisely the elements Habermas describes as required to create the appropriate cosmopolitan nature of the EU: equal rights, the rule of law, democratic decision-making, and civic solidarity.

Erik O. Eriksen's chapter, "On the *pouvoir constituent* of the European Union," addresses the issue of effective and legitimate EU institutions. Habermas argues that it is time to develop transnational democracy through a democratic multilevel political order. Eriksen, however, asks if his model is a viable method to provide legitimacy. He notes that Habermas is not clear regarding in what capacity Europeans are equal. Only a *pouvoir constituent*, or single authority, provides the proper legal system that can place the individual as the subject bearing rights.

Ultimately, these chapters can be read usefully in the wake of new challenges facing Europe, primarily those of the refugee crisis that reached historic proportions by the fall of 2015 and the Paris terror attacks of November 13, 2015. These two developments have led many European nations—EU members and not, Schengen signatories and not, but very importantly, including Germany itself—to reevaluate national identity vs. European identity, open borders vs. closed borders, and indeed, the very viability of the most recent attempt at European integration. From public spheres to human dignity; from trust, sacrifice, and identity to education, austerity, and integration: the terms with which this collection engages touch on issues that are at the heart of the EU and of Habermas' ideas. Germany's importance has not decreased in the wake of the events of late 2015. While this collection focuses on events before 2015, its arguments, like Habermas' theories of cosmopolitanism, remain relevant and salient.

Note

1 "the member states...enjoy a monopoly on the means for a legitimate use of force..." Habermas (2012: 54).

References

Charter of Fundamental Rights of the European Union (2010) Official Journal of the European Union, 2010/C 83/02, March 30, 2010. http://eur-lex.europa.eu/LexUriServ/LexUriServ.do?uri=OJ:C:2010:083:0389:0403:en:PDF (last accessed: March 2, 2016).

Habermas, Jürgen (2001a) "The Postnational Constellation and the Future of Democracy," in *The Postnational Constellation: Political Essays*. ed. and trans. Max Pensky. Cambridge, MA: MIT, pp. 58–112.

Habermas, Jürgen (2001b) "Why Europe Needs a Constitution," *New Left Review*, 11, pp. 5–26.

Habermas, Jürgen (2012) *The Crisis of the European Union: A Response*. Trans. Ciaran Cronin. Malden, MA: Polity Press.

Habermas, Jürgen (2013) "Democracy, Solidarity and the European Crisis," Lecture delivered April 26, 2013 at the KU Leuven. www.kuleuven.be/communicatie/evenementen/evenementen/jurgen-habermas/en/democracy-solidarity-and-the-european-crisis (last accessed: March 2, 2016).

Habermas, Jürgen (2014) "Democracy in Europe: Why the Development of the European Union into a Transnational Democracy is Necessary and How it is Possible." Lecture delivered in September 2014 at the University of Oslo ARENA Centre for European Studies. ARENA Working Paper 13/2014. www.sv.uio.no/arena/english/research/publications/arena-publications/workingpapers/working-papers2014/wp13-14.pdf (last accessed: March 2, 2016).

Habermas, Jürgen, and Jacques Derrida (2003) "February 15, or What Binds Europeans Together: A Plea for a Common Foreign Policy, Beginning in the Core of Europe," *Constellations*, 10(3), pp. 291–297.

Moravcsik, Andrew (1998) *The Choice for Europe: Social Purpose and State Power from Messina to Maastricht*. Ithaca, NY: Cornell University Press.

Van Gend en Loos (1963) Case 26/62. *European Court Report*, February 5. http://eur-lex.europa.eu/legal-content/EN/TXT/?uri=CELEX%3A61962CJ0026 (last accessed: March 2, 2016).

Part I
Foundations

1 Democracy as Ideal and Practice
Historicizing *The Crisis of the European Union*

Christian Bailey

Reactions to the Nobel Committee's decision to award the European Union (EU) its Peace Prize in 2012 were predictably mixed. What was perhaps less predictable was that the EU's own leaders would greet such news with feelings of foreboding and a profound sense of their own shortcomings. Yet this was the reaction of Martin Schulz, the socialist President of the European Parliament, when he joined European Council President Herman van Rompuy and European Commission President José Manuel Barroso to collect the prize in Oslo. Schulz was reminded of Thomas Mann's novel *Buddenbrooks* and its account of the decline of a great family business, squandered by the later generations who could not emulate the heroic deeds of their forefathers. Thinking back on the achievements of the first generation of postwar European statesmen, Schulz worried that present day leaders were similarly watching a great political project fall apart (Kripa 2012b).

Schulz's reflections are interesting for a couple of reasons: they indicate not only the current sense of crisis in the EU but also the enduring mythology of a great European project that has only recently gone off the rails. Jürgen Habermas' analysis of the crisis of the European Union offers a similar paradoxical mix of pessimism about the recent direction of EU policymaking combined with a strong belief in the underlying value of the postwar European integration project. This chapter seeks to historicize Habermas' arguments concerning the relationship between democracy and European integration. Rather than measuring current practice in European institutions against an ahistorical ideal of democracy, it recovers how democracy has been understood, conceptualized and practiced within the EU. As we will see, a variety of ideas about democracy, many of which appear irreconcilable with each other, have been invoked to support and extend, but also to critique and argue against, European integration across the second half of the twentieth century (Lacroix and Nicolaïdis 2010; Conway and Depkat 2010). Accordingly, any attempt to further democratize the EU will need to engage with the diverse understandings of democracy that have historically developed and been a factor in how Europeans have constructed an integrated Europe.

Habermas stresses three components in his proposed construction of the European Union as a transnational or cosmopolitan democracy. The first component is legal and involves the forming of "an association of free and equal citizens ... [with] rights which guarantee everyone equal private and civic autonomy." After this work of formulating a treaty or constitution has been agreed upon, the remaining tasks are political and cultural. Powers must be distributed "within an organization which secures the collective decision-making power of the association of citizens by administrative means," i.e., through an executive that is legitimized by a parliament. That is the political task. Then comes the cultural dimension: "civic solidarity" must be developed "within and across national borders ... [as] a necessary condition for joint political will-formation and hence for both the communicative generation of democratic power and the legitimation of the exercise of political authority" (Habermas 2012: 21–22). This chapter is concerned with the second and third components and focuses on Habermas' major concrete recommendations for democratizing the European project through politics and culture. These are: enhancing the role of the European Parliament (EP), strengthening the role of the political parties at a European level, encouraging a European civil society, and developing a transnational media. Clearly Habermas invests hopes in the democratizing potential of these institutions and sectors; accordingly, such hopes should be measured against the historical record of the EP, European political parties, civil society associations and the media (Habermas 2012: 12–17, 48–49, 135–136).

While the perspective offered is a pan-European one, particular attention is paid to how such developments look from a German perspective. Adopting such an approach should enable us to assess whether a distinctively German approach to Europe is discernible, or whether there is convergence between the peoples of Europe concerning how to deepen European integration. The question of German distinctiveness versus a common European sentiment is particularly urgent in light of Germany's commanding role in managing the Greek crisis and the ensuing outbreak of nationalist rhetoric in European newspapers and among populations. For even as Habermas has continued to advocate creating a European demos through institutional reform, national opinion formers have emphasized not a common European identity but national differences (Habermas 2015). And so, during a period when Germany's most popular tabloid, *Bild-Zeitung* exclaims "No more billions for the greedy Greeks" and Greece's *Dimokratia* newspaper presents Angela Merkel as a Nazi under a headline "Memorandum macht frei," we must ask whether and how Habermas' political union can emerge out of the present, seemingly intractable crisis (*Bild-Zeitung* 2015; Reilly 2012).

Reforming Democratic Practice in the EU

Over the last two decades, national politicians have turned to the use of plebiscites to justify policies agreed within EU bodies concerning the enlargement and deepening integration of the EU. They did so in 2005 in an effort to ratify the treaty establishing a constitution for Europe, but failed due to No votes in France and the Netherlands. Similarly, the Irish voted down the successor Lisbon Treaty in 2008, although by this time, most national political leaders had abandoned using such referenda. Most recently, the Greek government called a referendum in July 2015 to approve the latest bailout package proposed by EU leaders. On this occasion, though, these national politicians were seeking a national veto rather than go-ahead. Such efforts to legitimize (or challenge) decisions made in international summits through referenda suggest political leaders' doubts that commitments made by either EP parliamentarians or national politicians would be deemed legitimate by electorates. They also suggest a potential conflict between Europeans who seek to develop a European-wide cosmopolitan democracy that would entail delegating more powers to EP parliamentarians and those who clamor for more direct democracy addressed at citizens of individual nation states. One of the sources of conflict is the different national understandings and histories of democracy. Some of the newer entrants to the EU from Eastern and Southern Europe have come to prize unitary national sovereignty above all else, while other nations, such as Germany, have embraced more federal versions of democracy. Similarly, evidence from a comparative study of European newspapers suggests persistent differences even among the founding six countries: for instance, while Germans support strengthening the EP, French voters prefer to reinforce the role of national ministers in European decision-making by extending qualified majority voting (Medrano 2010: 325).

To complicate matters further, recent years have seen ever more bitter clashes between EP delegates and national parliamentarians, particularly but not exclusively in more Euroskeptic countries such as the UK and a number of Eastern European nations. National parliamentarians have often sought to win support by denying the rights of elected representatives in Strasbourg to interfere with their own nation's sovereignty (Judt 2005: 461–462). Perhaps this prizing of national over transnational or cosmopolitan democracy explains the increasing willingness of European statesmen to turn to referenda when seeking to push through European reforms. Yet, the increasing reliance on the approval of national majorities via referenda in some ways signals a departure from early postwar models of democracy. In countries such as Germany, leading statesmen turned to European integration after World War Two as a way of enshrining constitutional rights and safeguards across the European communities that could not be overturned by the popular will of any national majority. Habermas himself recognizes the value of such safeguards when he argues that European law must not be liable to change because of the will of a majority expressed at any given time (Habermas 2012: 8). Rallying cries to deepen democracy at the European level must thus be careful to make clear which aspects of democracy will thereby be strengthened and which restrained. And any deepening of democracy will require EU politicians to tackle the national differences in how democracy has been envisioned and experienced.

If European leaders (and populations) may have different ideas of what constitutes democracy, they nevertheless appear to agree that the European Union is not democratic enough. Even in the early 1990s, at a time when European enlargement was celebrated as the final step in a post-Cold War reunification of Europe, Helmut Kohl spoke of an emerging "democratic deficit" in the European Community (EC). He indeed argued before a CDU/CSU party conference audience in 1992 that the Maastricht Treaty would help to address this deficit (CDU 1992: 169). Concerns about a democratic deficit have intensified among policymaking elites in Europe over the last 20 years, with the European Commission noting that a declining minority of the "citizens of Europe" have voted in European elections. The decline in voter turnout is particularly worrisome given that the European treaties since the Single European Act of 1985/6 have consistently shifted power towards the elected representatives in the European Parliament (EP) and away from the appointed bureaucrats and national politicians who make decisions and negotiate treaties behind closed doors. Recognizing that the practice of democracy at a European level entails more than citizens simply voting, and perhaps looking for new ways to convince Europeans to even do that, European leaders have sought to encourage the growth of transnational civil society organizations that would bring Europeans together across national boundaries. For instance, a dialogue between the European Commission and special interest groups was initiated in 1992, leading to biennial talks between the Commission and a Social Platform group of over 1,000 social policy NGOs established in 1998 (Friedrich 2011: 90–91). But rather than regarding such initiatives as a viable means of creating a European society from the bottom up, critics have interpreted them as another way in which the most wealthy and well-organized insider lobbyists can continue to dominate the functioning of the EU (Kohler-Koch 2011: 13–15).

In spite of European elites encouraging civil society participation, it has also become apparent during the recent Eurocrisis that many of the most important decisions about distributing resources within the EU were made, not by representatives from transnational European institutions, but by national ministers or heads of state who negotiated within intergovernmental bodies (Kripa 2012a). This trend has led to criticisms that the most populous and prosperous nations, chiefly Germany, can impose an agenda on Europe that is tailored to the German national interest (Kaletsky 2012; Crossland 2012). Habermas has seen in the intergovernmental method of decision-making the potential for an "undermining of democracy" and a "template for a post-democratic exercise of political authority" by the "self-authorizing European Council of the seventeen" (Habermas 2012: viii). For Ulrich Beck and Daniel Cohn-Bendit the problem is even simpler: they see dominant national politicians such as Angela Merkel practicing a form of Machiavellian *Realpolitik* or "Merkiavellism" that manipulates European institutions in order to push forward a nakedly nationalist agenda (Beck and Cohn-Bendit 2012; Beck 2013). It might therefore seem that Alan Milward's influential analysis of the early postwar model of European integration continues to hold true: rather than understand the construction of the European Union as an incremental process towards a federal Europe, this supranational structure has continued to offer a means for national politicians to "save" their nation states by pooling a limited amount of resources and risk (Milward 2000).

Of course, the issues with which Habermas is grappling are not the same as those of the 1950s and 1960s with which the statesmen in Milward's analysis were confronted. Indeed, while the European treaties of the mid-1980s to late 1990s offered the prospect of a more genuinely federal EU, the extension of the EU into 28 countries presented a host of new problems. Many of the new members in the east of Europe were, in light of their recent history as Soviet satellites, justifiably skeptical of limiting their sovereignty in the name of a lofty internationalism. Such skepticism was, moreover, fanned by the rise of new nationalist, anti-EU parties. Accordingly, the incorporation of such new countries has broken down many of the areas of agreement that characterized EC politics in the latter twentieth century. For theorists such as Habermas, the problem once more is how to create "solidarity among strangers" and encourage a European "*Wir-Gefühl*" (shared identity) among a much wider and more diverse collection of communities and societies than had belonged to the EC for much of the latter twentieth century (Habermas 2001: 16; Winkler 2005). The route to such a *Wir-Gefühl* goes chiefly through strengthening the EP, pan-European civil society groups, and European media, all of which should, according to Habermas, enable Europeans to constitute themselves as a cosmopolitan people and society. This strengthening would mark a significant departure from the current model of "integration by stealth" and is deemed necessary by Habermas before the EU can build more European institutions (Müller 2008: 145). Habermas outlines several concrete proposals for achieving this new European consciousness, proposals that require an assessment of the actual, recent performances of the institutions and sectors that Habermas still believes capable of driving forward a revived European project.

The European Parliament and the Role of European Parties

Implying a belief that a European public might prove more eager than national politicians to support measures of European integration, Habermas has stressed how citizens can use the European Parliament (EP) to circumvent national political leaders. He has called for an enhanced role for the EP, not least in terms of the parliament's role in formulating and scrutinizing financial policy (Habermas 2012: 5). The question remains, though, how has the EP performed as an institution that embodies and promotes European integration? Of course, the EP cannot mimic or replace the role of national parliaments as it does not form a government and is not the initiator of European legislation. Since the 1970s the EP has, however, gained more powers and become more assertive in its interactions with the European Council and the European Commission. It was initially a body made up of national delegates who possessed no budgetary powers until 1970. Once its members became directly elected in 1979, they became more confident to question the authority of the other European institutions. Elected EP members rejected the budget proposed by the European Commission in 1980 and argued that deeper agricultural reforms were needed, signaling one of the first attempts to reform the Common Agricultural Policy (CAP). Since the Single European Act (SEA) in the mid-1980s, the EP has incrementally gained further powers and won certain symbolic victories, such as prompting the resignation of the Santer Commission in 1999 (Gfeller, Loth, and Schulz 2011: 5–7; Rittberger 2011). This incident saw clashes between the Commission and the EP and between the various party factions within the EP. It thus represented an important landmark, showing that European parliamentarians were willing to scrutinize and challenge the actions of appointed bureaucrats in the Commission and to contest policies along party lines.

It is nevertheless unclear whether the strengthening of the EP has served to increase the democratic legitimacy of the European project. In spite of its greater powers, voters have not sought to take part in deciding how it is constituted in greater numbers; quite the reverse. Voter turnout for EP elections between 1994 and 2014 has remained significantly lower than for national elections and has fallen in a number of countries. For instance, in Spain it has fallen from 59.1 percent to 43.8 percent across the period, while turnout for national elections has remained above 70 percent. In Greece the drop has been equally steep, going from 73.2 percent to 60 percent (turnout had fallen to 52.7 percent in 2009), while again the numbers for national elections have consistently been higher. It should also be noted that voter turnout in Greek national elections declined to 62.5 percent in 2012 and 63.6 percent in January 2015, perhaps suggesting a disengagement from voters who believed that national parliamentarians could exercise only a limited influence over their country's fate. The fall in "core countries" such as France has been comparable: the proportion of citizens voting in EU elections over this period has moved from 52.8 percent to 42.4 percent and remains below the average for national elections, which stands at over 70 percent. In Germany a similar change from 60 percent to 48.1 percent is significant because the biggest dip occurred between 1999 and 2009, indicating a steady waning in engagement, only arrested by the recent crisis. Comparing these figures with the turnout figures for national elections in Germany, it is again striking that the latter have remained at over 70 percent. Interestingly, the most noticeable increase in voter turnout for EP elections is in countries such as the Netherlands and the UK, where turnout was very low by the late 1990s and sentiment has recently become more Euroskeptic. In the Netherlands turnout rose from 30 percent in 1999 to 37.3 percent in 2014, while in Britain it climbed across the same period from 24 percent to 35.6 percent, a figure that matches the steady climb in turnout at national elections to 66.1 percent in 2015 (Eurostat IDEA 2015). These figures suggest, at the very least, that greater engagement does not necessarily lead to greater support for further measures of integration.

A potential cause of voter apathy regarding the EP, according to Habermas, is that transnational party groupings have not played a big enough role in creating cross-border agendas that could unite national delegates around transnational party platforms. These party alliances have thus failed to encourage European citizens to identify areas of common concern and to think less reflexively along lines of national interest. Habermas' worries seem to be shared by European political elites. For example, the co-decision-making procedure that was agreed as part of the Maastricht Treaty, whereby the EP and European Council have to agree on legislation before it is adopted, was designed to enhance the role of parties in debating and mobilizing support behind legislative measures. Further practical help for the parties was also offered in 2004 when a law was passed that allowed political parties within the EP to receive funds out of the EU budget (Jones, Menon, and Weatherill 2012: 369). Whether enhancing the role of transnational party groups within the EP has stimulated a European consciousness among the European electorate is nevertheless far from clear. The major transnational ideological groupings in the EP have certainly been easy to recognize and have functioned quite cohesively for at least the last three decades. Indeed, the Christian Democratic European People's Party (EPP) continued its dominance of the last two decades in the most recent European election in 2014, winning 221 seats, with the Progressive Alliance of Socialists and Democrats (S&D) gaining 191 delegates (see Figure 1.1).

As research by Simon Hix, Abdul Noury, and Gérard Roland on the period 1979–2001 has shown, strong and increasing group cohesion among these major party alliances is also visible in terms of voting records.

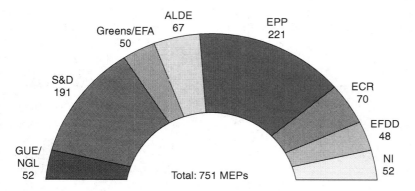

Figure 1.1 Distribution of Seats in the European Parliament by Transnational Party Groups (source: European Parliament, October 2014, accessible at www.bbc.co.uk/news/world-europe-29646414).

This trend led these political scientists to envisage EU political decision-making being reached through transnational party-political contestation rather than via the pre-existing intergovernmental model, whereby most major decisions are made by national ministers in the European Council (Hix, Noury, and Roland 2005). Such a conclusion now seems rather more doubtful given that at recent moments of crisis such as the bailout negotiations, agreements have been concluded between national finance ministers and representatives of the "Troika" (European Central Bank (ECB), European Commission (EC) and International Monetary Fund (IMF)) with EP delegates only able to hold hearings and conduct fact-finding missions (Manoli and Maris 2014: 79). The sidelining of the EU's parliamentary body at such pivotal moments, therefore, does provide evidence for Habermas' contention that the EP has failed to win more support from European populations because it has not been allowed to play a decision-making role when crucial negotiations about the allocation of EU resources have been held. But based on its past performance, how might have the EP have been likely to represent Europeans' views and interests had it been given a more prominent role?

Reviewing the data collected and analyzed from 1979 to 2001 shows that grand coalitions formed quite regularly between Christian and social democrats, with politicians from both parties voting very similarly, particularly in the late 1980s and early 1990s. It would appear that either such parties reflected a lack of polarization within European populations regarding questions of EU policy in the 1980s and 90s or that the spectrum of opinions among European publics was not being adequately represented by the groupings within the EP. Whatever is the case, it is clear that since the mid-1990s, the voting behavior of the Christian and social democratic parties have been diverging, while also increasingly failing to contain the dissent of individual delegates and national publics in the enlarged EU. A very public split between right-wing groups in the EP has occurred, with a breakaway group of parties made up of the British Conservatives; the Law and Justice, and Poland Comes First groups from Poland; and the Civic Democratic Party of the Czech Republic providing the leadership for a new, more Euroskeptic group: the European Conservatives and Reformists (ECR), which formed in 2009 (Almeida 2012: 128). The ECR can hardly be ignored; it is made up of around 71 MEPs, drawn from 16 countries. Furthermore, a Europe of Freedom and Direct Democracy Group (EFD) formed in 2009, proving to be more radically Euroskeptic and successfully recruiting 45 MEPs from seven countries, although it largely draws on two protest parties, the United Kingdom Independence Party (UKIP) and the Italian Five Star Movement.

While the centrist policies of the major political parties in the EP from core countries such as Germany have mimicked the centrist agendas of the major parties active within domestic politics, it is not clear whether this continuing centrism will persist within Germany, or will do anything other than serve to further alienate the "outsider" groups that are largely uniting only around negative, anti-integration measures. For instance, it was groups to the right of the CDU, such as the Free Democratic Party (FDP) and the hard-left grouping Die Linke ("The Left"), which proved most in favor of Greece leaving the euro in the light of the recent debt crisis (*Deutsche Presse-Agentur*, 2012). A more fundamentally anti-euro "Alternative for Germany" group also emerged in 2013, winning seven seats in the following year's European elections. It does not then appear that, through the enhanced role of the EP and the transnational party groupings within it, citizens are bypassing Euroskeptic national debates and forming a European consensus via directly elected European politicians. Rather, while party groupings are generally splintering within the EP, new ad hoc unities are being formed around negative agendas (Winkler 2005: 15). One recent and troubling example of such ad hoc unities is the fledgling Euroskeptic EP alliance, the "European Alliance for Freedom," that was established by far-right leaders including the French Front National leader Marine le Pen and the Dutch Party for Freedom leader Geert Wilders (Hebel and Schmitz 2013). It should be noted that such oppositional groups have often proved to be internally fractious. But they are arguably only designed to help rejectionist national parties to "win" back independence from supranational EU institutions.

The structure of how delegates of the EP are chosen may also have served to aggravate national rivalries and amplify differences between European nations, as smaller countries are much better represented than larger nations. For example, Malta is allocated one MEP per 82,500 citizens, whereas Germany receives one MEP per 830,000 citizens (Bundeszentrale für politische Bildung 2010). Such a weighted voting system, of course, illustrates the continuing sensitivity of European elites to citizens' concerns about the domination of the most populous and prosperous countries within Europe; a truly proportional allocation of votes would see the complete dominance of the larger nations. But equally, the current distribution of MEPs betrays a lack of trust among European elites that European citizens will regard each other first and foremost as fellow Europeans and not as members of nation states that seek to impose their respective national agendas on the other peoples of Europe.

Given the undeniable success of the transnational Christian democratic EPP grouping, it may appear that mainstream centrist parties can still thrive in the EP. Yet a complicating factor is the comparative lack of success of Christian democratic parties in Eastern Europe. In Eastern European countries such as the almost uniformly Catholic Poland, there was no breakthrough of a Christian democratic party that advocated the kind of federalist internationalism that has proved popular in (West) Germany since 1945. Christian parties from this region have rather eschewed the internationalism and assertively lay character of Christian democratic parties in Western Europe (Grzymala-Busse 2013; Bale and Szczerbiak 2008). Notable Christian politicians from Eastern Europe have also objected to the program of a Christian democratic EPP that stresses rights and equalities for minorities, such as same-sex couples, rights that they believe contravene Catholic teaching and mark a break with the Christian roots of Europe (Mach and Gora 2010; Bale and Hanley 2010). Such programs have been particularly unpalatable to right-wing Polish politicians who persuaded the Polish electorate to accept 70,000–80,000 directives in order to qualify for entry into the EU, arguing that they were returning to a European civilization they had historically helped to shape (Lange 2004: 3; Mach and Gora 2010: 227).

Enhancing the role of political parties in the EP has, therefore, not simply led to increased cohesion between European politicians or wider publics along ideological lines. Or if it has, agreement has increasingly been around programs dismissed as "populist" and anti-European by Habermas and other pro-European theorists, rather than around a postnational, cosmopolitan agenda. Equally worryingly, although a majority of MEPs responded to the Greek crisis by supporting initiatives to pool risk and debt through Eurobonds and a banking union—i.e., to solve the Eurocrisis through "more Europe"—national differences have started to supplant party loyalties when voting on these issues has taken place in the EP (Manoli and Maris 2014: 74–75). Furthermore, rather than gaining legitimacy, the EP may actually be losing ground to national parliaments during the recent crisis period. Since 2013, Conferences on Economic and Financial Governance have been held between representatives of national parliaments within the framework of the EU, suggesting that national parliamentarians rather than EP delegates have won a more prominent role as guarantors of democratic accountability in times of Eurocrisis (ibid.: 78).

As the EP appears to have lost influence in recent years, a variety of alternative means of providing popular legitimacy for the EU project have been proposed. Numerous outsider groups such as Italy's Five Star Movement and the German Alternative for Germany Party have advocated more direct democracy. Habermas' solution is different: he suggests strengthening a transnational European civil society that can educate and socialize a European citizenry that would then seek to rebuild European-wide democratic institutions. What then, are the prospects for cultivating such a European civil society? To answer this, we must turn again to the historical record.

A European Civil Society?

Not only theorists such as Habermas but also European policymaking elites have sought to cultivate transnational civil society bodies as a means of addressing the perceived democratic deficit in the EU and encouraging civic solidarity among Europeans. Civil society is understood here as the intermediate sphere between the private arena of the family and the public institutions of state. Within this sphere, common interests can form and impact on the political process. Habermas' and others' enthusiasm for civil society is partially due to the apparent success of fledging civil society groups in the Eastern bloc in the late 1970s and 1980s. These groups pushed forward a democratization process, even against the interests of an ageing and inflexible ruling nomenklatura (Glenn 2001: 25). Cultivating civil society at the European level has also appealed to pro-Europeans as a means of realizing the hopes of those federalists who provided inspiration for the European project in the early postwar period but who were marginalized by national statesmen in favor of a more limited form of European integration (Alliance des Démocrates et des Libéraux pour l'Europe 2010). Perhaps most importantly, the promotion of transnational civil society groups has been valorized by leading European institutions and intellectuals not only as a way of reviving a hollowed out European project but more profoundly of re-legitimizing the present day form of parliamentary democracy in Europe. For, as political scientists such as Dawid Friedrich have shown, today's parliamentary democracy in Europe has come to rely on limited participation on the part of unaligned citizens who vote in increasingly smaller numbers (Friedrich 2011: 5).

Works by Nancy Bermeo, Philip Nord, and Guido Müller have nevertheless illustrated that while the functioning of civil society associations presumes certain freedoms of association and expression alongside the existence of public discursive spaces free from political policing, such associations have not always promoted democratic political practice or a pluralist political culture (Bermeo and Nord 2000; Müller 2005). Indeed, associations have not always functioned as the "consensus-building little republics" that Alexis de Tocqueville described when he characterized them as the bedrock of democracy (Bermeo and Nord 2000: 102). In nineteenth-century Germany, they served to intensify confessional and class divides, working against the cohesion of wider society instead of functioning as a "transmission belt" between individuals and politicians (Steffek, Kissling, and Nanz 2007: 3). Similarly, in interwar Europe, organizations that formed to promote European integration did not all support an integrated democratic Europe along the lines envisaged by Aristide Briand, when he proposed Federal Union for Europe to the League of Nations in 1930. Alongside the plethora of Franco-German groups that aimed at reconciliation between First World War enemies within a democratic Europe, other groups such as the *Europäische Kulturbund* (European Cultural Alliance) agitated against democratic and republican constitutions and against the League of Nations. The *Kulturbund* was one of the most important pro-integration associations in Europe after 1918. It was made up of around 50 regional centers, producing one of the most influential interwar European journals, the *Europäische Revue* (European Review), and boasting a membership full of prominent political, business and cultural leaders such as Konrad Adenauer, Ignaz Seipel, Thomas Mann and many others. Yet, its agenda was very different to the kind of post-1945 liberal European project celebrated by Habermas among others. Its leading members attended the Volta Congress of 1932, organized by the Italian Fascists as an alternative Europeanist symposium to the Briand-inspired League of Nations talks. And its journal agitated for the overturning of the Versailles settlement, proposed the revision of democratic constitutions in Europe, celebrated ten years of fascist rule in Italy and advocated a reunification of a Greater Germany (Bailey 2013: 23–53).

Of course, if we turn to the post-1945 period, it is clear that the reviving of civil society organizations was an important part of the largely successful reintroduction of democracy into Western Europe. Many of the early postwar Europeanist civil society groups nevertheless conceived of their work as a means of taming the tyrannical potential of national parliamentary democracies to enforce a "dictatorship of the majority" (Kogon 1946). A large number also sought to remain politically unaligned, arguing that political parties did not clarify ideological differences through discussion, as Habermas has suggested, but amplified differences between citizens, stirring up enmities that could plunge Europe into another civil war (Paeschke 1947: 100–108; Müller 2011: 130). As recent research on Germany has illustrated, some of the most significant of these groups were not predominantly made up of those leftist federalists who had worked together in the wartime Resistance movements. They were, rather, nostalgic advocates of a united Europe as *Abendland* (Occident): a form of German-led European community based on pre-nationalist and pre-democratic traditions rooted in the experience of the Holy Roman Empire and the Habsburg Empire (Conze 2005; Bailey 2013). The histories of such groups suggest that support for a united Europe in civil society has been multivalent, even during the seemingly heroic first phase of postwar integration. Accordingly, we should not mythologize transnational associations or imagine that they will necessarily act to extend and deepen the current form of European integration, just because they are transnational bodies.

The Europe of the last two decades is not the Europe of the 1950s. The risk posed by the growth of transnational civil society bodies in recent years at first seems not so much that they would agitate against the current EU, but rather that they have quickly become cozy insiders that are hard to distinguish from the European bureaucratic elite. Due to concerns at the rapid interlocking of lobby groups with EU agencies in the previous decade, the European Commission launched a European Transparency Initiative in 2005 that aimed to uncover how lobbying and interest groups interacted with EU institutions (Friedrich 2011: 100). But alongside such insider groups, which seem unlikely to represent the bottom-up federalist agenda advocated by Habermas among others, other outsider groups have sprung up, the most prominent of which have been ad hoc groups such as those that emerged in France, the Netherlands and Ireland in order to lobby against the passing of a European constitution or the Lisbon Treaty.

While such groups have been less prominent in Germany, they have not been entirely absent. An independent Citizens' Initiative for a referendum on the EU constitution, which was active from 2008–2009, unlike many of the Euroskeptic groups, argued against the EU from a leftist position, promoting its cause in Marxist newspapers such as *Junge Welt* (Young World) and *Neues Deutschland* (New Germany) (Wangerin 2008). It linked up with other leftist groups in Austria and particularly in Ireland, where a coalition of trade unions, Sinn Fein, the Socialist Party and the Peace and Neutrality Alliance all lined up against the Lisbon Treaty. Crucially, the arguments it mounted against the European constitution were very much styled as protecting democracy. Among the Initiative's chief objections were: (i) that members of the European Constitutional Court would not be appointed by the legislature but by politicians within the executive; (ii) that an equivalent of the Basic Law's commitment to Germany being a social state was not included in the constitution; and (iii) that military obligations to the North Atlantic Treaty Organisation (NATO) were intrinsic to the constitution and thus threatened to involve German troops in military campaigns, in spite of the pacifism professed by much of the German public since 1945 (Heckmann 2009).

Groups such as the Citizens' Initiative may have been short-lived and marginal, particularly when compared to long-standing federalist groups such as the Europa-Union in Germany. The latter organization boasts 17,000 members and forms part of the larger Union Européenne de Fédéralistes (Union of European Federalists UEF), made up of hundreds of thousands of members across 22 countries (Union of European Federalists 2015). There is, however, little evidence that these more established groups are experiencing any great growth in support, or are functioning any more effectively as bridges between EU bodies and individual citizens, even in founding member countries like the Federal Republic. Rather, as a public opinion survey conducted in 2013 on behalf of the European Commission (known as the Eurobarometer survey) shows, Germans' views on the need for NGOs and civil society associations were towards the skeptical end of the EU-27 responses. Only a small majority believed that such organizations were necessary and only a minority of Germans—46 percent—thought they influenced EU policymaking. Germany was thus the fifth most skeptical country in the EU-27 regarding the value of civil society participation at the EU level (European Commission 2013: 7, 15).

It should be noted, nevertheless, that European and national elites, at least going on the evidence for Germany, have hardly been indifferent to whether a European civil society develops or not. The EU set aside €215 million for an initiative across the 27 member states called "Europe for Citizens," which ran from 2007–2013. As part of this program, meetings between Europeans in twinned towns, publications produced by civil society bodies, citizens' cafes, online forums, European Youth Parliaments, summer seminars and workshops were sponsored and advertised by participating government bodies such as the German Federal Ministry for the Family, Senior Citizens, Women and the Young (Wingert-Beckman 2010: 12–13). Between 2007 and 2010, 58 EU-funded projects were organized by German civil society groups alone, each attracting financial support from €10,000–60,000 (ibid.: 94–97). Furthermore, since December 2009, citizens have been encouraged to group together to propose legislation to the European Commission by the Citizens' Initiative, which places legislative proposals signed by at least one million European citizens before the Commission (Embacher 2010: 4). However, as yet, there seems little evidence that such civil society activity has led to a dramatic change of outlook or activity among the German electorate. While Germans were shown to be slightly more active in NGOs and other associations than the EU27 average, they were nowhere near as active as the less-integrated Nordic countries (European Commission 2013: 33). Such trends, therefore, suggest that European-wide civil society activity may not necessarily be affected by whether citizens have a pro-EU sensibility or not and may not, in turn, promote pro-EU sentiment.

Such a situation implies an inherent problem with Habermas' working assumption that an argumentative European-wide civil society would increase support for the kind of enlarged and more integrated Europe advocated in the 1990s and partially implemented in various stages over the last decade (Habermas 2012: 46–47). Habermas' optimistic assumptions about the Europhilia of active European citizens may well be based on the positive German experience in the EU. Certainly, the (West) German state has prospered and gained influence precisely by decentralizing and de-concentrating power in Germany, not least through European institutions (Bulmer, Jeffries and Paterson 2000: 6). And it was primarily the German *Länder* (states) that led the drive since the 1970s for a "Europe of the Regions" and promoted the EU as a means of redressing the inequalities that had emerged within nation states (Katzenstein 1993: 39). The congruence between German postwar interests and a more open and integrated Europe has not been altogether consistent though, and it is certainly not inevitable. Since the late 1990s, wealthy and independent-minded German regions such as Bavaria have witnessed how European enlargement has entailed the loss of jobs to competitors in neighboring countries such as the Czech Republic. Enlargement has also resulted in German workers, such as the Volkswagen staff at the Wolfsburg factory, having to accept an increase of their working week to 42 hours (without overtime) in order to remain competitive with their Eastern European colleagues (von Fröhlingsdorf et al. 2004).

Civil society groups in Europe have not only served to shape public opinion through discussion and lobbying. Social non-governmental organizations (NGOs) have also played a role as social service providers, not least in the new member-states. Such social activism is desirable, according to Habermas, who has argued that, "participation [in civil society] is only of democratic potential to the extent to which it politically influences the development of the formal to the material, the liberal to the social democracy" (Friedrich 2011: 35). Yet, civil society bodies in the former communist bloc, which have absorbed some of the responsibilities of former state bodies and thereby pushed forward decentralization and de-etatization, have faced challenges as they seek to deliver a European social model.

According to the Lisbon Agenda stipulations, they should offer a distinctive European alternative to the supposedly less generous and egalitarian American model, and promote "active social citizenship" (Saraceno 2009: 151). Evidence from the first half of the last decade would nevertheless suggest that they have received little help from more well-developed and well-funded equivalent bodies in prosperous Western nations such as Germany. Furthermore, the convergence between European welfare regimes that was supposed to occur as a result of the enlargement of the EU has not been particularly marked. The diversity between European nations has rather remained larger than that between the United States and an average of European nations when measured across the late 1990s and early 2000s (Alber 2006: 63–84). This suggests that European enlargement may not have reinforced the European social model in the way that its promoters have claimed.

Habermas' argument that one of the chief virtues of the European project is that it allows Europe to adapt to globalization without mimicking the neoliberal reforms piloted in the Anglo-American sphere since the 1980s may, therefore, appear somewhat exaggerated (Habermas 2001: 10–15). Perhaps as a result of civil society bodies failing to live up to the inflated role assigned them, a number of prominent examples from Eastern and Central Europe have lost the influence they gained in the late 1980s and early 1990s. For example, many of the fledgling civil society groups that played a pivotal role in pulling down the Iron Curtain in Europe, such as the liberal circles around Adam Michnik and his *Gazeta Wyborcza* (Electoral Gazette), have been in decline in recent years (Hoffmann 2007). They have been crowded out by more populist political parties led by figures such as former Czech President Vaclav Klaus, who, for instance, likened the EU to the Soviet-era Council for Mutual Economic Assistance (COMECON) in 2005 (von Beste et al. 2005: 98).

It would therefore appear that the growth of a European civil society is in evidence, although this civil society is not necessarily or ineluctably supportive of an ongoing program of wider and deeper integration. When analyzing civil society activity, we may accordingly want to avoid placing it within a teleological framework that describes Europe moving towards ever greater integration. We should instead recognize that the growth of an argumentative civil society does not predetermine the outcomes of the arguments that are made within it.

As Habermas has rightly pointed out, the media plays an important role in how European civil society functions and how its interactions are presented to the wider world. In order to understand how sentiment has been mobilized in the EU, we therefore also need to consider how the media has represented European issues and how European publics have used such media.

A European Media: Its Role in Creating a European Public Sphere

Developing the links that he first drew between a burgeoning public sphere and the emergence of a modern mass media in his 1962 work, *The Structural Transformation of the Public Sphere*, Habermas has stressed the potential for a transnational European media to help Europeans see their interconnectedness and ultimately build a common identity (Gripsrud 2007: 479–481). Forms of mass media, such as television and newspapers, can, according to his analysis, help to create a European identity by absorbing discussions occurring in various arenas of the public sphere and then presenting them before large audiences that are not necessarily in close geographical proximity to each other. According to this theory, the media should thereby increase transparency and encourage participation among European viewers and readers (Latzer and Sauerwein 2006: 13). One of the problems with the function of mass media in present-day Europe though, according to Habermas, is that it is largely organized along national lines. It therefore encourages European citizens to view even pan-European developments in terms of the various national interests. In order to address this state of affairs, Habermas has urged more support for transnational media ventures such as the French–German TV venture, Arte, a public service broadcaster (PSB) which is produced out of centers in France and Germany, receives EU funding, and offers a range of co-produced programs broadcast in both languages. As television has not received as much attention from researchers of the European public sphere as newspapers—even though 60 percent of respondents to a Eurobarometer survey of 2001 stated that they received most of their news about the EU via television—it seems pertinent to analyze whether transnational television has had the Europeanizing effects imagined by Habermas (Peter 2004: 150).

Arte may appear to be an unusually European media institution, given its explicit mission to represent a shared European culture (Luschny 2009: 30). Yet, transnational television in Europe is already quite vibrant and diverse with more than 100 transnational channels operating across the continent. And, paradoxically, the center of transnational TV in Europe is in the capital of Euroskeptic Britain, largely because the licenses that allow TV companies to broadcast there are extremely cheap, costing around $400. As has been well established by scholars of European media, most of the channels existing in this sector have not explicitly served a political agenda of pushing forward European integration. The most popular channels have either been American-owned sports, children's and music channels, or channels that have served specific diaspora communities (Chalaby 2002). The spread of at least 17 prominent pan-European channels—including Arte, various BBC channels, CNBC, Euronews, Eurosport, MTV, CNN International, and Fox Kids—nevertheless suggests how significant a market there is for such transnational television. Each channel has been distributed to at least five European nations, while on average these channels have been broadcast to 24 European countries, thereby reaching nearly 40 million European households. A number of such channels have also made significant strides to offer their content in a variety of languages. Euronews, for example, is dubbed into six languages and Eurosport into an impressive 18 (Chalaby 2002: 186, 193–194).

Undoubtedly, the emergence of such a vibrant transnational European TV sector was helped by the deregulation of television channels pushed through by national governments in the 1980s and 1990s. Growth was further promoted by the European Commission, which set out a "Television Without Frontiers" directive in 1991, preventing member states from restricting the transmission of broadcasts from other member states (Collins 1999). The rapid development of satellite and cable television technologies in the wake of such reforms certainly served to disrupt the dominance of national terrestrial channels, although with only rare exceptions such as the license fee-funded Arte did pan-European TV reach beyond the confines of pay television. Indeed, pan-European TV remained limited enough that as of 2002 fewer than half of EU households had access to such channels. Even a channel such as Arte, which is available to almost 62 million (or 89 percent of) French households via the fifth terrestrial channel, has usually gained viewing figures only in the tens of thousands, or around 3 percent of the viewing audience. In Germany, as of 2011, its market share was even smaller at 0.8 percent (*Hamburger Abendblatt* 2011).

With regard to Euronews, the 24-hour news channel that is produced by the European Broadcasting Union (EBU), a consortium owned by 11 member states from Europe, Jean Chalaby found its audience share to be even smaller, although Jostein Gripsrud, quoting figures taken from Euronews's website, claimed that it was reaching more European households (168 million) and attracting a larger daily audience (of 6.5 million) than either CNN or BBC World (Gripsrud 2007: 486; Chalaby 2002: 189). Interestingly, although the European Commission tripled its contribution to Euronews's €60 million running costs in 2011 to €15 million, which enabled the channel to open 11 new offices, viewing figures (based on Euronews' figures from 2012) have moved slightly downwards to a little under 5.4 million, rather than upwards since Gripsrud's 2007 study (Lloyd and Marconi 2014: 63). Such figures suggest that concerted political support for transnational European channels may not have the beneficial effects hoped for by Habermas. But it should also be noted that Euronews's figures suggest they are beating their nearest competitor, CNN, by almost four million viewers (Euronews 2012: 21). In addition, Euronews has established itself as the "world's no. 1 news media on YouTube," based on figures from December 2013 (Association for International Broadcasting 2014).

While the popularity of pan-European TV stations is thus debatable, their reach appears to be broad and growing. Interpreting the impact these channels make is, nevertheless, far from simple. To take Arte's flagship *Metropolis* as an example of a high-cultural program made by a PSB, this program's content and the makeup of the production teams are not quite as cosmopolitan as might be imagined. Rather, the vast majority of the individuals featured in this broadcast were from the production team's home nation: over 90 percent in the case of French program-makers and 85 percent in the case of their German counterparts (Rothenberger 2012: 165–166). Such trends may reflect abiding differences of production style or scarcity of resources; when it comes to commercial channels, however, the challenge for content providers has primarily been to make pan-European content appealing to audiences within the various nations. For instance, the commercial Eurosport network founded by the EBU has generally relied on dubbing as a way of making pan-European sporting events accessible to various European audiences. But the version broadcast in Britain restyled itself in 1999, responding to market surveys that suggested that the British viewing public regarded its European perspective as foreign. British Eurosport went on to ban foreign adverts, adopt the Union Jack as its logo, and send its own reporters to major sporting events so that they could report on them from a British perspective, rather than relying on a dubbed version of a pan-European commentary (Chalaby 2002: 194).

From these two examples of PSBs and commercial channels, it seems that transnational television networks do not necessarily promote a Europeanization of viewing habits or hybridization in terms of how news or cultural output is produced. Part of the reason may be that PSBs have traditionally been funded along national lines and have thus answered an agenda framed in terms of the national interest. And, as the case of British Eurosport shows, when it comes to commercial broadcasters, consumers do not necessarily wish to shop around in an international media market for their news or entertainment, but rather seek out channels that address their specific and distinctive linguistic or cultural capabilities and interests. One of the complexities in analyzing Habermas' claims for the mass media as a factor creating a European public sphere is that television channels operate according to at least two somewhat contradictory logics. On the one hand, they serve the kind of educative function with which PSBs tend to be charged: to disseminate information and provide perspective on political and cultural news as a means of educating a population according to a public mandate. On the other, particularly in the case of commercial broadcasters, they seek to win over the largest audience share, which does not necessarily entail that these broadcasters provide the most comprehensive coverage of political news and debate, particularly in a pan-European context (Latzer and Sauerwein 2006: 14–15). While Habermas has called for more cross-national PSBs to be funded, offering an alternative to commercial media ventures, it is not clear how the effectiveness of such PSBs could be measured. Certainly when it comes to assessing the role of Arte, media analysts tend to focus on viewership figures as they do with most national PSBs. They thereby follow the logic of the market. However, understanding the impact of TV programs on the views and even identities of viewers cannot be adequately done by simply counting up viewer figures; viewers may watch TV programs but that is no guarantee that they subscribe to any message or agenda implicit within these programs (Thomass 2004: 64–73).

Given the above analysis, it does not seem adequate to simply call for a more European media environment without understanding how European media have functioned and what political effects they have had. In spite of Habermas' praise for ventures such as Arte, the consensus on such cultural ventures is that they have not won the attention of more than an educated elite. If we turn our attention briefly to newspapers as a means of comparison, it would appear that the impact of Europeanist ventures may be similarly limited. Certainly prominent national broadsheets such as *Le Monde* and *Die Zeit* have increasingly showcased "European conversations" within which leading national politicians from different nations debate European issues with one another. Furthermore, when it has come to critical issues such as the French vote on the European constitution in 2005, the quality press in France (and in other European countries) uniformly instructed its citizens to vote yes. Yet the population obviously felt free to ignore such instructions (Ulrich 2010). In this important case the evidence for national media having had a decisive impact on Europeans' sentiments about EU policy is by no means overwhelming. It thus seems far from inevitable that transnational European media would result in more popular support for deepening European integration, even if they provided genuinely pan-European news and cultural content and were able to win a significant audience share.

Conclusions

Habermas' recommendations for a restructuring of the European project offer a bold vision for creating a new kind of cosmopolitan democracy in Europe. But the evidence presented in this chapter suggests that they do not fare particularly well against the historical record. The recent history of the European Parliament and the parties within it, the groups functioning in civil society, and pan-European television channels, suggests that, contrary to Habermas' diagnosis, the major cause for the EU's problems is not simply the absence or underdevelopment of adequate forums for debate. Rather, it seems that even the forums and institutions valorized by Habermas do not necessarily serve to promote a pro-integrationist consensus in European society. These European institutions instead continue to serve as battlegrounds within which European integration can be promoted but can equally be agitated against.

Habermas has sketched out a vision of a more democratic Europe than the current EU, which, at least in moments of crisis, seems to be dominated either by an intergovernmental clique or a closed off elite of technocrats.

By contrast, this chapter has drawn attention to the inherent tensions within the different understandings of democracy at play within Europe. For instance, some of the liberal rights—of minorities for instance—that are valorized in countries such as Germany are not necessarily seen as so intrinsic to democracy in eastern European countries such as Poland. Similarly, when measured against the historical record, civil society organizations and political parties do not appear to have always worked collaboratively to reinforce a democratic consensus in that way that Habermas envisages within his ideal type of the European public sphere.

The German postwar experience certainly does illustrate a way in which a nation state can strengthen its legitimacy and boost its economy as it federalizes power both downwards into the regions and upwards to supranational bodies. Yet, it is not clear that the historical experiences of other countries make them inclined or well positioned to follow Germany's path. It is also not entirely clear that the virtuous convergence that occurred between the various measures furthering integration, German economic progress, and political stability for much of the postwar era must continue in the Europe of the 28 or an even larger European Union.

More research into how democracy has already functioned at the national and European levels is clearly required. Such research would entail analyses of how civil society bodies have developed and operated, as well as how institutions such as the national and European parliaments have performed. Additional analysis would enable us to understand how European elites and publics have interacted, and to assess what kinds of outcomes have been promoted when Europeans have practiced democracy simultaneously at national and European levels. Without such research, the gap between optimistic visions of an ideal democratic and integrated Europe and critiques of how an at least partially democratic integrated Europe has functioned may continue to widen and perhaps even become unbridgeable.

References

Alber, J. (2006) "Überlegungen und Daten zur Idee eines "Europäischen Sozialmodells,'" from *Documentation of the conference The Future of the European Social Model: A German Perspective*, 3–4 November 2005. (ed. by Intitut fur Sozialpädagogik). Retrieved from www.soziale-dienste-in-europa.de/dokumente/Aktuelles/zukunft-esm-eine-deutsche-perspektive2005.pdf (last accessed: March 2, 2016).

Alliance des Démocrates et des Libéraux pour l'Europe (2010) *European Federalism*. Retrieved from www.learneurope.eu/files/5413/7457/7801/European_federalism.pdf (last accessed: March 2, 2016).

Almeida, D. (2012) *The Impact of European Integration on Political Parties: Beyond the Permissive Consensus*. Abingdon: Routledge.

Association for International Broadcasting (2014) Retrieved from www.aib.org.uk/euronews-record-viewing-figures-on-youtube/ (last accessed: March 2, 2016).

Bailey, C. (2013) *Between Yesterday and Tomorrow: German Visions of Europe, 1926–1950*. New York and Oxford: Berghahn Books.

Bale, T., and Hanley, S. S. (2010) "'May Contain Nuts?' The Reality behind the Rhetoric Surrounding the British Conservatives New Group in the European Parliament," *The Political Quarterly*, 81(1), pp. 85–98.
Bale, T., and Szczerbiak, A. (2008) "Why Is There No Christian Democracy in Poland—And Why Should We Care?" in *Party Politics*, 14(4), pp. 479–500.
Beck, U. (2013) *German Europe*. Cambridge: Polity Press.
Beck, U., and Cohn-Bendit, D. (2012) "Der grosse Sprung zurück," in *Die Zeit*, 25 October, retrieved from: www.zeit.de/2012/44/Replik-Beck-Cohn-Bendit (last accessed: March 2, 2016).
Bermeo, N., and Nord, P. (eds.) (2000) *Civil Society before Democracy: Lessons from Nineteenth-Century Europe*. Lanham: Rowman and Littlefield.
Bild Zeitung (2015) 'Nein! Keine weiteren Miliarden für die gierigen Griechen', in *Bild Zeitung*, 26 February, retrieved from: www.bild.de/politik/inland/griechenland-krise/keine-weiteren-milliarden-fuer-die-gierigen-griechen-39925224.bild.html (last accessed: March 2, 2016).
Bulmer, S., Jeffries, C., and Paterson, W. E. (eds.) (2000) *Germany's European Diplomacy: Shaping the Regional Milieu*. Manchester: Manchester University Press.
Bundeszentrale für politische Bildung (2010) *Mitgliedsstaaten der Europäischen Union*. Retrieved from www.bpb.de: file://userdata/documents2/cb24262/Downloads/4RT2SN.pdf (last accessed: March 2, 2016).
CDU, D. (1992) *Protokoll 3. Parteitag der CDU Deutschlands*, Dusseldorf, October 26–28. Retrieved from Konrad Adenauer Stiftung: www.kas.de/upload/ACDP/CDU/Protokolle_Parteitage/1992-10-26-28_Protokoll_03.Parteitag_Duesseldorf.pdf (last accessed: March 2, 2016).
Chalaby, J. (2002) "Transnational Television in Europe: The Role of Pan-European Channels," *European Journal of Communication*, 17(2), pp. 183–203.
Collins, R. (1999) "The European Union Audiovisual Policies of the UK and France," in M. Scriven, and M. Lecomte (eds.), *Television Broadcasting in Contemporary France and Britain*. New York and Oxford: Berghahn Books, pp. 198–221.
Conway, M., and Depkat, V. (2010) "Towards a European History of the Discourse of Democracy: Discussing Democracy in Western Europe, 1945–60," in M. Conway, and K. K. Patel (eds.), *Europeanization in the Twentieth Century: Historical Approaches*. Basingstoke: Palgrave Macmillan, pp. 132–156.
Conze, V. (2005) *Das Europa der Deutschen: Ideen von Europa in Deutschland zwischen Reichstradition und Westorientierung*. Munich: Oldenbourg.
Crossland, D. (2012) "The World from Berlin: Germany's Power 'Is Causing Fear' in Europe," in *Der Spiegel*, February 1, 2012. Retrieved from www.spiegel.de/international/europe/the-world-from-berlin-germany-s-power-is-causing-fear-in-europe-a-812715.html (last accessed: March 2, 2016).
Deutsche Presse-Agentur (2012) "Mehrheit der Deutschen hofft auf Sieg der Euro-Gegner," in *Die Ziet*, 7 September, 2012. Retrieved from www.zeit.de/politik/deutschland/2012-09/euro-skepsis-verfassungsklage (last accessed: March 2, 2016).
Embacher, S. (2010) *Zivilgesellschaft und Sozialdemokratie in Europa. Aktuelle Entwicklungen und normative Perspektiven*. Berlin: Friedrich-Ebert-Stiftung.
Euronews (2012) *Euronews: Media Kit 2012*. Retrieved from: www.euronews.com/media/download/mediapack/euronews_media_kit_2012_English.pdf (last accessed: March 2, 2016).
European Commission, T. P. (2013). *Flash Barometer 373: Europeans' Engagement in Participatory Democracy*. Retrieved from: http://ec.europa.eu/public_opinion/flash/fl_373_en.pdf (last accessed: March 2, 2016).

Eurostat IDEA [International Institute for Democracy and Electoral Assistance] (2015) *Voter turnout in national and EU parliamentary elections*. Retrieved from Eurostat: http://ec.europa.eu/eurostat/tgm/refreshTableAction.do?tab=table&plugin=1&pcode=tsdgo310&language=en (last accessed: March 2, 2016).

Friedrich, D. (2011) *Democratic Participation and Civil Society in the European Union*. Manchester: Manchester University Press.

Gfeller, A. É., Loth, W., and Schulz, M. (2011) "Democratizing Europe, Reaching to the Citizen? The Transforming Powers of the European Parliament," in *Journal of European Integration History*, 1 (2011), pp. 5–12.

Glenn, J. (2001) *Framing Democracy: Civil Society and Civic Movements in Eastern Europe*. Stanford: Stanford University Press.

Gripsrud, J. (2007) "Television and the European Public Sphere," *European Journal of Communication*, 22(4), pp. 479–492.

Grzymala-Busse, A. (2013) "Why There is (Almost) no Christian Democracy in Post-communist Europe," *Party Politics*, 19(2), pp. 319–342.

Habermas, J. (2001) "Why Europe Needs a Constitution," *New Left Review*, 11, pp. 5–26.

Habermas, J. (2012) *The Crisis of the European Union: A Response*. Cambridge: Polity Press.

Habermas, J. (2015) "Warum Merkels Griechenland Politik ein Fehler ist," *Süddeutsche Zeitung*, 22 June, 2015. Retrieved from: www.sueddeutsche.de/wirtschaft/europa-sand-im-getriebe-1.2532119 (last accessed: March 2, 2016).

Hamburger Abendblatt (2011) "Arte will mit Formatfernsehen mehr Zuschauer gewinnen," *Hamburger Abendblatt*, 15 November, 2011. Retrieved from www.abendblatt.de/kultur-live/article108170655/Arte-will-mit-Formatfernsehen-mehr-Zuschauer-gewinnen.html (last accessed: March 2, 2016).

Hebel, C., and Schmitz, G. P. (2013) "Euroskeptic Union: Right-Wing Populists Forge EU Alliance," *Der Spiegel*, November 13, 2013. Retrieved from: www.spiegel.de/international/europe/wilders-and-le-pen-plan-right-wing-populist-faction-in-eu-parliament-a-933340.html (last accessed: March 2, 2016).

Heckmann, J. (2009) "Wollt Ihr den totalen EU-Staat?!," *Neue Rheinische Zeitung*, 9 September, 2009. Retrieved from: www.nrhz.de/flyer/beitrag.php?id=14223 (last accessed: March 2, 2016).

Hix, S., Noury, A., and Roland, G. (2005) "Power to the Parties: Cohesion and Competition in the European Parliament, 1979–2001," *British Journal of Political Science*, 35(2), pp. 209–234.

Hoffmann, G. (2007) "Polnische Verkrümmung," *Die Zeit*, June 20, 2007. Retrieved from: www.zeit.de/2007/26/EU-Polen (last accessed: March 2, 2016).

Jones, E., Menon, A., and Weatherill, S. (2012) *The Oxford Handbook of the European Union*. Oxford: Oxford University Press.

Judt, T. (2005) *Postwar: A History of Europe after 1945*. London: Penguin.

Kaletsky, A. (2012) "Can the rest of Europe stand up to Germany?" *Reuters*, 20 June, 2012. Retrieved from: http://blogs.reuters.com/anatole-kaletsky/2012/06/20/can-the-rest-of-europe-stand-up-to-germany/ (last accessed: March 2, 2016).

Katzenstein, P. (ed.) (1993) *Tamed Power: Germany in Europe*. Ithaca and London: Cornell University Press.

Kogon, E. (1946) "Demokratie und Föderalismus," *Frankfurte Hefte 1*, 6(74), pp. 69–75.

Kohler-Koch, B. (2011) *The Role of Civil Society beyond Lisbon*. Retrieved from

Maastricht Monnet Paper Series, No. 2: www.mceg-maastricht.eu/pdf/2011(2)%20 Kohler-Koch.pdf (last accessed: March 2, 2016).

Kripa, M. (2012a) "Die Krisenausschuss," *Die Zeit*, October 31, 2012. Retrieved from: www.zeit.de/2012/45/Europa-Krise-Finanzminister-Waehrungsunion (last accessed: March 2, 2016).

Kripa, M. (2012b) "Im Schatten der Väter," *Die Zeit*, December 13, 2012. Retrieved from: www.zeit.de/2012/51/Europa-Schatten-der-Vaeter (last accessed: March 2, 2016).

Lacroix, J., and Nicolaïdis, K. (eds.) (2010) *European Stories: Intellectual Debates on Europe in National Context*. Oxford: Oxford University Press.

Lange, C. (2004) "Third-Sector Organizations in the Process of Regional Integration: EU Enlargement and Social NGOs—A German Perspective?" Paper presented at the *Sixth International Conference of the International Society for Third-Sector Research*, July 11–14, 2004. Retrieved from: www.istr.org/resource/resmgr/working_papers_toronto/lange.chris.pdf (last accessed: March 2, 2016).

Latzer, M., and Sauerwein, F. (2006) "Europäisierung durch Medien: Ansätze und Erkenntnisse Öffentlichkeitsforschung," in W. R. Langenbucher, and M. Latzer (eds.) *Europäische Öffentlichkeit und medialer Wandel. Eine tranzdisciplinäre Perspektive*. Wiesbaden: VS Verlag für Sozialwissenschaften, pp. 10–44.

Lloyd, J., and Marconi, C. (2014) *Reporting the EU: News, Media and the European Institutions*. London: I. B. Tauris.

Luschny, W. (2009) "Leben am Rhein: Europäisierung im Alltag am Beispiel Strasbourg/Kehl," in M. Vogt (ed.) *Europäisierung im Alltag*. Frankfurt a.M.: Peter Lang, pp. 23–35.

Mach, Z., and Gora, M. (2010) "Between Old Fears and New Challenges. The Polish Debate about Europe," in Lacroix, and Nicolaïdis (eds.) *European Stories*. Oxford: Oxford University Press, pp. 221–240.

Manoli, P., and Maris, G. (2014) "The role of the European Parliament in managing the international economic crisis," in S. Stavridis, and D. Irrera (eds.) *The European Parliament and Its International Relations*. New York: Routledge, pp. 70–91.

Medrano, J. D. (2010) "Europe's Political Identity: Public Sphere and Public Opinion," in Lacroix and Nicolaïdis (eds.) *European Stories*. Oxford: Oxford University Press, pp. 315–333.

Milward, A. (2000) *The European Rescue of the Nation state*. 2nd edn. Abingdon: Routledge.

Müller, G. (2005) *Europäische Gesellschaftsbeziehungen nach dem Ersten Weltkrieg: Das Deutsch-Französische Studienkomitee und der Europäische Kulturbund*. Munich: Oldenbourg.

Müller, J.-W. (2008) "'Our Philadelphia?' Understanding the (Apparent) Failure of the European Constitution," *The Journal of Modern European History*, 6(1), pp. 137–153.

Müller, J.-W. (2011) *Contesting Democracy: Political Ideas in Twentieth-Century Europe*. New Haven: Yale University Press.

Paeschke, H. (1947) "Verantwortlichkeit des Geistes," in *Merkur: Deutsche Zeitschrift für Europäisches Denken*, 1(1947), pp. 100–108.

Peter, J. (2004) "Kaum vorhanden, thematisch homogene und eher negativ—Die alltägliche Fernsehberichterstattung über die Europäische Union im internationalen Vergleich," in L. Hagen (ed.) *Europäische Union und mediale Öffentlichkeit. Theoretische Perspektiven und empirische Befunde zur Rolle der Medien im europäischen Einigungsprozess*. Cologne: Halem, pp. 146–161.

Reilly, G. (2012) "'Memorandum macht frei': how one Greek paper views the second bailout," *The Journal*, 10 February, 2012. Retrieved from: www.thejournal.ie/memorandum-macht-frei-how-one-greek-paper-views-the-second-bailout-351455-Feb2012/ (last accessed: March 2, 2016).

Rittberger, B. (2011) *Building Europe's Parliament: Democratic Representation beyond the Nation state.* Oxford: Oxford University Press.

Rothenberger, L. (2012) "ARTE—Problems of Creating a European TV. Intercultural Aspects at Micro, Meso and Macro Level at the European Cultural Channel Arte," *Communicación y Sociedad*, 25(2), pp. 145–174.

Saraceno, C. (2009) "Concepts and Practices of Social Citizenship in Europe: The Case of Poverty and Income Support for the Poor," in J. Alber, and N. Gilbert (eds.) *United in Diversity: Comparing Social Models in Europe and America.* Oxford: Oxford University Press, pp. 151–175.

Steffek, J., Kissling, C., and Nanz, P. (eds.) (2007) *Civil Society Participation in European and Global Governance: A Cure for the Democratic Deficit?* Basingstoke: Palgrave Macmillan.

Thomass, B. (2004) "Public Sector Broadcasting als Faktor einer europäischen Öffentlichkeit," in L. Hagen (ed.) *Europäische Union und mediale Öffentlichkeit.* Köln: Herbert von Halem Verlag, pp. 47–63.

Ulrich, B. (2010) "Nicht ohne Volk!," *Die Zeit*, 31 May, 2010. Retrieved from: www.zeit.de/2010/22/Habermas-Replik/komplettansicht (last accessed: March 2, 2016).

Union of European Federalists. (2015) *Europa Union Deutschland.* Retrieved from: www.federalists.eu/members/germany/ (last accessed: March 2, 2016).

von Beste, R., Dohmen, F., Leick, R., Puhl, J., Schlamp, H.-J., and Traufetter, G. (2005) "Europa im Jahre Null," *Der Spiegel*, 6 June, 2005, pp. 94–105.

von Fröhlingsdorf, M., Hawranek, D., Klawitter, N., Mahler, A., Martens, H., and Tietz, J. (2004) "Der Presis des neuen Europa," *Der Spiegel*, 26 April, 2004, pp. 100–114.

Wangerin, C. (2008) "Die Informationspflicht liegt bei der Regierung," *Junge Welt*, 16 May, 2008. Retrieved from: www.jungewelt.de/loginFailed.php?ref=/2008/05-16/031.php?sstr=referendum%7Clissabon%7Cvertrag (last accessed: March 2, 2016).

Wingert-Beckmann, C. (ed.) (2010) *Aktive europäische Zivilgesellschaft in Deutschland: Die Europäische Union fordert Projekte zivilgesellschaftlicher Organisationen.* Bonn: Kontaktstelle Deutschland "Europa für Bürgerinnen und Bürger."

Winkler, H. A. (2005) *Was hält Europa zusammen?* Retrieved from www.bosch-stiftung.de/content/language2/downloads/vortrag_winkler.pdf (last accessed: March 2, 2016).

2 Habermas on Human Dignity as the Origin of Human Rights and Egalitarian, Utopian Thinking

Jennifer Fredette

Jürgen Habermas' (2012b) *The Crisis of the European Union* includes a short essay meditating on human dignity as the secular origin of equality and human rights (75). In the essay, entitled "The Concept of Human Dignity and the Realistic Utopia of Human Rights," Habermas argues that human dignity brings an uncompromising and universal form of morality into the concrete, empirical world of positive law. Habermas claims that, due to its universality, the concept of human dignity surpasses individual nation states, thereby providing a shared justification for the protection of human rights across Europe that has the potential to generate deeper political integration.

In this way, human dignity is an integral part of Habermas' cosmopolitan hopes for the European Union. Eriksen (2013) maintains that "A minimal definition of cosmopolitanism is that the ultimate units of concern are *persons*–rather than groups, nations or states" (13, emphasis in original). And yet, cosmopolitanism is not purely individualistic: "Persons are ultimate units of concern for *everyone*" (ibid., emphasis in original). As Genna and Wilson point out in this book's introduction, a "cosmopolitan view of the world," according to Habermas, "sees an injustice done on one person as an offense against everyone's moral sensibility." Within this shared, cosmopolitan "we," the political units are individuals, but they are individuals who regard all other individuals within the transnational community as equals, and thus deserving of respect. Elsewhere, Habermas has suggested that "the European Union can be understood as an important step on the path toward a politically constituted world society" (Habermas 2012a: 336).

But there is no guarantee that the European Union will necessarily produce such cosmopolitan ends. *The Crisis of the European Union* is largely a critique of what Habermas sees as the European Union's "economistic narrowing of vision" during the financial crisis (Habermas 2012b: 3). The European Union, he laments, is turning toward a kind of "post-democratic executive federalism" that privileges financial markets and powerful nation states over the democratic will of the people while also undermining the very idea of a shared European citizenry (ibid.: 12).

In his essay on human dignity, Habermas argues that a renewed focus on dignity is the key to strengthening international cooperation and democratic commitments within the European Union. Human dignity certainly has transnational appeal across Europe, and it appears—at least, at first glance—to provide consistent universal interpretations of human rights. The attractiveness of such a concept for a European Union that is reeling from recession and increased Euroskepticism is obvious. When we examine the use of human dignity within jurisprudence across Europe, we see the moral gravity Habermas describes; we also see, however, profound inconsistencies in its legal application, both within and among nation states. Furthermore, while Habermas looks to human dignity to expand and deepen respect for human rights, courts have sometimes used the concept to justify violating human rights. The ambiguity of the concept in practice may threaten the international cooperation and cosmopolitan European solidarity that Habermas hopes it will inspire.

Despite these reservations, we still must contend with Habermas' argument about the utility of human dignity for the expansion of rights and equality. He is grappling with a central question of political philosophy: what government owes us, what we owe government, and what we owe one another. Habermas' answer is intended as a radically egalitarian one: we owe one another the fullest respect of our rights out of a recognition of everyone's equal worth and equal citizenship. Ultimately, however, additional work must be done to ensure that the concept of human dignity fulfills its egalitarian promise while also deepening integration and fostering European solidarity.

Habermas and the Concept of Human Dignity: "Kant-plus"

Habermas (2012b) acknowledges that human rights entered into national constitutions and the international legal lexicon prior to human dignity, but maintains it would be a mistake to assume that human dignity is a secondary concept, merely derived from human rights (73). In his view, human rights and dignity have always had a "close conceptual connection," but there is a clear directional relationship between the two: it is human dignity that provides the "moral 'source' from which all of the basic rights derive their sustenance" (ibid.: 75). When Habermas describes human dignity as "the moral source" of all basic rights, he is not referring to religious morality, but rather to the notion that human dignity is more than a political or legal invention. Policies and laws can be amended and suspended. For Habermas, human dignity is a "moral" value in the sense that it is a higher order of obligation: universal, authoritative, and unwavering. Habermas uses a litany of metaphors to describe the significance, and direction, of the relationship between human dignity and human rights: we are told human dignity is a "catalyst" in the construction of rights (ibid.); a "seismograph" that measures the importance of competing rights within democracies (ibid.: 81); a "portal" through which the moral commitment to equality is brought into law (ibid.); and a "hinge" connecting the moral value of equal respect to the legal world of human rights (ibid.: 81, 83).

Metaphors aside, what does Habermas actually mean by human dignity? His is a complex account; in part because it synthesizes what Jeremy Waldron (2009) describes as two divergent accounts of human dignity. Waldron proposes that "There are 'absolute worth' accounts of dignity and there are 'ranking status' accounts" (Waldron 2009: 222). The difference merits explanation because it helps us to understand what Habermas is attempting to accomplish with his theory of human dignity.

According to Waldron (2009), absolute worth accounts of human dignity suggest that all individuals have dignity by virtue of their humanity, which has been variously defined by different proponents of this view of human dignity. Within Catholic teaching, Waldron reminds us, humanity is defined by its likeness to God; because all humans are created in the image of God, they all have some irreducible worth (ibid.: 227–228).[1] For Immanuel Kant (2002), humanity also has absolute worth, but he locates its source in a different place than Catholic theologians: he defines humanity by its capacity for rational thinking (Kant 2002: 5). "Reason," he writes, "has been imparted to us as a practical faculty" (ibid.: 12). In his *Groundwork for the Metaphysics of Morals*, Kant develops a system of ethics[2] in which the morality of an action stems from its adherence to universal principles that humans can identify by virtue of this capacity for reason, and not from the consequences of the action (ibid.: 17). This means that everyone must be free to exercise his or her own rationality and thereby discover and choose to obey universal moral principles; to impede someone from doing so would deny his[3] rationality, and therefore worth and very humanity (ibid.: 48). Another way to say this is that humans should treat other humans as ends rather than means, as to do otherwise would subjugate the ends of one to the ends of another, which constitutes a failure to respect another's human rationality. This particular commandment—all humans must be treated as ends in themselves, with their own capacity for reason, and never as means to another's end—is sometimes referred to as the "categorical imperative" (ibid.: 37).[4]

We see in both the Catholic and Kantian examples that absolute worth accounts of human dignity are premised on the idea of an a priori moral belief in the fundamental sameness or worth (however defined) of all humans, and that this worth demands recognition. Waldron (2009) argues that the same is not true, however, for ranking accounts of human dignity.

Ranking status accounts of human dignity, according to Waldron (2009), remind us that the concept of "dignity" was initially developed in the decidedly non-egalitarian context of nobility. He highlights the presumption of hierarchy within ranking status accounts of dignity when he notes that those who were dignified through a noble title or rank had access to rights and privileges that others without that title or rank did not (ibid.: 230). In ranking status accounts of human dignity, the law extends the rights and privileges that were traditionally reserved for nobility to all persons.[5]

Kant (2002) adheres to an absolute worth account of human dignity grounded in a theory of morality; Waldron (2009) indicates that he favors the "ranking status" account that is made possible by the revolutionary extension of nobility through the law. And yet, in his essay on human dignity, Habermas (2012b) proposes that both absolute worth and ranking status accounts inform the concept of human dignity. Habermas describes the *moral* obligation of respect for human dignity in terms of "the absolute worth of the person" (ibid.: 89); he also states that today's *legal* concept of human dignity is "conferred by the status of democratic citizenship" (ibid.: 87). What Waldron describes as two separate interpretations of the concept of human dignity, absolute worth and ranking status, Habermas describes as two different modes of obligation to human dignity: moral and legal ("legal," as in, within positive law).

Habermas (2012b) describes human rights (those legal tools he believes were subsequently developed for the defense of the preexisting concept of human dignity) as having a "Janus face turned simultaneously to morality and to law" (ibid.: 82). It is the notion of human dignity, argues Habermas (ibid.), that makes this "improbable synthesis" of morality and law possible (ibid.: 83). The genealogy of human dignity that Habermas sketches reveals a concept that was initially rooted in rank and status but that, through the intervention of natural law thinkers like Kant, developed into a notion of the fundamental worth of individuals.[6] He concludes that human dignity continues to bear both connotations, and that this is what invests human rights with a universal moral charge to defend the equal worth of all individuals while securing the support of the state and its legal apparatus of positive law to do so. Perhaps the best summary of Habermas' concept of human dignity is that it is a moral sensibility animated by a belief in the fundamental, equal worth of all individuals, but expressed in the positive legal language of a status that demands equal recognition.

Habermas' essay urges the European Union to refocus on human dignity precisely because he believes its grand and universal moral charge (in addition to its legal power) can generate the kind of trust and mutual respect that is required for European cosmopolitanism. This is presented in stark contrast to what Habermas sees as the current, divisive focus on the economy. I would argue (along with Habermas, I believe) that a narrow focus on the economy also risks violating the Kantian categorical imperative by using certain nations as a means for the ends of others; we see this reflected in headlines musing about the need to "sacrifice Greece to save [the] Euro" (Elliot, Wintour, and Treanor 2012) or "sacrifice Greece to save Spain" (Nixon 2015).

There is no doubt that Habermas is deeply influenced by Kant's moral account for human dignity. Habermas (2012b) provides as an example of this Kantian view of human dignity in the German Constitutional Court's famous decision to overturn the Aviation Security Act of 2005 (ibid.: 72). In 2006, the German Federal Constitutional Court (FCC) determined that the government could not command the military to shoot down a hijacked plane, even if that plane would be maliciously flown into civilians below, because that would treat the doomed air passengers as a means rather than an end and thereby violate these passengers' human dignity (ibid.). The reasoning of the court, Habermas states, "unmistakably reecho[s] Kant's categorical imperative" in that it refuses to allow security forces to treat the passengers as a means to the safety of people on the ground (ibid.). Waldron (2009: 221) describes this case as "the legal use of a Kantian conception of dignity as a simple conception of human worth precluding trade-offs."[7]

And yet, Kantian ethics fall short of the true egalitarian ideal Habermas is pursuing. As stated earlier, Kant's account of human dignity is grounded in the notion of rationality. Judith Failer (2002) highlights the limitations of human dignity in Kant's account by focusing on the mentally ill, whom the state may place in civil commitment (despite their will and in violation of their rights) precisely because it has determined them to legally lack rationality. Failer notes there is a litany of other groups Kant believed lacked, or could not properly exercise without the assistance of others, the capacity for rationality, including women, servants, minors, "Indian smiths, tutors, and sharecroppers" (ibid.: 39).

One way to read Habermas' treatment of human dignity in *The Crisis of the European Union* is as an attempt to correct the shortcomings of Kant's work on the same concept. In an effort to be as inclusive as possible, Habermas (2012b) chooses to root human dignity within humanity itself—a category that humans cannot be excluded from as easily as rationality. In this way, Habermas bypasses Kant's problematic reliance on rationality as the ground for human dignity.

This egalitarian effort creates a daunting legal difficulty, however. In his essay, Habermas (2012b) is notoriously vague about the legal content of human dignity. We are told that it is universal, that everyone has it by virtue of being human, and that we know what it is because we all share it. Legal institutions, however, function in specifics; without guidance from Habermas as to the specific content of human dignity, how can we know when it has been violated?

My central contention is that Habermas' attempt to provide a truly universal moral basis for human dignity produces confusion as to its legal content, and hence his account of human dignity cannot provide answers about how the law and human rights must work to respect and defend it. This confusion, I will argue, is likely to weigh heaviest on the shoulders of those who are already marginalized within European society—quite the opposite of Habermas' goal. And yet, we should not be quick to jettison Habermas' efforts to ground human rights within what he describes as their progenitor, human dignity. As Habermas (2012b) persuasively argues within his essay, there is a competing view of human rights today, referred to as "minimalist," which stands to water down these legal protections. In the next section of this paper, I describe how Habermas' discussion of human dignity forces us to confront the shortcomings of minimalist conceptions of human rights. In the section that follows, I discuss the legal confusion that nevertheless arises within Habermas' account of human dignity. I then conclude by discussing why Habermas' account of human dignity is limited as a tool for building a cosmopolitan Europe.

Habermas' Account of Human Dignity as a Challenge to "Rights Minimalists"

One of Habermas' aims in his essay on human dignity is to challenge those contemporary theorists who propose an alternative, dignity-free narrative for the foundation of human rights. This alternative narrative of human rights is expounded by what Habermas calls human rights minimalists, a category that includes theorists like Michael Ignatieff (2003) and Kenneth Baynes (2009a; 2009b). They seek to peel rights away from natural law theory and morality and to provide far more modest, or pragmatic, foundations for human rights.

Ignatieff (2003) encourages us to shrink the list of human rights to only the most basic, such as the right to physical security. He posits that when grand and universal narratives about the source and content of human rights are applied to our multicultural world, those grand narratives, no matter how well intentioned, may amount to normative imperialism and censure those people and cultures who define the good life differently (ibid.: 74). Ignatieff also argues that certain democratic rights, like the right to self-determination, may ignite secessionist violence that disrupts the human right to bodily security; in other words, too elaborate a system of human rights may undermine the first and foremost right of security (ibid.: 29). The echoes of Isaiah Berlin's (1990) "Two Concepts of Liberty" are clear: human rights minimalists are deeply concerned about the incompatibility between different types of rights, and the tendency of expansive (or, as Berlin would say, "positive") conceptions of rights to reduce the level of protection given to the most basic (or "negative") rights.

Baynes (2009a) similarly argues for more pragmatic foundations for human rights, grounding them in international political and legal discourse. He argues we should locate the source of human rights in political debate and decision-making about who is a member of the community. In this view, the process of determining political membership produces the content and defines the borders of human rights (ibid.: 385). Baynes calls this a political conception of human rights; Habermas calls it minimalist. Either way, according to Baynes, this conception merely sets aside (rather than rejecting or forcing consensus on) divisive metaphysical questions. In his words, it is an "undertheorized agreement," one more prone to produce actual agreement and, hence, cooperation on the protection of rights (ibid.).[8]

Habermas complains that the minimalist view of human rights gets the human dignity–human rights equation backwards. Drawing on Baynes, Habermas (2012b) states that minimalists propose that "everyone is respected in his human dignity as a subject of equal rights" (ibid.: 99).

Herein lies the trouble, according to Habermas: in the minimalist conception of human rights, human dignity is respected because individuals have equal rights. Unfortunately, human rights, unlike Habermas' conception of human dignity, are not universal or equal. This could mean a variable respect for human dignity.

Furthermore, Habermas depicts the minimalist approach to human rights as a race to the bottom. Habermas concedes, along with minimalists, that human rights are often violated, but disagrees with the minimalist premise that limiting legal discourse to only those articulations of rights that are realistic or pragmatic will produce effective limits on state action. If we set the bar for human dignity at the level of human rights as they are currently respected throughout the international community, we debase human dignity, stripping it of what Habermas sees as its power as a moral obligation. In Habermas' (2012b) words, such a conception of human rights "relaxes the claim of human rights by cutting them off from their essential moral thrust, the protection of the equal dignity of every human being" (ibid.: 98).

Legal Confusion Within Habermas' Account of Human Dignity

Two paradoxes within Habermas' concept of human dignity raise questions about its application within legal institutions. On their own, they do not invalidate Habermas' argument. Still, they point to circumstances where human dignity may, contrary to Habermas' claims, justify the denial of human rights and hamper international cooperation. To develop a means of addressing these challenges, we must first identify them.

Paradox 1: How Do We Recognize Human Dignity—Through Reason or Feeling?

While Habermas is openly influenced by a Kantian view of human dignity as "fundamental worth," he does not derive rights in exactly the same way that Kant would. For Kant, the appropriate treatment of others derives from rational thought and adherence to universal laws, not intuition or feeling.[9] If we apply Kantian ethics to the political, we presumably would identify rights through a bloodless process of rational discovery. In a clarifying footnote of his translation of Kant (2002), Wood states "In the Metaphysics of Morals, Kant lists four feelings that are produced directly by reason and can serve as moral motivation. These are 'moral feeling,' 'conscience,' 'love of human beings,' and 'respect'" (ibid.: 17). Nevertheless, Kant seems hesitant to attribute to emotion the ability to correctly identify that which is morally right:

> Those who cannot think believe they can help themselves out by feeling when it comes to universal laws, even though feelings, which

by nature are infinitely distinguished from one another in degree, cannot yield an equal standard of good and evil, nor can one validly judge for others at all through his feeling.

(Kant 2002: 60)

Habermas, however, tells us that the emotional state of outrage is vital in alerting us to violations of dignity. In his words, "The appeal to human rights feeds off the outrage of the humiliated at the violation of their human dignity" (2012b: 75). With this reference to outrage, Habermas' Kantian take on the source of human rights takes a rather un-Kantian detour into the world of emotion. This is also apparent in Habermas' discussion of humiliation. Habermas states that "the background intuition of humiliation forces its way first into the consciousness of suffering individuals and then into the legal texts, where it finds conceptual articulation and elaboration" as new human rights (ibid.: 78). Outrage and humiliation appear to be central, for Habermas, to the recognition of violations of the supposedly universal concept of human dignity.

Why is this significant? Habermas speaks of human dignity as a universal concept, similar to how Kant does: it is "is one and the same everywhere and for everyone" (Habermas 2012b: 80). And yet, Habermas anchors human dignity in subjective feelings like outrage and humiliation. Even if we accept Habermas' premise that human dignity itself is universal, we are left to wonder whether its recognition, which is apparently driven by emotions, will be. Consider Martin Luther King, Jr.'s (1963) address at the March on Washington, when he claimed that children of color were "robbed of their dignity by signs stating: 'For Whites Only.'" Civil rights activists felt outrage at such violations of human dignity, but many other Americans, including elected officials, did not share in this sense of outrage and continued to defend segregation. Habermas states that outrage is what informs a demand for rights. But if we do not share the same sense of outrage experienced by those whose dignity we have violated and who demand rights to rectify the situation, we might remain unresponsive to their rights claims. Habermas does not describe for us the process whereby outrage or humiliation could potentially turn into political empathy.

This is particularly problematic because, as Essed (2009) points out, humiliation can be used as a tool for egalitarian struggles, or for the maintenance of hierarchy. She claims that while humiliation can be used by the oppressed "to take revenge" for the infliction of pain, it can also "discourage or … punish resistance against oppression" (ibid.: 132). She provides the example of what she describes as "humiliating tolerance" for ethnic minorities within the Netherlands, which has the effect of emphasizing the "otherness" of minorities and minimizing their demands for greater inclusion, all while celebrating the supposedly enlightened attitude of the Dutch toward difference (ibid.: 137). In short, the most concrete clue within Habermas' essay for the identification of human dignity and its violations proves to be of indeterminate use.

Paradox 2: What Happens When Two Visions of Human Dignity Collide Within the Courts? Four European Examples

Christopher McCrudden (2008) provides many examples of how human dignity is articulated differently in courts across Europe (and the world). One of the reasons for this heterogeneity, he observes, is that human dignity can be understood in individualistic and communitarian ways (McCrudden 2008: 699). Rao (2011) states that communitarian expressions of human dignity "require *living a certain way*" (italics in original) and, as such, are anchored in "ideas of appropriateness" (Rao 2011: 187). Unsurprisingly, there will sometimes be tension between human dignity "in the sense of advancing individual liberty based upon the choice of the individual" and the "use of dignity to express a communitarian ideal" (McCrudden 2008: 699). Habermas' account of human dignity does not help us navigate these situations. To illustrate this, I provide four examples of legal disputes in Europe that demonstrate the variable application of the concept of human dignity in the courts. This potentially poses a challenge for European legal integration and highlights the difficulty of using Habermas' concept to shape legal and political action.

In the 1990s, French citizen Manuel Wackenheim found employment working in bars and clubs in France (Kirby 2002). Outfitted in a protective, padded suit, Wackenheim, who has dwarfism, worked in a clubbing activity named "dwarf-tossing." Bar and club patrons paid money to see how far they could throw Wackenheim. The mayor of Monsang-sur-Orge demanded a ban on all dwarf-tossing in his municipality. Wackenheim sued, saying that the mayor was violating his right to earn a living: he had been unemployed previously, and this was an important source of income. Wackenheim also claimed the ban infringed on his right to private and family life, and his right to non-discrimination (Rosen 2012). France's highest administrative court, the Conseil d'État (Council of State), ruled in *27 Octobre 1995, Commune de Morsang-sur-Orge* that "the respect for human dignity is one of the components of public order" and that "the authority invested with municipal police power can, even in the absence of particular local circumstances, ban an attraction that threatens respect for human dignity." This was the first time the Council of State presented human dignity as part of the public order (Rogoff 2011). When Wackenheim's legal appeals failed, he sought out assistance from the European Court of Human Rights (ECtHR) and the UN Human Rights Committee; they both sided with France (Rosen 2012; Kirby 2002).

Wackenheim's case set an important, new legal precedent in France: it entered "human dignity" into the realm of public order considerations. Agents of the state endowed with public order police powers would henceforth be empowered to forbid those actions that they deemed to be in violation of the notion of human dignity. It should also be noted that the Council of State expresses here a communitarian notion of human dignity: the respect for human dignity needed to be shown not simply to Wackenheim by obtaining his consent for the job, but to the shared norms and values of the town that deemed such an activity to be an assault on human worth.

Wackenheim himself insisted that dwarf-tossing is not a violation of human dignity. We are stuck in the conundrum Habermas introduces: not all parties involved experience the same sense of outrage in the face of dwarf-tossing. Wackenheim claimed that there was no work in France for people of short stature, and that in banning dwarf-tossing, the commune of Morsang-sur-Orge scared event promoters away from hiring dwarf-tossing acts, effectively eliminating his most viable employment option. In his appeal before the UN Human Rights Committee (2002: sec. 3), Wackenheim argued that "his job does not constitute an affront to human dignity since dignity consists in having a job." Wackenheim turns the mayor's argument on its head by claiming that dwarf-tossing was salutary to his sense of fundamental worth as a human because it provided an otherwise evasive opportunity for paid employment.

While Habermas might bristle at this conflation of economics with human dignity, it can be argued that Wackenheim's economic claim relates to a very Kantian moral value: that of personal autonomy. Wackenheim identifies a relationship between employability and self-determination.[10] He is not alone in doing so: a key aspect of the European Union's human rights regime involves protecting the right to labor: after all, Article 15 of the Charter of Fundamental Rights of the European Union states "Everyone has the right to engage in work and to pursue a freely chosen or accepted occupation."

Wackenheim and French officials essentially disagreed about the meaning of human dignity. The mayor and the Council of State argued that human dignity means the equal worth of all persons, and that activities that derive their amusement from mocking the condition of dwarfism violate that notion of equal worth. No one individual has the right to engage in an activity that is deemed to violate this notion of his or her own equal worth. Wackenheim, however, argued that human dignity encompasses the right to work and earn, and the autonomy it brings; the ban effectively denied him that right and therefore his dignity as a human.

There is some disagreement among French legal experts, however, as to whether communitarian versions of human dignity always ought to override individual conceptions of human dignity. In 2010, the French National Assembly banned in public spaces throughout all of France the *niqab* and *burqa*, garments that cover the face and are worn by a very small percentage of Muslim women. One of the legal justifications was that the garments violated human dignity, and as such were an attack on public order (Conseil Constitutionnel 2010: sec. 4; Fredette 2014).[11]

Surprisingly, the Council of State warned politicians during the drafting of the law that the ban would violate multiple constitutional and European human rights and that it amounted to discrimination against Muslims (Conseil d'État: 2010). It offered an interpretation of human dignity that diverged considerably from what it had previously said in *Morsang-sur-Orge*:

"the principle of human dignity implies by its nature respect for individual freedom" (Conseil d'État 2010: 21). In other words, the legal protection of human dignity would not necessarily justify such a ban; it could also be interpreted as protecting a woman's right to choose to wear the *niqab* or *burqa*.

Why this shift? The Council of State warned that the jurisprudence of the European Court of Human Rights (ECtHR) links human dignity to the right to privacy guaranteed in the European Convention, as well as a right to "live according to our convictions and personal choices, even if it means putting ourselves at moral or physical risk, provided we do not harm anybody else" (Conseil d'État 2010: 21–22).[12]

Indeed: The ECtHR presents yet another model of what human dignity looks like. *KA and AD v Belgium* is a case from 2005 in which the ECtHR recognized, in the French Council of State's words, "the primacy of the principle of self determination over that of the protection of human dignity" (Conseil d'État 2010: 22). *KA and AD v Belgium* involved two men (KA and AD) who participated in sadomasochism with KA's wife. The Antwerp Court of Appeals had found KA and AD guilty of assault, as a video demonstrated KA's wife had pleaded with KA and AD to stop. In addition, the Antwerp court found KA guilty of "incitement to immorality or prostitution": he sought employment for his wife as a "slave" at a sadomasochism club and provided material support for her employment there (European Court of Human Rights 2005: sec. 1 para. 3). Important to the Antwerp court's reasoning was its conclusion that, in the words of the ECtHR (sec. 1 para. 5), "the practices in question were so serious, shocking, violent and cruel as to undermine human dignity." KA and AD maintained that the sexual activities were consensual, merely part of the sadomasochism experience, and held in a suitably private location. The ECtHR sided with Belgium, but only because it determined that KA and AD had failed to respect the "victim" when she rescinded her consent to the activities.

The ECtHR made a point of clarifying that sexual activity for which there is consent from all parties, sadomasochism included, should not typically be criminalized, and there need to be "particularly serious reasons" for interfering with the right to privacy that protects such consensual sexual activity (European Court of Human Rights 2005: sec. 3 para. 14). In other words, the Antwerp Court of Appeals was wrong to conclude that sadomasochistic practices are, in and of themselves, contrary to human dignity. If an individual chooses to give consent for such sexual behavior, he or she has the right to do so. The right to autonomy over one's own body includes the right to choose to engage in activities that others might look upon as undignified. While the Belgian community may feel "outrage" at sadomasochism, or even "humiliation" for the participants, that does not necessarily mean a rights violation is taking place. Once again, the use value of outrage for identifying human dignity and its violations is put into question: according to the ECtHR, outrage may simply be in the eye of the beholder. This hardly seems an adequate justification for the violation of individual rights, especially when they relate to individualistic conceptions of human dignity.

In citing *KA and AD v. Belgium* while considering the bill banning facial coverings, the French Council of State warned French legislators that there is a European legal norm on human dignity that runs contrary to France's. The French account of human dignity also seemed to clash with the German FCC's use of the categorical imperative in the Aviation case. In yet another example of the unpredictability of human dignity within the courts, however, not even German jurisprudence has been consistent on the nature of human dignity.

Siegel (2013) identifies within German jurisprudence three visions of human dignity: "dignity as liberty, dignity as equality, and dignity as life" (513). Dignity as liberty, she explains, is related to the idea of a right to develop one's own personality, referred to in Germany as *allgemeines persönlichkeitsrecht*. This is found in Article II of the German Basic Law.[13] According to Eberle (2012), the right to personality means "each person should be free to develop his own personality to the fullest subject only to restrictions arising from others' pursuit of the same" (Eberle 2012: 202). Dignity as equality, meanwhile, relates to "concerns about standing, status, and respect"; and finally, dignity as life requires the protection of human life (Siegel 2013: 513).

Siegel analyzes jurisprudence on abortion in Germany, observing how these different visions of human dignity—especially the personality rights of women and the duty to protect the potential life of the fetus—come into conflict. Similarly, Lepsius (2006) notes how in the German Constitutional Court's abortion decision of 1975, the court tied human dignity to the right to life and indicated that human dignity implies "constitutional 'duties to protect' or affirmative duties (*Schutzpflichten*)" (Lepsuis 2006: 773). In this instance, the court determined that the state had a duty to protect the human dignity (and potential life) of the fetus, at the cost of women's right to personality.

Interestingly, both Siegel (2013) and Lepsius (2006) note how German jurisprudence has over the years softened its call for the state to automatically privilege the protection of human dignity in terms of life over human dignity in terms of individual personality rights. Siegel comments on how German abortion jurisprudence in the 1990s did more to recognize "women's autonomy in making decisions about motherhood," thereby subtly altering the judicial balancing act and giving more weight to the personality rights of women who become pregnant (Siegel 2013: 517).[14] In a related fashion, Lepsius notes that the FCC's Aviation decision curiously did not invoke the duty of the state to protect human dignity in terms of life. Instead of focusing on the state's duty to protect the lives of the innocent passengers on the plane, the FCC read the case through the Kantian categorical imperative to treat individuals as ends in themselves. According to Lepsius, "the duties to protect have seen their heyday and rather must confront their jurisprudential death" (Lepsius 2006: 774).

If human dignity is supposed to be universal, and of an absolute worth that cannot be balanced against other values or interests, what do we make of the inconsistent application of the concept across courts in nations of Europe or of the shifts within German jurisprudence on the subject? Or the balancing of an individual's human dignity against communitarian understandings of human dignity? Did some of these courts incorrectly identify human dignity; was German jurisprudence right one day and wrong the next? And if so, how could we know? Because Habermas wants to recover human rights from minimalists by emphasizing the utopian value of the moral side of human dignity, he does not want to define its content in advance; yet this means that his theory has no answers for us regarding how to best use rights to protect human dignity in particular circumstances. If this is to be a "realistic utopia," we need to know more about the legal mechanisms for its realization. Without this, we are left with a morally compelling concept that has the potential to empower the state to write laws that violate individual rights—especially those of minority or marginalized groups.

Conclusion

Habermas speaks of human dignity as if it were an indivisible whole, easily identified whenever our sense of outrage or humiliation is stirred. The cases discussed here, however, demonstrate that human dignity can be used to limit individual freedom, reject non-dominant articulations of rights, and reduce certain individuals to a single condition of their life or facet of their identity ("dwarfism," "pregnant woman," "veiled Muslim woman"). Furthermore, we see in these cases that outrage and humiliation are subjective. Wackenheim felt humiliation at losing his job; some Muslim women who veil their faces are outraged by what they perceive as their nation rejecting them (Open Society Foundations 2011: 75). These emotional yardsticks for measuring violations of human dignity do not help us negotiate the sometimes clashing accounts found within the previously discussed cases.

Even in those cases where humiliation is recognized as such, there is no guarantee that emotions like outrage will be translated into an effective challenge to humiliation. Eriksen (2013) argues that "The manner in which the eurozone crisis has been tackled has brought humiliation back in—not merely in the form of economic and social exclusion but in the form of executive, *intergovernmental dominance*" (Eriksen 2013: 118, emphasis in original). While Eriksen maintains that this humiliation has triggered "*strong emotions*," we must acknowledge that these emotions are, at best, slow to develop into action to challenge austerity policies (ibid.: 119, emphasis in original).

If Habermas' concept of human dignity fails to address those moments when two competing visions of human dignity collide, or when few, if any, protest the humiliation of others, it is because he overestimates the universality of the concept while underestimating the work that still must go into building the cosmopolitan "we" of Europe. Such a political project requires the work of collective and democratic norm construction. The consensus must be built together, rather than discovered.

Notes

1 Waldron (2009) points out, however, that this is not purely an "absolute worth" account because it depends on an implicit ranking of humans above other living creatures (228).
2 This is often referred to as "deontological ethics."
3 As will be discussed later, the omission of "or her" is purposeful.
4 Technically, it is the "second formula" of Kant's (2002) three-part Categorical Imperative, which he believes is the universal and pure basis for all morality (xviii). The first formula urges us to "Act only in accordance with that maxim through which you can at the same time will that it becomes a universal law" (37). The third formula mirrors the first by depicting "the will of every rational being as a will giving universal law," thereby encouraging us to both follow universal principles and act as if we were *creating* (or "legislating") them for the universe as well (49).
5 Waldron (2013) elsewhere describes this power of law to grant dignity with the following: "In law, a status is a particular package of rights, powers, disabilities, duties, privileges, immunities, and liabilities accruing to a person by virtue of the condition or situation they are in" (24).
6 Habermas himself does not provide a lengthy discussion of this genealogy, but others have: see Waldron (2009) and McCrudden (2008).
7 Waldron (2009) maintains that this is not the only reading of Kantian human dignity, and argues for an alternative reading that depicts Kantian dignity as a ranking account, not one of fundamental worth. He concedes, however, that the fundamental worth reading is the predominant one in the discipline. It also appears to be the one Habermas is using.
8 Joshua Cohen (2004), along with Habermas, is a critic of the "minimalist" approach to human rights. He is particularly troubled by Ignatieff's claim that human rights must be reasonably linked to dominant ethical traditions at the domestic level, accusing Ignatieff of ignoring the contestation of tradition that may be happening at the domestic level. This criticism is similar to the one powerfully made by Seyla Benhabib (2002) in *The Claims of Culture* when she argues that participants in any given culture are constantly renegotiating and debating the boundaries of their own culture and the content of its traditions.
9 This is what Hannah Arendt (2006) describes, when discussing Adolf Eichmann's fondness for Kant, as the belief that "a law was a law, there could be no exceptions" (137).
10 So does Shklar (1989), who discusses the link between citizen standing (part of the ranking status account of human dignity) and gainful employment.
11 The French Constitutional Council stated in its decision that women who wear facial coverings "are placed in a situation of exclusion and inferiority that is manifestly incompatible with the constitutional principles of liberty and equality"; as such, it is acceptable to intervene in the name of protecting the public order (Conseil Constitutionnel 2010: sec. 4). While the Constitutional Council does not use the language of "human dignity," the reference to "inferiority" as an assault on public order that justifies intervention suggests an implicit acceptance of the *Morsang-sur-Orge* argument.
12 This right actually sounds similar to the German Basic Law's right to personality, discussed below.
13 "Every person shall have the right to free development of his personality insofar

as he does not violate the rights of others or offend against the constitutional order or the moral law."

14 A system of mandatory counseling was justified by the court as "trying to win [the pregnant woman] over as an ally in the protection of the unborn," a gesture to the autonomy of women and the need to show some degree of respect for their freedom to shape their own lives (in Siegel 2013: 521).

References

Anderson, Joel (2011) "Autonomy, agency, and the self," in B. Fultner (ed.) *Habermas: Key Concepts*. Durham, NC: Acumen Press, pp. 90–111.

Arendt, Hannah (2006) *Eichmann in Jerusalem: A report on the banality of evil*. New York: Penguin Classics.

Baynes, Kenneth (2009a) "Toward a political conception of human rights," *Philosophy and Social Criticism*, 35(3), pp. 371–390.

Baynes, Kenneth (2009b) "Discourse ethics and the political conception of human rights," *Ethics and Global Policy*, 2(1), pp. 1–21.

Benhabib, Seyla (2002) *Claims of Culture: Equality and diversity in the global era*. Princeton, NJ: Princeton University Press.

Berlin, Isaiah (1990) *Four essays on liberty*. New York, NY: Oxford University Press.

Cohen, Joshua (2004) "Minimalism About Human Rights: The Most We Can Hope For?" *The Journal of Political Philosophy*, 12(2), pp. 190–213.

Conseil constitutionnel (2010) Decision n° 2010–613 DC of October 7, 2010: *Act prohibiting the concealing of the face in public*, www.conseil-constitutionnel.fr/conseil-constitutionnel/root/bank/download/2010613DCen2010_613dc.pdf (last accessed: March 2, 2016).

Conseil d'État (2010) "Study of Possible Legal Grounds for Banning the Full Veil." Report adopted by the Plenary General Assembly of the Conseil d'État. March 25, 2010. www.conseil-etat.fr/content/download/1910/5758/version/1/file/etude_voile_integral_anglais.pdf (last accessed: March 2, 2016).

Eberle, Edward J. (2013) "Observations on the Development of Human Dignity and Personality in German Constitutional Law: An Overview," *Liverpool Law Review*, 33, pp. 201–233.

Ebert, Rainer, and Reginald M. J. Oduor (2012) "The Concept of Human Dignity in German and Kenyan Constitutional Law," *Thought and Practice: A Journal of the Philosophical Association of Kenya (PAK)*, 4(1), pp. 43–73.

Elliott, Larry, Patrick Wintour, and Jill Treanor (2012) "Germany Might Have To Sacrifice Greece To Save Euro, George Osborne Suggests," *Guardian*, June 12, 2012. Available at www.theguardian.com/business/2012/jun/12/germany-sacrifice-greece-save-euro-george-osborne (last accessed: March 2, 2016).

Eriksen, E. (2013) *The Normativity of the European Union*. Basingstoke: Palgrave MacMillan.

Essed, Philomena (2009) "Intolerable humiliations," in Graham Huggan and Ian Law (eds.) *Racism Postcolonialism Europe*. Liverpool: Liverpool University Press.

European Court of Human Rights (2005) "Press release issued by the Registrar Chamber Judgment, *K.A and A.D. v Belgium*." Available at https://wcd.coe.int/.

Failer, Judith (2002) *Who qualifies for rights? Homelessness, mental illness, and civil commitment*. Ithaca: Cornell University Press.

Fredette, Jennifer (2014) "Becoming a Threat: The *Burqa* and the Contestation

Over Public Morality Law in France," *Law and Social Inquiry*. doi: 10.1111/lsi.12101.

Genna, Gaspare and Ian Wilson (2016) "Introduction: Europe at the Crossroads," in Gaspare Genna, Thomas O. Haakenson, and Ian W. Wilson (eds.) *Jürgen Habermas and the European Economic Crisis: Cosmopolitanism Reconsidered*. New York and Oxford: Routledge.

Habermas, Jürgen (2012a) "The Crisis of the European Union in the Light of a Constitutionalization of International Law," *The European Journal of International Law*, 23(2), pp. 335–348.

Habermas, Jürgen (2012b) *The crisis of the European Union*. Maldon, MA: Polity Press.

Ignatieff, Michael (2003) *Human rights as politics and idolatry*. Princeton, NJ: Princeton University Press.

Kant, Immanuel (2002) *Groundwork for the metaphysics of Morals*. Edited and translated by Allen W. Wood. New Haven: Yale University Press.

King, Martin Luther Jr. (1963) "I have a dream…" Washington, DC. Available at www.archives.gov/press/exhibits/dream-speech.pdf (Last accessed: March 2, 2016).

Kirby, Emma Jane (2002) "Appeal for 'dwarf-tossing' thrown out." *BBC News*, September 27, 2002. Available at http://news.bbc.co.uk/2/hi/europe/2285348.stm (Last accessed: March 2, 2016).

Lepsius, Oliver (2006) "Human Dignity and the Downing of Aircraft: The German Federal Constitutional Court Strikes Down a Prominent Anti-Terrorism Provision in the New Air-Transport Security Act," *German Law Journal*, 7, pp. 761–776. Available at www.unodc.org/tldb/pdf/EssayCivilAviation2.pdf 6 (last accessed: March 2, 2016).

McCrudden, Christopher (2008) "Human Dignity and Judicial Interpretation of Human Rights," *European Journal of Human Rights*, 19(4), pp. 655–724.

McCrudden, Christopher (2013) "Dignity and religion," in Robin Griffith-Jones (ed.) *Islam and English Law*. Cambridge: Cambridge University Press.

Nixon, Simon (2015) "Why the Eurozone may need to sacrifice Greece to save Spain," *The Wall Street Journal*, January 28, 2015. Available at www.wsj.com/articles/europe-file-eurozone-may-not-blink-first-in-confrontation-with-greece-1422488136 (last accessed: March 2, 2016).

Open Society Foundations (2011) "Une voile sur les réalités: 32 musulmanes de France expliquent pourquoi elles portent le voile intégrale," *At Home in Europe Project*. New York, NY: Open Society Foundations.

Rao, Neomi (2011) "Three concepts of dignity in constitutional law," *Notre Dame Law Review*, 86(1), pp. 183–271.

Rogoff, Martin A. (2011) *French Constitutional Law: Cases and materials*. Durham, NC: Carolina Academic Press.

Rosen, Michael (2012) *Dignity: Its History and its Meaning*. Cambridge, MA: Harvard University Press.

Shklar, Judith N. (1989) "American citizenship: The quest for inclusion," *Tanner Lecture on Human Values* presented at the University of Utah, Salt Lake City, May 1–2, 1989. Available at http://tannerlectures.utah.edu.

Siegel, Reva (2013) "Dignity and the duty to protect unborn life," *Proceedings of the British Academy*, 192, pp. 513–527.

UN Human Rights Committee (2002) Manuel Wackenheim v France, Communication No 854/1999, U.N. Doc. CCPR/C/75/D/854/1999.

Waldron, Jeremy (2009) "Dignity, rank, and rights," *Tanner Lectures on Human Values* presented at the University of California, Berkeley, April 21–23, 2009. Available at http://tannerlectures.utah.edu.

Waldron, Jeremy (2013) "Is dignity the foundation of human rights?" New York University School of Law Public Law and Legal Theory Research Paper Series, Working Paper no. 12–73. Available at http://ssrn.com/abstract=2196074 (last accessed: March 2, 2016).

Part II
Values

3 Cosmopolitanism, Trust, and Support for European Integration

Gaspare M. Genna

Cosmopolitanism is an idea that links various nationalities together. Instead of holding exclusive national identities, individuals broaden their affiliation so that people from neighboring countries, or perhaps the entire world, are also included in the same group. The existence of a cosmopolitan view deepens the integration of nations because leaders' decisions consider a wider set of individuals (Habermas 2012). It must be said, however, that connecting the idea of cosmopolitanism and the idea of Europe is not new. The ideas behind the various treaties that make up EU law draw on the spirit of cosmopolitanism. What is interesting would be to discover if the average European adopted the cosmopolitan ideal when they evaluate the European Union. To explain why cosmopolitanism is so important for European integration, we need to discuss why individuals would accept others outside of their nationality into a political community. The foundation of this community is the development of positive perceptions among fellow Europeans because such perceptions broaden intergroup trust.

Due to the European economic crises mentioned in the book's introduction, many individuals have questioned the ideas behind European integration as evidenced by the rise in Euroskepticism (Ray 2007). Questions arise concerning the wisdom of providing economic assistance to struggling economies. Other critics question the merit of austerity in exchange for assistance. Adding to the complex picture is the geographic concentration among those that ask these questions. The economic aid providers are from the wealthier north and the recipients are in the south and east. Much of this debate is often tied to perceptions regarding the economic motivations of giving and the conditions of receiving. I argue that the skepticism boils down to trust: If each side trusts that the motives of the other are mutually beneficial, then tensions can be reduced. The application of trust is at the heart of cosmopolitanism.

We need an explanation regarding how individuals' perceptions of others impact support for integration. In other words, are Europeans bonded into a political community? A political community promotes a significant degree of support for a political system's institutions and politicians (Easton 1965: 189). Karl Deutsch refers to a political community as a "people who have learned to communicate with each other and to understand each other well beyond the mere interchange of goods and service" (Deutsch 1953: 61). A political community is, in other words, a cohesive set of individuals who have developed a social-psychological attachment with one another through greater communication and understanding. What some refer to as a "we feeling" (Deutsch et al. 1957: 36) is also found in other, more general, renditions of community (Taylor 1972; Harrison 1974). Interpersonal trust is the foundation of a political community (Putnam 1993).

This chapter empirically supports the theoretical connection between the level of trans-European political cohesion and support for integration. The proposed model will explain the association between trust in individuals from various parts of Europe and public support for integration. The remaining sections will detail the importance of in-group membership for an individual's motivation to support integration. I test the hypotheses using ordered logistic regression analysis and data from the *European Election Study* (2004). The data include a representative sample of individuals from 24 EU member-states.[1] I end by briefly illustrating the model using the 2015 German–Greek tensions regarding the latter's debt bailout negotiations.

Self-interest, Trust, and Cooperation

David Easton's (1965; 1975) theoretical work views public support as diffuse or specific/utilitarian. Individuals provide utilitarian support when the state provides acceptable outputs, which can be economic or non-economic gains for the individual (Easton 1965: 157). The research regarding utilitarian support of European integration builds on the conceptualization of self-interest, which is one cornerstone of political decisions (Olson 1965).

Researchers point out that motivations for utilitarian support increase with the EU's ability to provide benefits and minimize any negative effects (Anderson and Reichert 1996). Werner J. Feld and John K. Wildgen's (1976) work shows a connection between support levels in the four core countries of the European Economic Community (EEC) and welfare increases in the early years of integration. The attempt at explaining support continued with David Handley (1981) who notes that the economic downturns of the 1970s dramatically lowered support levels for the EEC. Richard C. Eichenberg and Russell J. Dalton (1993) refined the testing of Handley's argument by looking at the various material influences on support levels, and confirmed his results. Others have also built upon utilitarian theory with analogous findings (Anderson and Kaltenthaler 1996). Moreover, others have taken a more refined approach and predicted the probability of support given an individual's socio-economic position and the expected effects of market integration (Anderson 1991; Gabel and Palmer 1995; Anderson and Reichert 1996; Gabel and Whitten 1997; Gabel 1998).

Other individual motivations, while associated with self-interest in nature, are not necessarily economic. The founders of European integration were driven by the memories of catastrophic wars and hoped that regional integration would be a vehicle for a permanent peace (Deutsch et al. 1957; Haas 1958; Etzioni 1965; Mitrany 1966). Europeans also supported integration, in integration's early years, in part for its promise to prevent war (Hewstone 1986). However, with the passing memory of the world wars and the end of the Cold War, physical security is a diminishing factor in an individual's decision to support integration (Gabel 1998). Other benefits include a more effective form of governance at the supranational level because the individual lacks such a form at the national level due to underdeveloped welfare benefits and high levels of corruption (Sánchez-Cuenca 2000).

These studies provide insights into utilitarian support levels, but answer only a narrow range of questions and provide, at best, short-term explanations. Business cycles that would influence self-interest motivations help to explain utilitarian support, but these variables do not explain how psychological factors, such as in-group/out-group dynamics, would also influence support. Such dynamics would explain how Europeans' views of fellow EU nationalities relate to support, and can serve as a more stable explanation because views on fellow nationalities are deep-seated.

In contrast to specific or utilitarian support, diffuse support is "a reservoir of favorable attitudes or good will that helps members to accept or tolerate outputs to which they are opposed or the effect of which they see as damaging to their wants" (Easton 1965: 273; 1975: 444). David Easton goes on to say that such support "is an attachment to a political object for its own sake, it constitutes a store of political good will. As such, it taps deep political sentiments and is not easily depleted through disappointment with outputs" (Easton 1965: 274). What "an attachment" refers to is not quite clear. Easton does mention that it is associated with a "sense of community" (ibid.: 325) but the concept of "community" also lacks specificity by leaving its definition as "the degree of solidarity" (ibid.: 184). In the simplest formulation, diffuse support occurs after a period of time when specific support is present (Easton 1965).[2] Diffuse support enters the picture when the political system has a "communal ideology" that promotes a common interest (ibid.: 333). However, common interest is not entirely separate from self-interest. It is possible for a collection of individuals to have similar interests; however, the summation of these interests does not necessarily define a common interest. Habermas (2012) points to common interests that arise from a coordination of similar self-interests and leads to collaboration. Collaboration is more likely at higher rates of political cohesion, as measured by trust in others. Common interest develops because there is a "sense of community" where individuals strongly identify with one another (Easton 1965: 326).

A Political Cohesion Model for EU Support

Research that looks at common interest motivations for individual support for integration has mainly focused on the factors that would impede the formation of the political community. They echo the claim by Robert Dahl (1989) that an attachment allows for easier rule because attachment adds legitimacy to those that govern by the governed. Lauren McLaren (2002) demonstrates that hostility towards other cultures effects attitudes towards the EU. Sean Carey (2002) agrees when he demonstrates that a strong national attachment lowers the probability that an individual will support regional integration. In addition, Kees Van Kersbergen (2000) explains support for the EU by examining the role integration has in forming primary national allegiances. The research demonstrates that these different attitudes lower the chances of supporting the EU. In developing a political cohesion model of public support, I focus attention on individuals' direct evaluations of members of the trans-European society. Support for integration improves with higher levels of cohesion because transnational social cohesion lowers the barriers to collective action. As pointed out by Habermas (2012), collective action is needed to solve problems facing Europeans.

Political cohesion is closely associated with the establishment of a common identity. Through a common identity, individuals can rationalize that individual problems are actually collective problems and that societies need to forge links, by way of integration, if collective problems are to be solved. A common European identity is not necessarily associated with a foundational mythos, ethnic affiliation (Obradovic 1996), common language, or shared customs (Smith 1992), or any characteristic that we usually associate with national identities (Zetterholm 1994; Cederman 1996; McKay 1996). However, a common European identity does have a similarity with national identities in that it is "imagined" and develops through the construction of a society (Anderson 1991). The notion of "imagined" affiliations speaks to the malleable nature of identity. Identity is constructed in order to adapt to new political and/or economic realities. Individuals make choices as to who can and cannot belong to a specific identity. In fact, individuals may also choose to belong or not to belong given the characteristics of those who already claim the identity. I will demonstrate that in-group/out-group identity, who is and is not a member of a group, is important in the social-psychological dynamics within and among such groups in a political community.

Many view European identity as part of a common belief in liberal-democratic values (Moravcsik 1993; Beetham and Lord 1998). Also, all citizens of member states are also citizens of the EU, thereby giving them a codified European identity. However, the average EU citizen may not have this level of sophisticated understanding of identity given that they are not well informed. A more reasonable approach in explaining support for integration is through the psychology of common interest evaluations. Jean Piaget (1965) stated that building attachments to groups is part of normal human behavior. These attachments promote cohesion among group members and are associated with the social-psychological phenomena of in-group bias and subjective images. Individuals become members of the in-group because the group fulfills some need (Tajfel 1982). At the level of national identity, individuals form attachments because they see the nation as the embodiment of what is important (DeLamater, Katz and Kelman 1969). Also individuals will interact with others who are members of another group if the other group's members share some commonalities with in-group members (Brewer 1968). The members of both groups are more trusting of each other and are therefore more likely to cooperate with each other.

One often-cited definition of trust is "the probability of getting preferred outcomes without the group doing anything to bring them about" (Gamson 1968: 54). That is, group members will not need to monitor each other because there is confidence that interests are aligned. In other words, one will not take advantage of the other because everyone has the interest to cooperate effectively. Robert Putnam (1993) shows, in the Italian case, that the level of trust one has for others produces effective institutional performance because of the higher probability of obtaining cooperation. It lowers the costs of association because of the perception that individuals will not cheat or defect. Paraphrasing Ronald Wintrobe (1995: 46), trust yields a stream of future returns on exchanges that would not otherwise take place because trust makes behavior predictable and stable. Therefore, individuals may develop overlapping group memberships or an integrated identity when trust is present. When trust is not present, overlapping memberships do not occur and group status becomes exclusive.

How is political cohesion, as measured by trust levels, associated with support for European unification? Why would geographic heterogeneity among member states from the north, south, and east partially explain the variation of support of the EU? Social identity theory helps us answer these questions by focusing on in-group and out-group biases. In-group bias is a social condition in which individuals tend to favor members of their group versus others who are not members (the out-group members) (Tajfel 1978). In early psychological experiments, individuals tended to give more rewards and side with other members of their group because of their affiliation. These biases occurred even when test subjects were only recently informed that they belonged to a particular group and had neither met nor interacted with other in-group members (Tajfel 1978, 1982; Turner 1978; Brewer 1979; Brewer and Kramer 1985; Messick and Mackie 1989).

The cause of in-group bias, as put forth by Henri Tajfel (1981, 1982), is due to the positive evaluations individuals have for members of their group. Members join and identify with such groups because, as stated above, the group symbolizes a set of values. By associating with similar-valued individuals, self-esteem improves because values are reinforced. Self-esteem further improves when individuals make favorable comparisons between the in-group and out-groups. Not only are individuals part of a subjectively valued group, the in-group is also subjectively judged as better than the out-groups. Therefore, by tying an individual's social identity to the importance of the in-group, group maintenance or cooperation for group survival becomes important. To this end, individuals will tend to give favorable biases to fellow group members.

Out-group bias, in contrast, is a social condition in which individuals tend to favor members of out-groups instead of members of their own in-group. Out-group bias occurs when individuals perceive that the two groups are of differing social status (Tajfel 1978; Tajfel and Turner 1986). In this instance, individuals from the lower status group will have negative evaluations of members of their group when compared to the higher status out-group. The negative evaluations stem from their lower status and are tied to their self-esteem. The relative evaluations lead members of the lower status group to have positive evaluations of higher status members and thereby extend favoritism to them. The phenomenon of out-group bias also occurs when the lower status group feels that the higher status group is legitimately in their higher status position and that the status hierarchy is stable. That is, neither group will change their status (Turner 1978). However, the members of the higher status group will continue to exhibit in-group biases because they have positive evaluations of their members and negative evaluations of the members from the out-group. The in-group bias exhibited by members of the out-group stems simply from the differing social status of the groups (ibid.).

Since cohesiveness is a function of in-group evaluations associated with identity, it is important to revisit the possible phenomenon of overlapping in-groups. Overlapping in-groups are important in the context of integration because the formation of a European identity is not theorized to replace national identities but to coexist with them (Deutsch et al. 1957). It is important to note that the recognition of overlapping identities is based on perceptions. Perceptions are simply the images individuals carry. Kelman states that image:

> Refers to the organized representation of an object in an individual's cognitive system. The core of an image is the perceived character of the object to which it refers—the individual's conception of what this object is like. Image is an inferred construct, however, rather than a mere designation of the way the object is phenomenally experienced.
> (Kelman 1965: 24)

William Scott, more succinctly, claims that "an image of a nation (or of any other object) constitutes the totality of attributes that a person recognizes (or imagines) when he contemplates that nation" (Scott 1965: 72). In addition, such images are subjective (Kelman 1965: 27). Individuals can use perceptions of other groups to formulate likes and dislikes for, and positive or negative stereotypes of, out-groups (Druckman et al. 1974; Hewstone 1986; Druckman 1994).

A positive perception develops the likelihood that multiple identities form as members of in-groups view the values of out-group members as similar and therefore compatible. Groups can tie themselves together in a unifying identity, much like individuals do with one another in forming group attachments. Recall that individuals tend to form groups, in part, because of the importance of the group's values. If a subset of such values is present in other groups, then a broader identity will form without necessarily dissolving prior identities. We see evidence of this as Europeans simultaneously hold subnational, national, and supranational identities (Fitjar 2010; Chacha 2013). The individuals in the broader group, one that includes two or more in-groups, can now operate with similar cohesiveness as the individual in-groups. However, if such values are not present, then the in-group and out-group biases will manifest, leading to a lack of cohesiveness.

In the context of Europe, I hypothesize that individuals support integration when they hold a positive image of other EU nationalities. The positive perception may result from evaluations of similarity on a number of issues and thus an individual will tend to view other nationalities as more in line with the in-group versus an exclusive, out-group identity. Where there are similarities, a cohesive political community can develop. Subjectively perceived dissimilar values would produce less trust and lower the probability of supporting integration.

Studies show that individuals can perceive differences along a north-south-east divide. Jan Delhey (2007) demonstrates that underlying the geographic divide are stark differences in economic development and cultural characteristics.[3] Perceptions of southern nationalities as lesser developed economically due to their values are prevalent in the minds of some. The eastern countries' economic development is also low and coupled with views regarding the legacies of communist rule and less experience with democracy. Finally, a more economically developed north can point to significant differences among the peoples of Europe. The level of economic development is perceived as an outcome of commonalities specific to the northern, southern, and eastern sub-regions.

The idea that culture can explain differences in the levels of economic development linger in the minds of the average European and can help decipher the variation of trust in nationalities. Oskar Niedermayer (1995) observed that there is a variation in trust among the first 12 EU nationalities. On average, individuals reported more trust in northern nationalities than in southerners. What is not clear from Niedermayer's research is the association between varying trust levels of northern and southern Europeans and support for integration, but it does make a case for looking at trust in community building. Delhey (2007) demonstrated that trust among EU nationalities does vary along geographic divides and that this variation of trust does have implications for the social cohesion of Europe. The empirical work reveals a link between variation in trust among the EU nationalities and general support for integration.

The logic of social identity theory in the context of the EU leads to the following testable hypotheses. First, there is a positive association between the overall level of trust for fellow EU nationalities and support for integration. I assume that trust reflects the positive images of European nationalities in the mind of the individual. Second, trust in eastern nationalities, followed by trust in southern nationalities will have a larger explanatory value than trust in northern nationalities. Eastern and southern nationalities comprise the lower-status groups because they come from countries with lower economic development. The lower status would promote biases, resulting in exclusion from the broader European in-group by northerners. Therefore, to support integration, individuals will need to trust the lower-status groups before members of groups enter into a collaborative relationship.

Data Description and Testing Procedures

The public opinion data for the analysis come from the *European Election Study 2004* (Schmitt et al. 2009).[4] I use a weighting variable so that no national population will be over or under represented in the data; all tests are at the individual level. The weighting variable also adjusts for any over or under representation of socio-economic groups.

Dependent Variable

The dependent variable is support for European integration. The survey question asks:

> Some say European unification should be pushed further. Others say it already has gone too far. What is your opinion? Please indicate your views using a 10-point-scale. On this scale, 1 means unification 'has already gone too far' and 10 means it 'should be pushed further'. What number on this scale best describes your position?

Higher values indicate a greater support for the progress towards unification. One can interpret the lower values (<5) as less support and the midpoint (=5) as satisfaction with the status quo.

Independent Variables

The following are the explanatory variables, each of which measures the respondents' trust in fellow EU nationalities. To measure trust, I use a series of questions asking the respondents to gauge their trust in other EU nationalities:

> Now I would like to ask you a question about how much trust you have in people from various countries. Can you please tell me for each, whether you have a lot of trust of them or not very much trust.

The respondents assign a level of trust to each EU nationality. The original values were transformed so that 1 = "have a lot of trust of them" and 0 = "not very much trust." I will conduct an analysis to validate the hypothesized grouping of the individual trust variables along a north-south-east division.

Control Variables[5]

The analysis requires the use of various other variables so that the results are understood in the light of some prevailing hypotheses.

Institutional Trust. Political trust is closely related to regime legitimacy (Hooghe and Zmerli 2011) and can be operationalized as trust in governmental institutions (Marien 2011). I therefore control for trust in two of the most visible and therefore well-known EU institutions: the European Parliament and European Commission. The survey measures trust in these two institutions by using the following question:

> Please tell me on a score of 1–10 how much you personally trust each of the institutions I read out. One means that you do not trust an institution at all, and 10 means you have complete trust.

One other political body that the respondents are asked to evaluate is their home governments. Support for integration can be negatively associated with trust in the respondents' governments (Sánchez-Cuenca 2000). If respondents strongly trust their home governments, supporting European integration can be a risky trade-off.

Democratic Satisfaction. The democratic deficit is a widely talked about problem in EU politics (McCormick 1999; Schmitter 2000). Like trust in the respondents' home governments, satisfaction with democracy in the respondents' country is negatively associated with support for integration (Sánchez-Cuenca 2000). The following question captures the degree to which individuals are satisfied with democracy in their country:

> On the whole, how satisfied are you with the way democracy works in [c.]?
>
> 1. Very satisfied
> 2. Fairly satisfied
> 3. Not very satisfied
> 4. Not at all satisfied.

The values were recoded so that higher values indicate higher levels of satisfaction.

Ideology. Prior research demonstrates the negative effect nationalism has on both European identity formation and support for integration (McLaren

2002; Carey 2002). One method to measure this possible effect is through left-right self-evaluations.[6] The respondents were asked to place themselves on a left-right continuum. The range is one to ten with ten being the most extreme rightist ideology. The more rightwing the respondents, the less supportive they will be of integration for reasons given in studies by Lauren McLaren (2002) and Sean Carey (2002).

Education. To measure education, the study uses a standard question that attempts to standardize educational achievement across Europe: *How old were you when you stopped full-time education?* Individuals who are still studying are recoded into their appropriate age group based on responses to the question on age. Although they have not completed their studies, this method captures the amount of their education at the time of the survey.

Income. Respondents were asked to provide the "total wages and salaries per month of all members of this household; all pensions and social insurance benefits; child allowances and any other income like rents etc." The survey researchers categorized the responses into "quintiles of income." Individuals in higher income quintiles will be more supportive of integration because their skills allow them to better take advantage of the opportunities offered by economic integration (Gabel 1998).

Age. Respondents were asked to list the year of their birth. I subtracted the response from 2004 in order to achieve the age at the time of the survey.

Geographic Effects. Geographic variables are included in each of the models. These variables control for effects that are specific to the countries' region: north, south, or east. They are constructed as "dummies" meaning that a value of one is tabulated if the respondent is from a specific European region. For example, respondents from Denmark are coded one for north but zero for south and east. I omit the variable representing the east in each regression.

Explaining Support for the EU

The overall results of the analysis below show that political cohesion is an important factor in explaining support for the EU. The first step is to determine if the trust variables measured the latent dimensions described in the theoretical section. Trust in the EU nationalities measures political cohesiveness. This trust is thought to be divided along a north-south-east dimension. Table 3.1 displays the results of the principle component factor analysis (varimax rotation). A factor analysis will tell us if the variables can be grouped together given our theorized latent variable. The analysis produced three factors, as hypothesized. Trust in the eastern nationalities loaded into the first factor, followed by trust in the northern nationalities, and then trust in the southern nationalities. The weakest factor value among the "trust in

Table 3.1 Principle Component Factor Analysis for Trust in EU Nationalities (Varimax Rotation)

Trust in:	Factor loading	Factor loading	Factor loading
Lithuanians	**0.811**	0.248	0.043
Latvians	**0.799**	0.294	0.036
Slovakians	**0.785**	0.115	0.198
Slovenians	**0.778**	0.172	0.186
Estonians	**0.776**	0.311	0.046
Czechs	**0.705**	0.146	0.223
Hungarians	**0.665**	0.274	0.213
Cypriots	**0.633**	0.191	0.306
Poles	**0.601**	0.059	0.238
Maltese	**0.590**	0.367	0.260
Danes	0.248	**0.801**	0.134
Finns	0.325	**0.753**	0.108
Swedes	0.222	**0.767**	0.184
Dutch	0.176	**0.745**	0.234
Luxembourgers	0.237	**0.691**	0.278
Belgians	0.223	**0.673**	0.285
Irish	0.318	**0.624**	0.218
Austrians	0.243	**0.598**	0.207
Germans	0.094	**0.533**	0.430
British	0.191	**0.375**	0.299
Italians	0.228	0.214	**0.718**
French	0.080	0.375	**0.637**
Spaniards	0.201	0.338	**0.623**
Portuguese	0.315	0.369	**0.557**
Greeks	0.430	0.269	**0.511**

$\chi^2 (276) = 1.2 \times 10^5$; $p < 0.000$
Trust in northern nationalities reliability $\alpha = 0.889$
Trust in southern nationalities reliability $\alpha = 0.807$
Trust in eastern nationalities reliability $\alpha = 0.915$

Note
European Election Study 2004.

the northern nationalities" variables is "trust in British" (0.375). However, the value is higher than the 0.300 threshold for inclusion and will therefore not be omitted from the scale (DeVellis 1991; Acock 2013). "Trust in the French" is strongly loaded into the southern nationalities factor. I calculated three new variables—trust in northern, southern, and eastern nationalities—based on the factor loadings. Reliability alphas tell us if we can be reasonably sure that grouping the trust in the three categories is not a random occurrence. In other words, if we were to conduct the survey again using a different sample, will we get similar results? The reliability alphas for the three scales range from 0.807 to 0.915, indicating very good reliability for the latent variable (DeVellis 1991).

Table 3.2 presents the first results of the ordered logit regression. Model one tests the relationship between trust for all EU nationalities and

Table 3.2 Ordered Logit Model: Support for European Unification on Trust for Europeans

Independent variables	Model 1		Model 2	
Trust variables	Coefficient	S.E.	Coefficient	S.E.
Trust in all EU nationalities	0.306***	0.025	–	–
Trust in northern nationalities	–	–	0.076***	0.025
Trust in southern nationalities	–	–	0.158***	0.023
Trust in eastern nationalities	–	–	0.265***	0.023
Control variables				
Trust in the European Parliament	0.105***	0.015	0.106***	0.015
Trust in respondents' government	−0.037***	0.010	−0.037***	0.010
Trust in the European Commission	0.168***	0.015	0.167***	0.015
Satisfaction with democracy in respondents' country	0.182***	0.032	0.176***	0.032
Left/Right self-placement	−0.036***	0.009	−0.030***	0.010
Northern country dummy	−0.695***	0.082	−0.589***	0.084
Southern country dummy	−0.295***	0.077	−0.221**	0.078
Demographic variables				
Education	0.003***	0.001	0.003***	0.001
Income	0.015	0.009	0.013	0.009
Age	0.003*	0.001	0.003*	0.001
τ^1	−1.05	0.140	−0.979	0.141
τ^2	−0.592	0.139	−0.517	0.140
τ^3	−0.065	0.138	0.009	0.139
τ^4	0.335	0.138	0.411	0.139
τ^5	1.35	0.130	1.434	0.140
τ^6	1.78	0.140	1.868	0.140
τ^7	2.35	0.141	2.434	0.141
τ^8	3.04	0.142	3.130	0.143
τ^9	3.34	0.144	3.426	0.144
χ^2 (degrees of freedom)	1,068.65 (11)***		1,098.98(13)***	
log likelihood	−13,533.9		−13,565.9	
N	6,431		6,454	

Notes
*** $p \leq 0.001$;
** $p \leq 0.010$;
* $p \leq 0.050$;
European Election Study 2004.

support. The trust for all EU nationalities variable is the average value of the individual trust components. The sign of the coefficient is positive and significant, indicating that the more an individual trusts members of other EU nationalities, the higher levels of support. Since the models include other variables that hope to explain support for integration, we can say that the result holds even while controlling for the other variables. While holding the control values at their means, support for integration increases steadily as the trust for all EU nationalities goes from its minimum to its maximum value: aggregating the dependent variable's response values of six or greater together, respondents are about 24.5 percentage points more likely to support integration as we move from the lowest to the highest level of trust in fellow EU nationalities.

The second model in Table 3.2 substitutes the trust in all EU nationalities variable with those that measure trust in the northern, southern, and eastern nationalities. The results fall along expected lines. All three variables are positive and have high levels of statistical significance. The coefficient for the trust in eastern nationalities variable is the largest, followed by the southern variable. Trust in northern nationalities has the smallest coefficient. Given these results, the largest percentage point change in support for European integration is with the trust in eastern nationalities variable, followed by trust in southerners, and then northerners. This means that trust in eastern nationalities has greater explanatory value, followed by trust in southerners and leaves trust in northerners with the least explanatory value. As the trust in eastern nationalities variable goes from its minimum to its maximum value, support for integration increases by 27.2 percentage points. The increase for trust in southerners is 24.6, while the increase for trust in northerners is only 10.2.

Figure 3.1 plots the marginal percentage point change as the various regional trust variables increase from their minimum to their maximum values among the German respondents. Each bar represents a different

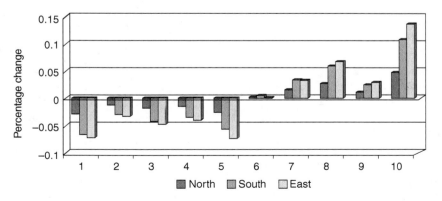

Figure 3.1 Percentage Point Change for European Integration Support by Political Trust Category for Germans.

combination of trust levels for each category of trust. I isolate these respondents given Germany's central role in current economic crises. I also wish to highlight Habermas' (2012) argument that it is critical for Germans to adopt a cosmopolitan attitude in order to have a viable solution to the financial crisis. Therefore, it would be interesting to see how German views fit with the general model. The trend is similar to the general model: as trust goes up for each of the groups, so does the percentage point change in the likelihood of supporting European integration. Also, as the bars indicate, the explanatory value becomes larger as we go from trust in northerners, to trust in southerners, and then to trust in easterners. As the trust in eastern nationalities variable goes from its minimum to its maximum value, support for integration increases by 26.8 percentage points. The increase for trust in southerners is 23.2, while the increase for trust in northerners is only 10.3.

German and Greek Trust

Cosmopolitanism is especially important during times of economic crisis. The fiscal crisis experienced by a few eurozone countries, mostly in the southern part of Europe, required solidarity from less economically vulnerable member states, like Germany. Solidarity in this case would be the extension of loans and other finical benefits. According to the cohesion model, individuals are more likely to support integration when they trust the less economically developed nationalities. Trust is assumed to result from positive images that bridge group identities. The quarrels between Germany and Greece in 2015 over continuing loan bailouts and austerity provides a good illustration of the model presented in this chapter.

Tensions between Greece and the EU began shortly after the electoral victory of the Syriza Party and the appointment of its leader, Alexis Tsipras, as prime minister in late January 2015. Syriza ran on an anti-austerity platform and also demanded the renegotiation of Greek public debt. Tsipras argued that austerity harmed the economy and that the mismanagement of previous administrations produced the high debt. Syriza therefore reasoned that the government cutbacks and higher taxes required by the austerity package in return for further loans were unfair to the Greek people.

The rhetoric hit a feverish pitch when Germany and its chancellor, Angela Merkel, were targeted as villains. Anti-austerity demonstrations were festooned with Nazi-era symbols and remembrances of the German occupation of Greece during World War II.[7] Protestors also re-imaged Merkel in placards with a Hitler-like mustache.[8] The protestors, many of whom were Syriza supporters or party members, attempted to send a message that the imposition of austerity on the Greek people by the current German government bore a strong resemblance to the Nazi brutal occupation. The image that linked the current crisis to the Nazi past also included demands that the Germans give the Greeks war reparations. Tsipras made an official request for reparations in the first half of 2015, 70 years after the fact.[9]

The manner in which the Syriza government targeted Germany, and Germany's reaction, displayed clear in-group and out-group dynamics. By casting Germany as the villain, the government questioned Germany's motivation for exchanging bailout loans for austerity. Greeks attempted to cast Germany's image as no different from its terrible past. In other words, according to the Greeks, Germany is not behaving like a member of modern Europe. Germany for its part argued that Greeks needed to live within their means. Further, they implied that Greek fiscal behavior would drag the rest of the EU into economic crisis. It demanded that Greece behave responsibly, cut back on government spending, and live up to its financial obligations. In other words, the Germans viewed Greece as not behaving like a good member of modern Europe.

To what degree do the German–Greek tensions matter with regards to support for integration? Support for integration would be critical because if support decreases among Germans, then German desire to support Greece economically would also decrease. Admittedly, the two are not perfectly correlated. However, while it is possible to support integration but not economic support for Greece or austerity, it is unlikely to support the latter two without supporting integration.

The data used in this chapter is very useful since researchers executed the survey prior to the economic crisis. This allows us to gauge the effect trust has on support without worrying if the crisis itself had an effect on both trust and support. I reran the model using only the German sample and substituting "trust in Greeks" variable for the other trust variables. The resulting coefficient for the trust variable is 0.562 (se = 0.222; p = 0.012). This means that the German likelihood to support integration increases by 13.6 percentage points when they trust Greeks. However, the results were completely different when we examine the relation trust in Germans has on support for integration for the Greek sample. Trust in Germans is not statistically significant.[10] This further supports the hypothesis that trusting nationalities from lesser economically developed member states is the critical variable in explaining support for integration, more so than trusting nationalities from more economically developed member states.

The results using the German and Greek samples has important implications for the bailout negotiations. For the Greeks, it is important that the Germans trust them. Higher levels of trust in the Greek people mean that Germans are more supportive of integration, and, by implication, are more willing to help. If Germans on the whole are less trusting of Greeks, then they will be less supportive of Greek bailouts. For the Germans, it is not important that the Greeks trust them with regard to European integration. The models indicate that Greek support for integration does not hinge, on average, on trusting the German people. In other words, Greeks, on average, do not use trust in Germans as their reason for supporting integration.

Conclusion

The findings indicate that the idea of cosmopolitanism as a way to deepen integration is valid, yet complex. Political cohesion developed from trusting various national groups can aid in explaining the probabilities for supporting European integration. Given the lower level of economic development among the southern and eastern countries, individuals that trust these nationalities are more likely to see the common interests involved in building a united Europe. Common interests are necessary when considering the economic divide among member states and the special needs of the less economically developed states during times of crisis. The German–Greek example also demonstrated the value of the direction of trust.

Two important issues must be considered with regard to these results. Neither of these issues would necessarily put into question the results found in this paper, but are important enough to consider. First, we need up-to-date data so that we can further validate the association between trust among Europeans and support. Unfortunately, at the time of writing, such survey data do not exist. However, there is nothing in the model's logic that makes the arguments any less salient today.

Second, the survey occurred at the time Europe expanded eastward. This fact may not necessarily add complexity to model. One can argue that the findings of the trust variables may be an artifact of the current expansion and have less to do with economic development. In other words, it may reflect the "newness" of the eastern members. The results showing the impact of trust in southern nationalities, as demonstrated through the data, puts this argument in doubt. The southern trust scale included two of the original members of the EU. If time of entry were the underlying factor, then we should see trust in the French and Italians factor together along with the older members. Also, trust in the British factored into the northern grouping, even though it joined later. These points lead to the conclusion that heterogeneous economic development is the key factor in understanding why trust in southern and eastern nationalities has greater explanatory value.

Notes

1 Individuals from Malta were not included in this survey. Bulgarian and Romanian respondents were also not included because these countries were not yet EU members.
2 See Baker, Dalton, and Hildebrandt (1981) for the evidence of this process in the case of post-war Germany.
3 See also Gerritsen and Lubbers (2010).
4 The data utilized in this publication were originally collected by the 2004 European Election Study research group. This study has been made possible by various grants. Neither the original collectors of the data nor their sponsors bear any responsibility for the analyses or interpretations published here. The data are available from the homepage of the European Election

Study (http://eeshomepage.net/) and from the Archive Department of GESIS (the former Central Archive for Empirical Social Research (ZA) at the University of Cologne, Germany.

(www.gesis.org)

5 I made every attempt to include controls for alternative explanations.
6 McLaren (2002) and Carey (2002) used survey questions that directly measured nationalism. I use the left-right self-evaluations as a proxy given that the survey used in this chapter does not have direct measures.
7 "Protesters rally as Merkel voices support for austerity-hit Greece," CNN, October 9, 2012. www.cnn.com/2012/10/09/world/europe/greece-merkel-visit/.
8 "Merkel tells irate Greeks painful reforms will pay off," Reuters, October 9, 2012. http://in.reuters.com/article/2012/10/09/greece-merkel-idINDEE898087 20121009.
9 "Greece Nazi occupation: Athens asks Germany for €279bn," BBC, April 7, 2015. www.bbc.com/news/world-europe-32202768.
10 Trust in Germans coefficient is 0.264 (se = 0.197; $p = 0.179$).

References

Acock, Alan C. (2013) *Discovering Structural Equation Modeling Using Stata*. College Station, TX: Stata Press.
Anderson, Benedict (1991) *Imagined Communities: Reflections on the Origin and Spread of Nationalism*. New York: Verso Publishers.
Anderson, Christopher J., and M. S. Reichert (1996) "Economic Benefits and Support for Membership in the EU: A Cross-national Analysis," *Journal of Public Policy*, 15(3), pp. 231–249.
Anderson, Christopher J., and Karl C. Kaltenthaler (1996) "The Dynamics of Public Opinion toward European Integration 1973–93," *European Journal of International Relations*, 2(2), pp. 175–199.
Baker, Kendall L., Russell J. Dalton, and Kai Hildebrandt (1981) *Germany Transformed: Political Culture and the New Politics*. Cambridge, Massachusetts: Harvard University Press.
Beetham, David, and Christopher Lord (1998) *Legitimacy and the European Union*. London: Longman Publishers.
Brewer, Marilynn B. (1968) "Determinants of Social Distance among East African Tribal Groups," *Journal of Personality and Social Psychology*, 10(3), pp. 279–289.
Brewer, Marilynn B. (1979) "In-Group Bias in the Minimal Intergroup Situation: A Cognitive-Motivational Analysis," *Psychological Bulletin*, 86(2), pp. 307–324.
Brewer, Marilynn B., and Roderick M. Kramer (1985) "The Psychology of Intergroup Attitudes and Behavior," *Annual Review of Psychology*, 36, pp. 219–243.
Carey, Sean (2002) "Undivided Loyalties: Is National Identity an Obstacle to European Integration?" *European Union Politics*, 3(4), pp. 387–413.
Cederman, L. (1996) *Nationalism and Integration: Merging Two Literatures in One Framework*. Oslo: European Consortium for Political Research.
Chacha, Mwita (2013) "Regional Attachment and Support for European Integration," *European Union Politics*, 14(2), pp. 206–227.
Dahl, Robert A (1989) *Democracy and its Critics*. New Haven, CT: Yale University Press.
DeLamater, John, Daniel Katz, and Herbert Kelman (1969) "On the Nature of National Involvement: A Preliminary Study," *Journal of Conflict Resolution*, 13(3), pp. 320–357.

Delhey, Jan (2007) "Do Enlargements Make the European Union Less Cohesive? An Analysis of Trust between EU Nationalities," *Journal of Common Market Studies*, 45(2), pp. 253–279.

Deutsch, Karl W. (1953) *Nationalism and Social Communication: An Inquiry into the Foundations of Nationality*. New York: Technology Press of Massachusetts Institute of Technology and Wiley.

Deutsch, Karl W., Sidney A. Burrell, Robert A. Kann, Maurice Lee Jr., Martin Lichterman, Raymond E. Lindgren, Francis L. Loewenheim, and Richard W. Van Wagenen (1957) *Political Community and the North Atlantic Area: International Organization in the Light of Historical Experience*. Princeton: Princeton University Press.

DeVellis, Robert F. (1991) *Scale Development: Theory and Applications*. Applied Social Research Methods Series, Vol. 26. Newbury Park, CA: Sage Publications.

Druckman, Daniel (1994) "Nationalism, Patriotism, and Group Loyalty: A Social Psychological Perspective," *Mershon International Studies Review*, 38(1), pp. 43–68.

Druckman, Daniel, Faisunisa Ali, and J. Susana Bagur (1974) "Determinants of Stereotypy in Three Cultures," *International Journal of Psychology*, 9(4), pp. 293–302.

Easton, David (1965) *A Systems Analysis of Political Life*. New York: John Wiley & Sons.

Easton, David (1975) "A Re-assessment of the Concept of Political Support," *British Journal of Political Science*, 5(4), pp. 435–457.

Eichenberg, Richard C., and R. J. Dalton (1993) "Europeans and the European Community: The Dynamics of Public Support for European Integration," *International Organization*, 47(4), pp. 507–534.

Etzioni, Amitai (1965) *Political Unification*. New York: Holt, Rinehart, and Winston.

Feld, Werner J., and John K. Wildgen (1976) *Domestic Political Realities and European Unification*. Boulder: Westview.

Fitjar, Rune D. (2010) "Explaining Variation in Sub-state Regional Identities in Western Europe," *European Journal of Political Research*, 49(4), pp. 522–544.

Gabel, Matthew J. (1998) *Interests and Integration: Market Liberalization, Public Opinion, and European Union*. Ann Arbor, Michigan: The University of Michigan Press.

Gabel, Matthew J., and Harvey Palmer (1995) "Understanding Variation in Public Support for European Integration," *European Journal of Political Research*, 27(1), pp. 3–19.

Gabel, Matthew J., and Guy D. Whitten (1997) "Economic Conditions, Economic Perceptions and Public Support for European Integration," *Political Behavior*, 19(1), pp. 81–96.

Gamson, William (1968) *Power and Discontent*. Homewood, IL: Dorsey.

Gerritsen, Debby, and Marcel Lubbers (2010) "Unknown is unloved? Diversity and Inter-population Trust in Europe," *European Union Politics*, 11(2), pp. 267–287.

Haas, Ernst B. (1958) *The Uniting of Europe*. Stanford: Stanford University Press.

Habermas, J. (2012) *The Crisis of the European Union: A Response*. Cambridge: Polity Press.

Handley, David H. (1981) "Public Opinion and European Integration: The Crisis of the 1970s," *European Journal of Political Research*, 9(4), pp. 335–364.

Harrison, R. J. (1974) *Europe in Question*. London: George Allen & Unwin.

Hewstone, Miles (1986) *Understanding Attitudes to the European Community: A Social-psychological Study in Four Member States*. Cambridge: Cambridge University Press.

Hooghe, Marc, and Sonja Zmerli (2011) "Introduction: The Context of Political Trust," in Marc Hooghe and Sonja Zmerli (eds.) *Political Trust: Why Context Matters*. Colchester, UK: ECPR Press.

Kelman, Herbert C. (1965) "Social-Psychological Approaches to the Study of International Relations," in Herbert C. Kelman (ed.) *International Behavior: A Social-Psychological Analysis*. New York: Holt, Rinehart, and Winston, pp. 565–607.

Marien, Sofie (2011) "Measuring Political Trust Across Time and Space," in Marc Hooghe and Sonja Zmerli (eds.) *Political Trust: Why Context Matters*. Colchester, UK: ECPR Press, pp. 13–46.

McCormick, John (1999) *Understanding the European Union: A Concise Introduction*. New York: Palgrave.

McKay, David (1996) *Rush to Union: Understanding the European Federal Bargain*. Oxford, UK: Clarendon Press.

McLaren, Lauren (2002) "Public Support for the European Union: Cost/Benefit Analysis or Perceived Cultural Threat?" *Journal of Politics*, 64(2), pp. 551–566.

Messick, David M., and Diane M. Mackie (1989) "Intergroup Relations," *Annual Review of Psychology*, 40, pp. 45–81.

Mitrany, David (1966) *A Working Peace System*. Chicago: Quadrangle Books.

Moravcsik, Andrew (1993) "Preferences and Power in the European Community: A Liberal Intergovernmentalist Approach," *Journal of Common Market Studies*, 31(4), pp. 473–524.

Niedermayer, Oskar (1995) "Trust and Sense of Community," in Oskar Niedermayer and Richard Sinnott (eds.) *Public Opinion and Internationalized Governance*. Oxford, UK: Oxford University Press.

Obradovic, D. (1996) "Policy Legitimacy and the European Union," *Journal of Common Market Studies*, 34(2), pp. 191–221.

Olson, Mancur, Jr. (1965) *The Logic of Collective Action*. Cambridge: Harvard University Press.

Piaget, Jean (1965) *The Moral Judgment of the Child*. New York: Free Press.

Putnam, Robert D. (1993) *Making Democracy Work: Civic Traditions in Modern Italy*. Princeton: Princeton University Press.

Ray, Leonard (2007) "Mainstream Euroskepticism: Trend or Oxymoron?" *Acta Politica*, 42(2), pp. 153–172.

Sánchez-Cuenca, Ignacio (2000) "The Political Basis of Support for European Integration," *European Union Politics*, 1(2), pp. 147–171.

Schmitt, Hermann, Stefano Bartolini, Wouter van der Brug, Cees van der Eijk, Mark Franklin, Dieter Fuchs, Gabor Toka, Michael Marsh, and Jacques Thomassen (2009) *European Election Study 2004* (2nd edition). GESIS Data Archive, Cologne. doi:10.4232/1.10086

Schmitter, Philippe C. (2000) *How to Democratize the European Union ... and Why Bother?* Lanham, Maryland: Rowman & Littlefield Publishers.

Scott, William A. (1965) "Psychological and Social Correlates of International Images," in Herbert C. Kelman (ed.) *International Behavior: A Social-Psychological Analysis*. New York: Holt, Rinehart, and Winston.

Smith, Anthony (1992) "National Identity and the Idea of European Unity," *International Affairs*, 68(1), pp. 55–76.

Tajfel, Henri (1978) "Interindividual Behaviour and Intergroup Behaviour," in Henri Tajfel (ed.) *Differentiation between Social Groups: Studies in the Social Psychology of Intergroup Relations*, London: Academic Press, pp. 27–60.

Tajfel, Henri (1981) *Human Groups and Social Categories: Studies in Social Psychology*. Cambridge: Cambridge University Press.

Tajfel, Henri (1982) "Social Psychology and Intergroup Relations," *Annual Review of Psychology*, 33, pp. 1–39.

Tajfel, Henri, and John Turner (1986) "The Social Identity Theory of Intergroup Behavior," in Stephen Worchel and William Austin (eds.) *Psychology of Intergroup Relations*. Chicago: Nelson-Hall, pp. 7–24.

Taylor, Paul (1972) "The Concept of Community and European Integration Process," in M. Hodges (ed.) *European Integration*. Harmondsworth, UK: Penguin Press.

Turner, John (1978) "Social Comparison, Similarity, and Ingroup Favouritism," in Henri Tajfel (ed.) *Differentiation between Social Groups: Studies in the Social Psychology of Intergroup Relations*, London: Academic Press.

Van Kersbergen, Kees (2000) "Political Allegiance and European Integration," *European Journal of Political Research*, 37(1), pp. 1–17.

Wintrobe, Ronald (1995) "Some Economics of Ethnic Capital Formation and Conflict," In Albert Breton, Gianluigi Galeotti, Pierre Salmon, and Ronald Wintrobe (eds.) *Nationalism and Rationality*. Cambridge, UK: Cambridge University Press, pp. 43–70.

Zetterholm, S. (1994) *National Cultures and European Integration*. Oxford, UK: Berg Publishers.

4 European Reform from the Bottom-Up

The Presence and Effects of Cosmopolitan Values in Germany

Aubrey Westfall

The European Union is an international anomaly: Its powers extend beyond the state, making it more than an international organization but not yet a functioning sovereign system. The recent financial crisis and controversy over the Greek bailout reveal some of the starkest differences in the competencies of the state versus the European Union; and the struggle over how to manage the crisis has disintegrated into conventional power politics of bargaining between states, especially between Greece and Germany. Jürgen Habermas is very vocal in his disapproval of using conventional politics to reform the non-conventional ethos of the European Union. He argues the economic crisis in the European Union has inappropriately directed political energies towards intergovernmental economic reforms that reinforce state sovereignty at the expense of increased regional cooperation and democratization. Instead, Habermas argues, resources should be directed at reinforcing the values of human rights through democratization.

Habermas wants the EU to expand notions of democracy beyond the state into a form of cosmopolitan democracy. Cosmopolitanism encompasses the idea that all humans should be equal citizens in a single (usually global) community; it requires democratic institutionalization beyond the state to resolve the tension between current forms of state-based democracy and human rights. As Habermas conceives it, the European Union represents a step in the process of institutionalizing a cosmopolitan world society, but only the first step. In order for the process of integration to continue, national governments must abandon preconceptions of governance tied to notions of national sovereignty and readjust their priorities with reference to humanitarian solidarity. As such, the future of the European Union rests in the ability of its members to expand notions of sacrifice and solidarity beyond national borders and to view all members of the union as having equal claims to the rights and privileges conventionally granted to national citizens.

Beck and Grande agree:

> If Europe wants to overcome its current crisis, it urgently needs to develop a new political vision and a new concept for political integration.... Our

argument is that we need not less Europe, but more—but we need a different, more cosmopolitan Europe.

(Beck and Grande 2007: 69)

They go on to emphasize the definition of cosmopolitanism provided by Christoph Martin Wieland in 1788 "[the cosmopolitan individual] means his own country well; but he means all other countries well too, and he cannot wish to establish the prosperity, fame and greatness of his own nation on the outsmarting or oppression of other states" (Wieland, in ibid.: 70). For Habermas, the most appropriate test of European solidarity is how a strong member of the European community, like Germany, treats other suffering members of the European community, like Greece, Italy or Portugal. However, appropriately socialized civic solidarity should exist beyond international (or European) policy, and should manifest domestically. In fact, given the bottom-up nature of democratic politics, it is logical to assume sustainable solidarity should first manifest in interpersonal relationships at the local level, rather than at the international level, which, as Habermas argues, is largely dominated by elites with little connection to the European population. A more immediate test of the potential for improved and sustainable solidarity is found in the values and opinions held by the public. Do Europeans embrace values of cosmopolitanism?

Germany presents the most critical context for an examination of cosmopolitan values. Since the beginning of the economic crisis in 2008, Germany has been identified as the "reluctant hegemon" of Europe (*The Economist* 2013). Germany is disproportionately powerful when compared to other European countries, and that power is largely founded in Germany's economic strength: Germany's unemployment is half the European average, its budget is balanced, and its debt is falling. Germany is also the eurozone's biggest creditor, giving it the biggest say in the Euro's future. Therefore, any discussion about the future of the European must begin and end with reference to Germany.

The economic power of Germany translates into substantial political power; most analysts agree that leadership in the European Union must come from Germany (*The Economist* 2013). However, the ability to act does not necessarily translate into a will for action, which Germany has not yet exhibited. Germany continues to shy away from taking the helm of leadership for several possible reasons. The first reason relates to the destructive legacy of Germany's European leadership (particularly relating to Germany's role in the two world wars of the twentieth century), and their desire to remain politically modest; the second reason is a desire to avoid the consequences of moral hazard; and the third reason has to do with concerns over the need for fiscal responsibility and potential free-riding by the Mediterranean states (ibid.). While these considerations may be legitimate, Habermas suggests an interest in civic solidarity should override these concerns. Solidarity works with the principle of predictable reciprocity: I'll scratch your back if you scratch mine. In a speech at KU

Leuven on April 26, 2013, Habermas argued that Germany (and the other European nations) should be naturally drawn to notions of European solidarity because it discourages the kind of semi-hegemonic political status that led Germany into regular conflicts in the twentieth century (Habermas 2013). Furthermore, Germany's post-war reconstruction was completed with deliberate and systematic reference to humanitarian and inclusionary principles, both of which form the basis of institutionalized solidarity. Germany therefore has both philosophic and practical reasons for forging the path towards cosmopolitanism, leading to the assumption that if solidarity can be found anywhere, it should be found in Germany. This makes Germany an ideal case for examining the existence of aggregate levels of cosmopolitanism across residents of Germany. More importantly, Germany's central role in directing the development of the European Union gives the implications of German solidarity greater weight. From Habermas' perspective, if the German public displays elevated levels of cosmopolitanism, which are translated to the German leadership of the European Union, the probability of successful and sustainable reforms to the European Union should be enhanced. Conversely, if the German public does not display characteristics of cosmopolitanism, the consequences for German leadership could be a move away from cosmopolitanism and Habermas' suggested reforms.

In what follows, I test two hypotheses that relate to Habermas' theory: 1) Levels of individual adherence to values of cosmopolitanism exist and are increasing; and 2) Adherence to cosmopolitan values is associated with increased support for European integration. I use data from the European Social Surveys to examine indicators of individual cosmopolitanism in German residents, and move to an examination of opinions relating to immigration and immigrants, arguing that openness towards immigrants provides a difficult test case for cosmopolitanism. I then quantitatively examine the relationship between values of cosmopolitanism and support for European unification after grounding the relationship in the literature. I find some empirical support for Habermas' assertion that cosmopolitan values exist and are empirically associated with support for European integration, with a few caveats. The final section discusses the implications of the findings.

Support for Cosmopolitan Principles

In order to evaluate the levels and effect of cosmopolitan values, I rely on data from the European Social Survey (ESS). The ESS is a cross-national social survey intended to track the relationships between changing European institutions and the beliefs, opinions, and behaviors of European citizens over time. It is an academic survey, directed by a core scientific team from the Centre for Comparative Social Surveys at City University, London, and managed by several universities and research institutions in Europe. The ESS was established in 2001 and is in its sixth biennial round, surveying people from more than 30 nations. In order to examine the presence of cosmopolitanism and assess its power in shaping support for European integration, I use data from the six most recent waves of the ESS in Germany, which has been completed every two years between 2002 and 2012. The survey of German residents includes responses from an average of 2,907 people per year.

General Support for Cosmopolitan Principles

For sustainable cosmopolitanism, the values of human rights and universal equality must be held by the people and practiced in everyday life. The ESS provides many useful indicators for gauging the extent to which the German population embraces cosmopolitanism. In particular, responses to the descriptions listed in Table 4.1 indicate values aligning with the idea that all humans are equal citizens in a community and have the right to be protected under the law because they are human beings (not only because they are citizens of a state).

The first description relates directly to the values of cosmopolitanism because it relates to the notions of equal rights despite citizenship or personal attributes. The second and third statements extend beyond a narrow definition of cosmopolitanism and describe an individual's orientation towards others. The second statement relates to a personality trait of openness, which corresponds to concepts of democracy, multiculturalism and civil liberties, and the third statement relates to collective responsibility and humanitarianism.[1] Because Habermas is deliberately expansive in what he considers to be cosmopolitanism, it is appropriate to incorporate notions of democracy and humanitarianism into his examples of cosmopolitan behavior.

Figure 4.1 illustrates the percentage of German European Social Survey respondents that identify with the cosmopolitan descriptions. Most Germans identify with these values, suggesting high levels of cosmopolitanism in general.

Because each indicator described above captures an important component of cosmopolitanism, it is appropriate to combine them into an

Table 4.1 Descriptions of Cosmopolitanism

Here we briefly describe some people. Please read each description and tick the box on each line that shows how much each person is or is not like you:

- S/he thinks it is important that every person in the world should be treated equally, S/he believes everyone should have equal opportunities in life
- It is important for her/him to listen to people who are different from her/him, even when s/he disagrees with them s/he wants to understand them
- It is important for her/him to help the people around her/him, s/he wants to care for their well-being.

European Reform from the Bottom Up? 81

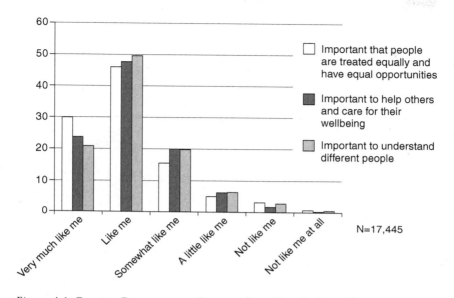

Figure 4.1 German Responses to Cosmopolitan Descriptions (data source: European Social Survey, Rounds 1–6).

index. This index provides a single measure of an individual's cosmopolitanism based on their affirmative responses to the three questions relating to Habermas' conceptualization of cosmopolitanism.[2]

German support for cosmopolitan ideas varies over time. Figure 4.2 illustrates the changing levels of cosmopolitan values in the last decade. The figure includes the average scores on the cosmopolitan index, along with the percentage of people expressing support for the individual indicators of cosmopolitan values. While most Germans in the sample hold cosmopolitan values, the levels of support increased substantially between 2002 and 2012.[3]

The improving trend in cosmopolitanism in Germany is echoed throughout Europe, where the average scores on the cosmopolitan index increased from 74.9 in 2002 to 80 in 2012. Germany surpasses the EU average in the cosmopolitan index when data from all years is considered together (European average = 75.6, German average = 77), and by 2012, the German average in the cosmopolitan (80) index surpasses the EU average (76.2), as illustrated in Figure 4.3.

In general, the German public appears to embrace values of cosmopolitanism, and their support of cosmopolitanism has increased in recent years. If Habermas' theory is correct, these findings provide hope for increased Europeanization under German leadership, provided that the cosmopolitan values are translated from the public to the elites. However, support for cosmopolitanism in theory may not extend to support for cosmopolitanism

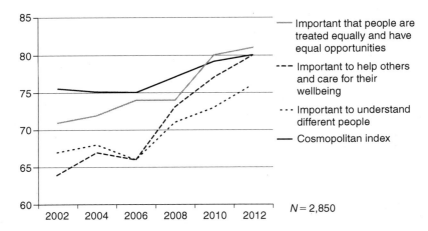

Figure 4.2 Support for Cosmopolitan Values in Germany Over Time (data source: European Social Survey, Rounds 1–5).

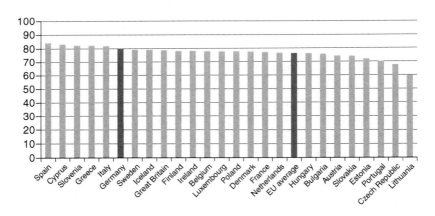

Figure 4.3 Average Scores in Cosmopolitan Index by EU Country, 2012 (data source: European Social Survey, Round 6).

Note
Due to missing data in Round 6, data for Greece are drawn from Round 5, Austria from Round 6, and Luxembourg from Round 4.

in practice, especially when someone is expected to extend cosmopolitan generosity to a particularly difficult or different population. The following section turns to an evaluation of whether Germans maintain their support for cosmopolitanism when immigrants are the potential beneficiaries of their cosmopolitan value system.

European Reform from the Bottom Up?   83

Cosmopolitanism as Public Support for Immigration and Immigrants

Habermas argues that the European Union should be preserved because it represents an important step in the process of institutionalizing a cosmopolitan world society. Further,

> The goal of a democratic constitution of world society calls for the creation of *world citizens* ... who insist on equal opportunity and equal distribution, confront the relatively conservative reasons of *national citizens* who insist on maintaining the freedoms they already enjoy at the national level.
>
> (Habermas 2012: 58)

Therefore, national commitment to cosmopolitanism, human rights and humanitarian solidarity can be tested by whether a government or legal system treats foreign and national citizens (i.e., world citizens) equally. At the individual level, the presence of cosmopolitanism should be strongest where people accept and appreciate those most different from them. In most societies, immigrants are a population identified as distinct from the native population due to ethnic, religious, cultural and social differences, making openness or support for immigrants the most difficult test case for the presence of cosmopolitanism. Habermas himself identifies this logic when he says:

> A common European identity will develop all the quicker, the better the dense fabric of national culture in the respective states can integrate citizens of other ethnic or religious origins ... there can be no integration without a broadening of our horizons, and without a readiness to tolerate a broader spectrum of odors, thoughts, and what can be painful cognitive dissonances [created by the presence of immigrants].
>
> (Habermas 2006)

The European Social Survey provides several indicators that are useful for testing the depth of cosmopolitan values as they relate to immigrant populations. Figure 4.4 illustrates the responses from Germany to the question "To what extent do you think Germany should allow people of this group to come and live here?" from the European Social Survey. This question was asked in reference to three groups: immigrants of the same race/ethnic group as native Germans, those that are of different race or ethnic groups, and those from poorer countries outside the European Union. The most cosmopolitan responses should be open (favorable towards allowing more immigrants) and should not differentiate according to the racial, ethnic or economic origins of the immigrants.

In general, the German survey respondents lean towards openness to immigration, especially when compared to the rest of the European sample.

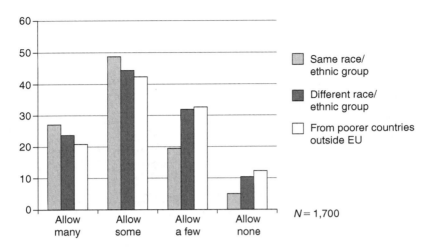

Figure 4.4 German Responses to The Question "To What Extent Do You Think Germany Should Allow People of this Group to Come and Live Here?" As A Percent of the Total Responses (data source: European Social Survey, Rounds 1–6).

Seventy-six percent of German respondents favor allowing many or some immigrants of the same ethnic group, compared to 64.7 percent of European respondents favoring ethnically similar immigration. Fifty-eight percent of German respondents favor allowing many or some immigrants from a different ethnic group, compared to 49.6 percent of EU respondents, and 55 percent of Germans are in favor of allowing many or some immigrants in to Germany from poorer countries outside the European Union, while only 46.4 percent of EU respondents feel the same way.

While Germany is generally open to immigrants when compared to the EU sample, there are signs that the German population embraces more cosmopolitan immigration preferences over time. Figure 4.5 illustrates the German preferences for very open immigration policy in 2002, 2004, 2006, 2008, 2010, and 2012.

Over this period of time, the number of people favoring the most open immigration policy has increased, with the most noticeable jump manifesting between 2006 and 2008, and with a small decline between 2008 and 2010, though it is worth noting that the preferences reported in 2010 remain more open than those expressed in 2002, 2004, or 2006.

Germany appears to be open and accepting of many different types of immigrants. However, from a cosmopolitan perspective, the most noticeable feature of the responses is the gap between the preferences for immigrants belonging to the same ethnic group and for those who are different ethnically. On average, there is an 8.96 percent gap between the German responses relating to the same race or ethnic group and those referring to a

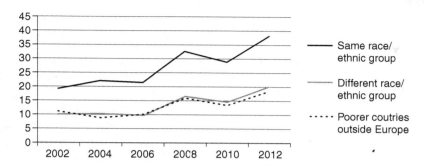

Figure 4.5 German Responses to the Question "To What Extent Do You Think Germany Should Allow People of This Group To Come And Live Here?" As A Percent of the Total Responses Over Time (data source: European Social Survey, Rounds 1–6).

different ethnic group, with a preference expressed for immigrants from the same ethnic group. The presence of this gap suggests that the German population may not universally embrace principles of cosmopolitanism, which would disallow treating people differently because of racial characteristics.

Survey respondents from Germany prefer the most restrictions against immigrants from poorer countries outside the EU. Because forming preferences based on principles of economic inequality can be considered as a pragmatic response to economic conditions, this preference may not offend the principles of cosmopolitanism as much as racial differentiation. However, the discriminatory act of preferring ethnically similar migrants to those from poorer countries does still violate the principles of solidarity, especially for Habermas, who believes solidarity should manifest itself in shared (economic) suffering: "A Europe-wide civic solidarity cannot develop if social inequalities between the member states become permanent structural features, and hence reinforce the fault lines separating rich and poor countries" (Habermas 2012: 53).

A second measure of cosmopolitanism is created by measuring the gap in preferences for immigration policy, based on the immigrants' race/ethnicity or the economic status of the country of origin. Survey respondents are asked if they would prefer many, some, a few, or no immigrants with the following characteristics: (1) the same race/ethnicity as the majority of Germans, (2) a different race/ethnicity than the majority of Germans, and (3) coming from a poor country outside the European Union. Responses were ranked from 0–3, with three representing the most open policy preference. The gap in responses is measured by subtracting the score for the policy preference relating to immigrants of a different ethnicity from the score for the policy preference referring to immigrants of the same ethnicity. The resulting number measures how much divergence there is in a policy preference.[4] This process was repeated by subtracting the score for the policy preference relating to immigrants from a poor country outside the EU from the score for the policy preference referring to immigrants of the same ethnicity. In Germany, the gap between openness to immigrants from the same race/ethnic group and those from either a different ethnic group or a poor country from outside of the European Union has grown over time, as illustrated in Figure 4.6.

Compared to the full EU sample, German residents are more likely to distinguish between the desirability of immigrants based on their race or the wealth of their country of origin. In the full EU sample, 28 percent of respondents distinguished between immigrants ethnically compared to 36 percent of German residents, and 36 percent of EU respondents distinguished between them economically compared to 43 percent of German residents. These findings suggest that while German residents are becoming more open to immigrants over time, the openness does not necessarily correspond with cosmopolitan values of universal equality and rights when compared to other European populations. Still, according to the data examined here, a majority of German residents do not theoretically discriminate about the desirability of immigrants based on their ethnicity (63.9 percent) or the economic status of the immigrant's host country (56.9 percent), further confirming the finding that most German residents might support notions of cosmopolitanism regarding the equal treatment of immigrant groups.

In sum, compared to the rest of the European population, German residents appear to be committed to the fundamental ideas of cosmopolitanism, and this corresponds with a general openness to many different types of immigrants. Further, German adherence to cosmopolitan values and open attitudes towards immigration are increasing over time. However, some German survey respondents appear to abandon the cosmopolitan principles of equality and favor discriminating against hopeful immigrants by virtue of the immigrant's race/ethnicity or economic context. These results suggest that theoretical values are not always transferring into preferences with reference to potentially challenging populations.[5] These results

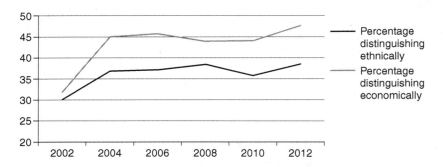

Figure 4.6 Percentage of Respondents Who Distinguish Between Desirability of Immigrants (data source: European Social Survey, Rounds 1–6).

suggest that while German cosmopolitanism is well developed theoretically, there are social issues that have the potential to compromise the values of cosmopolitanism and the principles of global citizenship.

The Relationship Between Cosmopolitanism and Support for European Unification

According to the ESS data, Germans ascribe to values of cosmopolitanism. But does adherence to these values contribute to support for increased development of a world society through the institutions of the European Union, as implied by Habermas? The following section examines the importance of cosmopolitan values in explaining varying support for European integration in Germany.

Habermas is not the first to associate cosmopolitanism with support for European integration. Inglehart argues postmaterialists (those prioritizing democratic values of equality and expression over materialistic values such as physical and economic security—values consistent with Habermas' cosmopolitanism) should be more comfortable with the abstract, value-oriented and communal concept of European integration (Inglehart 1977).[6] Janssen empirically tests Inglehart's theory and does not find evidence that postmaterialism leads to support for European values (Janssen 1991). However, he relies primarily on cross-tabulations of public opinion data, which cannot control for the full range of other relevant factors. In subsequent years, a rich body of empirical and quantitative research investigating public attitudes towards the European Union has developed, though the effects of cosmopolitanism remain underexplored.

Many scholars assert that support for European integration is based on a rational or utilitarian calculation of the costs and benefits of membership at the individual level. Individuals expecting to economically benefit from membership (i.e., those with more developed job skills, higher education levels and higher incomes, and living in border areas) are generally more likely to support EU membership (Anderson and Reichert 1995; Gabel 1998a; Gabel 1998b). Similarly, Anderson and Reichert (1995) show that evaluations and perceptions of the economic climate predict support for the European Union. At the same time, the national political climate provides important cues for individuals deciding whether to support unification. Janssen (1991) finds involvement in politics is commonly associated with more support for the European Union at the individual level, on the premise that familiarity with politics and the political process reduces threats associated with political change (in other words, those who are less familiar with the political process have a fear of the unknown when it comes to political change). Many other scholars develop this thesis, suggesting that experiences with the national government either serve as a proxy for experience with European institutions (Anderson 1998) or directly influence support for integration (Franklin et al. 1994; Franklin et al. 1995; Van der Eijk and Franklin 1996).

Concerns over individual and national identity are also important determinants of EU attitudes. Taggart argues Euroskeptic individuals see the EU as undermining the integrity of the nation state, which is an individual's point of reference for identity (Taggart 1998), and many others have likewise found nationalism to be important in determining support for the European Union (Carey 2002; Marks et al. 2002). As illustrated using the case of Turkish membership in the EU, citizens who are strongly attached to their nations are more likely to experience hostility or antipathy towards other cultures, especially if they perceive foreign cultures as threatening their native culture, and people experiencing these sentiments are more likely to disapprove of European Integration (McLaren 2002; 2007; van Spanje and de Vreese 2011).

Measurement

Previous research on support for European integration informs the selection of several variables drawn from the European Social Survey in an attempt to develop a comprehensive explanatory model of support for European integration.[7] The dependent variable is derived from a question asking survey respondents the following: "Some say European unification should go further; others say it has already gone too far. What number of the scale describes your position?" Respondents are then asked to place their own position on a scale from 0–10, with zero representing the opinion that European unification has already gone too far, and 10 representing the opinion that European Unification should go further.[8] Unfortunately, this question was only asked in the 2004, 2006, 2008, and 2012 surveys, limiting analysis to those years.

Several independent variables are also derived from the ESS. The primary independent variables measure cosmopolitanism. As previously described, the cosmopolitan index measures affirmative responses to three questions relating to Habermas' conceptualization of cosmopolitanism. A second measure of cosmopolitanism is created by measuring the gaps in preferences for immigration policy, based on the immigrants' race/ethnicity or the economic status of the country of origin (described above). The two gap scores are added together to produce the immigration discrimination index, which is standardized on a scale ranging from 0–1, with 1 representing the most discriminatory preferences.[9]

The model includes several control variables based on the relevant literature discussed above. Economic status, measured by household income, and completed years of education test the utilitarian hypothesis, which suggests an individual's economic status predicts support for the European Union (Anderson and Reichert 1995; Gabel 1998b). The model also controls for the influence of national politics on public opinion through controlling for political ideology, political interest, and political involvement (Janssen 1991; Franklin et al. 1994; Franklin et al. 1995; Van der Eijk and Franklin 1996; Anderson 1998; Hooghe et al. 2002;

Marks et al. 2002). Political ideology is measured by self-placement on an 11-point scale ranging from left to right. Political interest is measured with a four-point scale ranging from "not at all interested" to "very interested." Political involvement is measured with an additive index of whether an individual has contacted a politician or government official, worked in a political party or action group, worked in a political organization or association, worn a campaign badge/sticker, signed a petition, participated in a public demonstration, or boycotted products (Reliability alpha = 0.65).

The model also includes an indicator of the perceived threat to national or individual identity with a measure of anti-immigration attitudes.[10] Anti-immigration attitudes are measured with an index of three items: Is it generally bad or good for Germany's economy that people come to live here from other countries? Would you say that Germany's cultural life is generally undermined or enriched by people coming to live here from other countries? Is Germany made a worse or a better place to live by people coming to live here from other countries?[11]

Both the utilitarian and the political hypotheses predict that an individual's evaluation of the current state of the economy and government should predict support of the European Union. The extent of an individual's satisfaction with both is measured with a satisfaction index, which is created by summing self-placement on an 11-point scale in reference to the following questions: "On the whole, how satisfied are you with the present state of the economy in Germany?" and "Thinking about Germany's government, how satisfied are you with the way it's doing its job?"[12]

Finally, additional socio-demographic variables are included in the model. Sex is measured with a dummy variable representing females and age is measured in years. Definitions and summary statistics for all variables in all four years are displayed in Table 4.A.1, and Pearson's R correlations coefficients illustrating the relationships between the independent variables are displayed in Table 4.A.2 (see Appendix).

Results

Table 4.2 displays four ordered probit models predicting support for European unification among German residents. The first is a pooled model, followed by models limited to a single year in 2004, 2006, 2008, and 2012. The single-year models are included to explore potential temporal changes in the relationships illustrated by large shifts in the values of the primary independent variables between the years 2004 and 2012, hinted at in Figures 4.2 and 4.5. As illustrated in Appendix B, none of the independent variables are highly correlated, reducing the threats to the validity of the model caused by multicollinearity. While only two variables are consistently significant across all the years, the relationships between the independent and dependent variables offer some support for the cosmopolitan hypothesis and largely confirm the previous literature.

Table 4.2 The Effect of Cosmopolitan Values on Support for European Unification

	Pooled	2004	2006	2008	2012
Cosmopolitan index	0.424**	0.604**	0.382*	0.664**	0.325
	(0.088)	(0.182)	(0.177)	(0.177)	(0.176)
Immigration discrimination index	0.019	0.470**	-0.124	-0.035	-0.292*
	(0.060)	(0.119)	(0.121)	(0.121)	(0.120)
Left-right scale	-0.025**	-0.039**	-0.041**	-0.019	-0.015
	(0.006)	(0.013)	(0.014)	(0.013)	(0.012)
Political interest	0.027	0.112**	0.002	-0.055	0.046
	(0.016)	(0.034)	(0.033)	(0.034)	(0.031)
Political involvement	0.006	0.009**	0.041*	0.003	-0.005
	(0.009)	(0.019)	(0.020)	(0.018)	(0.017)
Satisfaction index	0.799**	0.998**	0.811**	1.044**	1.159**
	(0.062)	(0.136)	(0.132)	(0.133)	(0.132)
Anti-immigration attitudes	-2.071**	-2.217**	-2.227**	-1.972**	-1.904**
	(0.070)	(0.143)	(0.147)	(0.143)	(0.134)
Income	0.067	-0.029	0.129	-1.973	0.013
	(0.053)	(0.143)	(0.154)	(0.143)	(0.084)
Education	0.002	-0.009	-0.001	0.001	0.010
	(0.004)	(0.008)	(0.008)	(0.101)	(0.007)
Female	-0.014	-0.066	0.024	-0.006	-0.019
	(0.024)	(0.050)	(0.050)	(0.049)	(0.044)
Age	-0.001	-0.003	-0.004**	-0.0004	0.002
	(0.001)	(0.002)	(0.002)	(0.001)	(0.001)
N	7,896	1,832	1,810	1,963	2,291
Adj. R^2	0.05	0.06	0.06	0.05	0.05

Notes
Standard errors for coefficients are in parentheses;
** $p<0.01$;
* $p<0.05$.

The cosmopolitan index is positively and significantly associated with support for European unification in the pooled model, in 2004, 2006, and in 2008, though the relationship is weakest in 2006, and it approaches significance in 2012 ($p=0.064$). In the pooled sample of all data from 2004–2012, the average change in the probability of fully supporting EU unification between a respondent with minimum levels of cosmopolitanism compared to one with maximum cosmopolitanism is 5 percent. This finding affirms Habermas' assertion that a commitment to cosmopolitanism corresponds with the values used to justify European unification.

However, the weakly significant relationship between cosmopolitanism and support for EU unification in 2006 and the absence of a relationship in 2012 raise questions about the consistency of the relationship. While the data cannot directly confirm what is contributing to the change in the relationship during these years, it may relate to periods of crises within the European Union. In 2005 the EU was undergoing a political crisis following the failed European Constitutional Treaty, and in 2012, it was still reverberating from the shock of the European debt crisis, which started in 2009 and continues through the time of this writing. The weakened finding during these periods suggests that perhaps cosmopolitanism values only carry weight in EU preference formation when they are not confronted with great practical opposition in the form of political or economic difficulty.

The disconnect between cosmopolitanism and support for EU unification in times of difficulty are echoed in the findings relating to the alternative measure of cosmopolitanism via the immigration discrimination index (measuring whether the respondent discriminates against immigrants based on their ethnicity or the economic condition of their country of origin), which does not share a consistently significant relationship with support for European unification. The generally insignificant findings suggest that this measure does not usually predict support for European unification in the same way as the cosmopolitan index. This difference is likely due to disconnect between cosmopolitanism (or European integration) in theory, and the concepts applied to a specific group of people. As suggested by the low and negative correlation between the cosmopolitan index and the discrimination index ($B=-0.03$), German individuals are not necessarily connecting the ideas like "every person in the world should be treated equally ... everyone should have equal opportunities in life" to a consistent immigration policy preference that does not discriminate against people based on their race, ethnicity, or country of origin. Similarly, while the general values of cosmopolitanism are apparently associated with ideas of European unification, the same connection is not made between nondiscriminatory practice in immigration policy (applied cosmopolitanism) and European unification.[13]

The immigration discrimination index does gain significance in 2004 and 2012, but the positive direction of the relationship in 2004 implies that the more discriminatory individuals are more likely to support unification, contradicting my hypothesis. In 2012, however, the significant relationship is negative, as expected. This finding, combined with the lost significance of the relationship between cosmopolitanism and support for EU integration, further supports the idea proposed above, where the more benevolent ideas of cosmopolitanism are compromised in times of crisis, and conversely, the more discriminatory or economically conservative ideas gain predictive power in determining support for further EU integration.

Several theories from the previous literature are confirmed in the models. National and individual politics appear to influence support for European unification in several ways. The satisfaction index is consistently associated with support for unification; it shares a positive relationship in all four years and in the pooled sample. In the pooled sample, the average change in the probability of fully supporting EU unification between a respondent with minimum levels of satisfaction compared to one with maximum satisfaction is 11 percent. This finding confirms those who view the national government as a proxy for EU institutions (Anderson 1998) or who theorize that one's experience with the national government directly influences support for integration (Franklin et al. 1994; Franklin et al. 1995; Van der Eijk and Franklin 1996).

Individual politics (which are closely related to national politics, as an individual's political opinions and activities are often localized) sporadically predict support for European unification. Individual political interest is positively associated with support for unification in 2004, and political involvement is significant in 2004 and 2006. These findings could be interpreted as affirming Janssen's theory that familiarity with politics reduces perceived threats from the European Union, though the inconsistency of the findings questions the continued relevance of these determinants (Janssen 1991). Political ideology measured with the left–right scale shares a significant and negative relationship with support for European unification in the pooled model, 2004, and 2006. While the magnitude is not extremely large (the shift in the probability of support for European unification between the most left-wing and right-wing individuals is negative 3 percent), this finding offers support for literature affirming the influence of national ideological differences on European integration (Hooghe et al. 2002). This finding also offers support for the identity hypothesis, where nationalism is expected to be important in determining support for the European Union (Carey 2002). Though the ESS does not contain measures of nationalism to confirm this association directly, nationalistic sentiment and the preservation of the national community is largely the purview of conservative or right-wing ideological positions.

The models offer the strongest support for the identity hypothesis, which predicts that hostility towards other cultures should influence support for European integration (McLaren 2007; Azrout et al. 2011). The anti-immigration index is significantly and negatively associated with support for European unification in all four years and in the pooled model. These relationships exhibit the largest magnitude of any in the model: the probability of an individual with the most anti-immigrant attitudes is 14 percent less likely to support for unification on average than an individual with the most pro-immigrant attitudes; and the probability of the most anti-immigrant person supporting the highest level of support for unification is 28 percent less than someone who accepts immigration.

Interestingly, the models do not offer strong support for the utilitarian hypothesis that an individual's economic status and evaluations predict support for the European Union. Income and education do not share a significant relationship with the dependent variable in any of the models. As mentioned previously, the satisfaction index (containing measures of satisfaction with the economy) does share a consistently positive relationship with support for unification. However, the insignificance of the other economic indicators and the significant relationships between many of the political indicators and support for European unification suggests that the satisfaction index is likely a measure of political satisfaction, rather than a reflection of the respondent's individual condition.

In sum, the results largely confirm the previous literature and especially support the identity theories of support for European integration, though they do not offer strong support for the utilitarian hypothesis. In addition, the consistently significant relationship between cosmopolitanism and support for European integration suggests the need for additional study of the importance of cosmopolitanism in fomenting support for Europe and the inclusion of cosmopolitan values in future models predicting support for European unification. The evidence presented here provides some empirical support for Habermas' assertion that cosmopolitan values are associated with the fundamental notions of European integration. However, the general lack of a statistical relationship between the immigration discrimination index (the test of cosmopolitanism applied to a concrete population) and European unification, suggests differentiation between cosmopolitanism at the philosophical and practical level. Furthermore, the changed relationship in the 2012 data suggests an impermanence to the relationship between cosmopolitanism and EU unification, where the connection between values and preferences is compromised in times of difficulty or crisis.

Conclusions

Habermas argues that the future of the European Union must be secured through the encouragement and preservation of European solidarity, which should motivate every citizen of Europe to look upon every other citizen as equal and valuable members of a democratic European community. According to Habermas, this solidarity must be built upon the theoretical foundations of cosmopolitanism. This chapter investigates the stability of this foundation through examining support for cosmopolitan values in Germany, and then empirically tests the relationship between cosmopolitanism and support for European unification.

The evidence that cosmopolitanism exists at the individual level in Germany is mixed. Most Germans adhere to general principles of cosmopolitanism, but when the values of cosmopolitanism are tested with reference to the specific population of immigrants, the opinions of German residents are more divided. Similarly, the regression models usually show a significant relationship between cosmopolitan values and support for European unification (though not in 2012), but the relationship is absent when cosmopolitanism is measured in terms of discriminatory preferences in immigration policy. These results suggest a lack of consistency in the power of cosmopolitanism to form preferences of EU integration and a separation between theory and application, both in support for cosmopolitan values and in making the connection between cosmopolitanism and European unification.

Despite these mixed results, there is evidence of change. In recent years, a greater percentage of German residents report adhering to cosmopolitan values. These changes extend to opinions relating to immigration policy. German respondents expressed more open policy preferences in 2012 than at any other time in the decade, despite substantial economic pressures.

If we look only at theoretical support for cosmopolitanism and the link between cosmopolitanism and European unification, it appears that the theoretical foundation for a European Union based on solidarity does exist. Habermas suggests that the next step must be democratization, depending on the cosmopolitanism of the public to further the cause of the European Union from the bottom-up. However, the mixed results presented here should give pause. The inconsistency in the relationship between cosmopolitanism and support for EU unification and the disconnect between theory and application in the relationship between cosmopolitanism and European unification may suggest that the expected relationship between cosmopolitanism and Europeanism will persist only as long as European unification is framed at the abstract theoretical level. As soon as the political reality of unification becomes obvious or uncomfortable, the power of cosmopolitanism in driving unification will be lost, and there is some risk that it already has been in the current crisis. This leaves Europhiles with two options: (1) over-emphasize the theoretical links between cosmopolitan values and European unification in hopes of dominating the rhetoric surrounding unification (Habermas' current strategy), (2) make more explicit connections between cosmopolitan values and their real-life applications. The first option risks irrelevance as European unification becomes increasingly involved in policymaking, and the second risks backfiring if people prioritize their policy preferences over their cosmopolitan values (the magnitude of the relationship between anti-immigration attitudes and support for European unification suggests that they may), leading to destructive populism. Given these risks, democratization is a viable option for the European Union only if it is implemented alongside a continual socialization campaign promoting cosmopolitan values and democratic safeguards to protect vulnerable populations from the populist impulse.

This chapter focuses on the resident German population due to the dominant position Germany has in directing the future of the European Union. The findings suggest that Germany is an appropriate leader for promoting the values of cosmopolitanism in a democratizing Europe; the public is generally supportive of cosmopolitan principles and usually exhibits a connection between their values and European unification. However, German endorsement is only the beginning. Because the data here is limited to residents of Germany, the results are not yet transferable to the rest of the European population and it is not guaranteed that the rest of the European population feels the same affinity for these values (though Figure 4.3 suggests that most of them do). Nor is it obvious that all Europeans connect cosmopolitanism to Europeanization. Therefore, there is the risk that cosmopolitan German leadership could impose a vision of Europe that is not endorsed by the whole European public. Further research should be conducted to evaluate the levels of cosmopolitanism across the European Union and their application to the European project. Should the same patterns appear, the task of German leadership should be made easier and more rapid democratization could follow, thereby fulfilling Habermas' dream of a more democratic Europe built on a foundation of human solidarity.

Appendix

Table 4.A.1 Descriptive Statistics of Dependent and Independent Variables for Years 2004, 2006, 2008, 2012

Variable	Definition	N	Mean	S.D.	Range
Dependent Variable: Support for European integration	Response to following question: Some say European unification should go further; others say it has already gone too far. What number of the scale describes your position?	2,764 2,796 2,643 2,881	5.20 4.74 5.19 5.45	2.78 2.81 2.82 2.79	0–10
Cosmopolitan index	Additive index measuring affirmative responses to descriptions of cosmopolitan values.	2,808 2,864 2,726 2,927	0.75 0.75 0.77 0.75	0.14 0.15 0.14 0.14	0–1
Immigration discrimination index	Additive index measuring discrimination in immigration policy preferences.	2,765 2,828 2,676 2,896	0.17 0.17 0.16 0.17	0.20 0.20 0.20 0.19	0–1
Left-right scale	Response to following question: In politics people sometimes talk of "left" and "right". Where would you place yourself on this scale where 0 means the left and 10 means the right?	2,590 2,600 2,536 2,820	4.50 4.41 4.54 4.51	1.80 1.83 1.86 1.90	0–10
Political interest	Response to the following question: How interested would you say you are in politics? Not at all interested, hardly, quite or very?	2,865 2,912 2,751 2,958	1.61 1.60 1.74 1.79	0.87 0.88 0.82 0.81	0–3
Political involvement	Additive index with a code of 1 being applied to political activities.	2,852 2,892 2,737 2,939	1.02 0.98 1.19 1.35	1.28 1.29 1.36 1.38	0–7

Variable	Description	N	Mean	SD	Range
Satisfaction index	Additive index of satisfaction with national government and the current state of the economy	2,753 / 2,789 / 2,625 / 2,848	0.34 / 0.39 / 0.41 / 0.53	0.19 / 0.20 / 0.20 / 0.19	0–1
Anti-immigration attitudes	Additive index of placement on scale from 0–1 with 1 being the most anti-immigrant responses.	2,653 / 2,695 / 2,614 / 2,865	0.51 / 0.50 / 0.46 / 0.42	0.21 / 0.20 / 0.20 / 0.19	0–1
Income	Household's total net income annually. Coded by range in Euros in 2004 and 2006, by percentile in 2008, standardized on scale from 0–1	2,177 / 2,173 / 2,286 / 2,553	0.55 / 0.55 / 0.45 / 0.55	0.18 / 0.17 / 0.25 / 0.28	0–1
Education	Years of full-time education completed	2,811 / 2,872 / 2,737 / 2,946	12.92 / 13.19 / 13.63 / 13.81	3.23 / 3.42 / 3.39 / 3.36	0–25 / 0–36 / 2–45 / 0–35
Female	Coded 1 if female	2,870 / 2,916 / 2,751 / 2,958	0.52 / 0.51 / 0.47 / 0.50	0.50	0–1
Age	Age in years	2,806 / 2,870 / 2,725 / 2,951	46.84 / 48.00 / 48.96 / 48.70	17.87 / 18.08 / 17.43 / 18.57	15–96 / 15–96 / 15–91 / 15–99

Table 4.A.2 Pearson's R Correlation Coefficients the Independent Variables in Table 4.2, Pooled

	1	2	3	4	5	6	7	8	9	10
1 Cosmopolitan index	1.00									
2 Immigration discrimination index	-0.08	1.00								
3 Left-right scale	-0.13	0.10	1.00							
4 Political interest	0.09	0.04	-0.04	1.00						
5 Political involvement	0.12	-0.06	-0.10	0.30	1.00					
6 Satisfaction index	0.01	0.02	0.15	0.13	0.07	1.00				
8 Anti-immigration attitudes	-0.15	0.18	0.13	-0.26	-0.26	-0.34	1.00			
9 Income	-0.01	-0.02	0.06	0.16	0.20	0.24	-0.22	1.00		
10 Education	0.06	-0.06	-0.09	0.24	0.28	0.11	-0.32	0.30	1.00	
11 Female	0.13	-0.02	-0.06	-0.20	-0.05	-0.09	0.04	-0.07	-0.08	1.00
12 Age	0.03	0.09	0.05	0.25	-0.05	-0.01	0.06	0.03	-0.13	-0.01

Notes

1 For all three questions measuring cosmopolitanism, each survey respondent placed themselves on a six-point scale according to whether the individual described is not like them at all, not like them, a little like them, somewhat like them, like them, or very much like them.
2 Principle component factor analysis (varimax rotation) confirms the relationship between these three variables, as they strongly load on a single factor with an eigenvalue of 2.04 explaining 93 percent of the variance between variables (all three variables have a factor loading number above 0.7). The reliability alpha for the index is 0.627, suggesting the internal consistency of the latent construct is borderline acceptable according to common practice. Though this reliability score is lower than the ideal, it is not unexpected. A smaller number of items in an Alpha test can often deflate the value of an alpha, and in this case only three items are being examined. The additive index results in a scale from 0–15, which is then standardized to a range of 0 to 1.
3 This change is statistically significant ($p < 0.01$).
4 For example, if an individual indicates that she would prefer to allow some immigrants of the same ethnic group into Germany, but no immigrants of a different ethnic group, her gap score would be a 2. There are occasionally negative gap scores, when an individual expresses a preference for immigrants of a different ethnicity or from poor countries outside the EU. These scores still represent discrimination, so the absolute value of the score was included in the measure.
5 For example, 28 percent of German survey respondents from 2002–2012 who strongly identify with the idea that it is important that every person in the world should be treated equally and have equal opportunities in life also distinguish between immigrants on the basis of their ethnicity, and 36 percent distinguish economically.
6 The main difference is that postmaterialism may be tied to cultural contexts or communities (i.e., nations), whereas cosmopolitanism would not expect a cultural community to apply to the relevant intellectual values.
7 Most previous research on support for European unification has relied on the Eurobarometer survey, a cross-national survey managed by the European Commission and dating back to 1973 (see Boomgaarden et al. 2011 for a comprehensive discussion of studies using the Eurobarometer). While the Eurobarometer survey typically contains a range of indicators about the European Union, the questionnaire is not consistent over time, making valid multivariate analysis over time very difficult. By contrast, the ESS has been consistently implemented in the same form over the last decade.
8 In using a single scalar measure of support for European integration, I continue the practice of oversimplifying the perspectives of the European public. Boomgaarden et al. (2011) correctly criticize this practice and illustrate the multidimensionality of EU public opinion. In this instance, data limitations prevent a more nuanced analysis, as the ESS contains few EU-related indicators.
9 The reliability alpha for the index is 0.81, suggesting good internal consistency of the latent construct.
10 Threats to identity are discussed in Taggart (1998), Carey (2002), McLaren (2002), Kritzinger (2003), McLaren (2007), and Azrout et al. (2011).
11 In the survey, responses to the three immigration questions are given on an 11-point scale, with 10 representing the most anti-immigration attitudes. Principle component factor analysis (varimax rotation) confirms the relationship between these three variables, as they strongly load on a single factor with an eigenvalue of 1.82 (all three variables have a factor loading number above 0.75). To construct the index of anti-immigrant attitudes, the responses were

added together and standardized on a scale from 0 to 1. The reliability alpha for the index is 0.85, which indicates good internal consistency of the latent construct.
12 Though these questions capture distinct aspects of the political and utilitarian hypotheses, their high correlation (Pearson's $R = 0.64$) justifies the creation of a single measure to reduce the occurrence of multicollinearity in the model. The reliability alpha for the index is 0.78, suggesting good internal consistency of the latent construct. To construct the satisfaction index, the responses were added together and standardized on a scale from 0 to 1.
13 The discrepancy could be a feature of measurement. The discrimination index is an indicator of whether or not individuals differentiate between the desirability of immigrants based on their ethnicity/race or the economic status of their country of origin. It is therefore possible that an individual could be virulently but equally anti-immigrant, and by this measurement would be considered more cosmopolitan to an individual who is open, but more open to some groups than others. The anti-immigration index and the discrimination index are not highly correlated ($R = 0.12$), but the possibility of measurement error could account for the insignificance of the relationship.

References

Anderson, Christopher J. (1998) "When in Doubt, Use Proxies Attitudes toward Domestic Politics and Support for European Integration," *Comparative political studies,* 31(5), pp. 569–601.

Anderson, Christopher J., and M. Shawn Reichert (1995) "Economic benefits and support for membership in the EU: A cross-national analysis," *Journal of Public Policy,* 15, pp. 231–250.

Azrout, Rachid, Joost van Spanje, J., and Claes de Vreese, C. (2011) "Talking Turkey: Anti-immigrant attitudes and their effect on support for Turkish membership of the EU," *European Union Politics,* 12(1), pp. 3–19.

Beck, Ulrich, and Edgar Grande (2007) "Cosmopolitanism Europe's Way Out of Crisis," *European Journal of Social Theory,* 10(1), pp. 67–85.

Boomgaarden, Hajo G., Andreas Schuck, Matthijis Elenbaas, and Claes de Vreese (2011) "Mapping EU Attitudes: Conceptual and Empirical Dimensions of Euroscepticism and EU Support," *European Union Politics,* 12(2), pp. 241–266.

Carey, Sean (2002) "Undivided Loyalties Is National Identity an Obstacle to European Integration?" *European Union Politics,* 3(4), pp. 387–413.

ESS Round 5: European Social Survey Round 5 Data (2010). Data file edition 3.0. Norwegian Social Science Data Services, Norway—Data Archive and distributor of ESS data.

ESS Round 4: European Social Survey Round 4 Data (2008). Data file edition 4.1. Norwegian Social Science Data Services, Norway—Data Archive and distributor of ESS data.

ESS Round 3: European Social Survey Round 3 Data (2006). Data file edition 3.4. Norwegian Social Science Data Services, Norway—Data Archive and distributor of ESS data.

ESS Round 2: European Social Survey Round 2 Data (2004). Data file edition 3.3. Norwegian Social Science Data Services, Norway—Data Archive and distributor of ESS data.

Franklin, Mark N., Michael Marsh, and Lauren McLaren (1994) "Uncorking the bottle: Popular opposition to European unification in the wake of Maastricht," *JCMS: Journal of Common Market Studies,* 32(4), pp. 455–472.

Franklin, Mark N., Cees Van der Eijk, and Michael Marsh (1995) "Referendum outcomes and trust in government: Public support for Europe in the wake of Maastricht," *West European Politics*, 18(3), pp. 101–117.

Gabel, Matthew J. (1998a) "Economic integration and mass politics: Market liberalization and public attitudes in the European Union," *American Journal of Political Science*, 42(3), pp. 936–953.

Gabel, Matthew J. (1998b) "Public support for European integration: An empirical test of five theories," *Journal of Politics*, 60(2), pp. 333–354.

Habermas, Jürgen (1995) "Address: multiculturalism and the liberal state," *Stanford Law Review*, 47(5), pp. 849–853.

Habermas, Jürgen (2006) "Opening up Fortress Europe. Jürgen Habermas on Immigration as the Key to European Unity," *Signandsight.com*, November 16, 2006. Accessed August 17, 2013: www.signandsight.com/features/1048.html.

Habermas, Jürgen (2010) "Leadership and Leitkultur," *New York Times*, October 28, 2010. Accessed August 16, 2013: www.nytimes.com/2010/10/29/opinion/29Habermas.html.

Habermas, Jürgen (2012) *The crisis of the European Union: A response*. Cambridge: Polity Press.

Habermas, Jürgen (2013) "Democracy, Solidarity and the European Crisis," Lecture delivered by Professor Jürgen Habermas on 26 April, 2013 in Leuven. Accessed August 16, 2013 from: www.kuleuven.be/communicatie/evenementen/evenementen/jurgen-habermas/en/democracy-solidarity-and-the-european-crisis.

Hooghe, Liesbet, Gary Marks, and Carole Wilson (2002) "Does Left/Right Structure Party Positions on European Integration?" *Comparative Political Studies*, 35(8), pp. 965–989.

Inglehart, Ronald (1977) *The Silent Revolution: Changing Values and Political Styles Among Western Publics*. Princeton: Princeton University Press.

Janssen, Joseph I. (1991) "Postmaterialism, Cognitive Mobilization and Public Support For European Integration," *British Journal of Political Science*, 21(4), pp. 443–468.

Kritzinger, Sylvia (2003) "The Influence of the Nation State on Individual Support for the European Union," *European Union Politics*, 4(2), pp. 219–241.

Marks, Gary, Carole Wilson, and Leonard Ray (2002) "National Political Parties and European Integration," *American Journal of Political Science*, 46(3), pp. 585–594.

McLaren, Lauren M. (2002) "Public Support for the European Union: Cost/Benefit Analysis or Perceived Cultural Threat?" *Journal of Politics*, 64(2), pp. 551–566.

McLaren, Lauren M. (2007) "Explaining Opposition to Turkish membership of the EU," *European Union Politics*, 8(2), pp. 251–278.

Taggart, Paul (1998) "A touchstone of dissent: Euroscepticism in contemporary Western European party systems," *European Journal of Political Research*, 33(3), pp. 363–388.

The Economist (2013) "The Reluctant Hegemon," *The Economist*, June 15, 2013. Accessed August 15, 2013, from: www.economist.com/news/leaders/21579456-if-europes-economies-are-recover-germany-must-start-lead-reluctant-hegemon.

Van der Eijk, Cees, and Mark Franklin (eds.) (1996) *Choosing Europe? The European electorate and national politics in the face of union*. Ann Arbor: University of Michigan Press.

van Spanje, J. H. P., and C. H. de Vreese (2011) "So What's Wrong with the EU? Motivations Underlying the Eurosceptic Vote in the 2009 European Elections," *European Union Politics*, 12(3), pp. 405–429.

Part III
Tools

5 Reason, Faith, and Europe
Two German Perspectives on What is Europe?

James M. Skidmore

What is Europe? It seems like a simple question, but it can be—and has been—answered from multiple perspectives: geographic, ethnic, political, religious, linguistic. Even today the issue of identity lies at the heart of the debates that face the European Union as it evolves and defines—or redefines—itself. And as Anthony Pagden points out in his introduction to a collection of essays about the idea of Europe, the experiment that is Europe is still ongoing: "no one has any clear idea of the outcome" (Pagden 2002).

A successful outcome may seem even less likely in light of the Greek debt crisis and the threat it has posed to both the euro as a stable currency and the larger European Union as a stable multinational political formation. As of July 2015 an agreement among the government of Greece, the Eurogroup, and the so-called Troika (the European Central Bank, the International Monetary Fund, and the European Commission) was reached, though without much jubilation on anyone's part. The Greek government, having just won a national referendum empowering it to reject the austerity measures being sought by the Eurogroup and the Troika, agreed to new restrictions on its fiscal policies that closely resembled the proposed austerity program. Germany's Finance Minister Wolfgang Schäuble continued to muse publicly about Greece exiting voluntarily, if only temporarily, the eurozone. Various commentators, among them Paul Krugman of the *New York Times*, assailed Greece's creditors for their "betrayal of everything the European project was supposed to stand for" (Krugman 2015). Or as Neil Irwin, writing in the same newspaper, put it, Europe's response to Greece reflects "a deep aversion to government spending as a tool to fight economic slumps and faith in deregulated labor markets. It is a vision of austere, market-based policies that are a break with Europe's past" (Irwin 2015).

The recent financial troubles facing the eurozone that, by extension, have shaken the European Union itself are not solitary irritants. Mass drownings of refugees in the Mediterranean in the 2010s have also underscored weaknesses in Europe's attempts to act in a unified fashion. The nations of Europe cannot be held responsible for the civil wars in Syria and Libya, but their response to the new waves of refugees from these and other areas of civil unrest and economic strife have shown European solidarity, in the words of The Economist (2015), to be "flimsy." When these economic and social problems are considered within a larger framework that takes into account political, social, historical, and cultural issues, one must truly wonder whether Europe, regardless of whose Europe it is, can maintain any semblance of a unified identity. This is ironic because in one sense the continent has never been more integrated than it is today. Europe has been unified in the past, but always under the rule of one man, be it Caesar, Charlemagne, Napoleon, or Hitler. Today's European Union, the latest iteration of a commonwealth of nations that began with the Treaty of Paris (1951)—establishing the Coal and Steel Community—and the Treaty of Rome (1957)—establishing the Economic Community—is not an empire but a freely agreed upon union, one with flaws, but democratic nonetheless. Though not a country, Europe has become a state-like entity with courts and parliaments and councils and even an internet domain—.eu—all of which lend it at times an integrated presence both within its member states and on the larger world stage.

One thing Europe does not have is a constitution. A constitution defines a state's governing structures, but it is also often burdened with the extra duty of establishing the raison d'être of that state. The treaty establishing a constitution for Europe faltered after it was rejected in public referenda in France and the Netherlands in 2005. An indefinite period of reflection was then called to allow member states more time to consider and debate the proposed constitution, or to put ratification procedures on hold. It became clear, however, that a sweeping constitutional process would not work, so European leaders reverted to the incremental approach, ratifying the Treaty of Lisbon in 2007. This treaty amends previous treaties in such a way as to attain many of the organizational goals set out in the delayed constitutional process.

While the European Union may not have a constitution per se, neither do some of its member countries, for that matter: The United Kingdom has a constitutional tradition but no actual written document that could be called a constitution; Germany has a Basic Law that was intended to be provisional yet which has taken on the role of a constitution. Unlike Europe as a whole, the continent's constituent countries often have more cohesive histories and shared cultural traditions that provide a raison d'être for communal governance. In the absence of broadly shared political or cultural traditions, a constitution—a legal framework—would seem necessary to establish common governance of Europe and a resulting shared definition of European identity. But one can also argue that a constitution may not be the source for a common European identity: as the European Union develops its governmental structures and works out the practice of federal governance, a constitutional tradition should be able to develop over time as shared and common practices and histories emerge. This, as we shall see below, is an essentially Habermasian understanding of the role of law enshrined by a constitution.

One of the issues that caused a stir in the early 2000s had been the absence of any mention of God in the proposed constitution's preamble. In his apostolic exhortation "Ecclesia in Europa" from June, 2003, Pope John Paul II addressed challenges facing the Roman Catholic Church in Europe, specifically "the loss of Europe's Christian memory" (John Paul II 2003). He advocated a re-evangelization of the continent, and called upon the drafters of the constitution to "include a reference to the religious and in particular the Christian heritage of Europe" (ibid.). They did not. Instead a formulation was arrived at referring to "the cultural, religious and humanist inheritance of Europe," and it would be taken over by the Lisbon Treaty. A decidedly secular preamble, this wording bases Europe's constitutional legitimacy on rational human values. No primacy to a religious legacy, Christian or otherwise, is given.

Is the rational secularism that was enshrined in the failed constitution enough to sustain an entity like Europe? Many view the Enlightenment of the eighteenth century as the turning point in human history towards modernity, when the Western world gained the wherewithal to shake off in a consequential manner the fetters of religious dogma and rely on *ratio* to manage human affairs. One could say, tongue firmly in cheek, that some countries—France comes most readily to mind here—made a religion out of this secularist approach. It is no exaggeration to claim that contemporary Europe sets an example of a society governed along rational-secular principles. Human reason, not divine intervention, has allowed this loosely connected society to determine what is right, proper, and good, though it is clear that in many countries of Europe Christian religious doctrine in the areas of marriage and family still holds considerable legal sway. The European Union has enshrined these self-evident truths in its Charter of Fundamental Rights, first adopted in 2000 and, since the Treaty of Lisbon, part of the canon of law informing the decisions of the European Court of Justice. As the Charter's preamble observes:

> The peoples of Europe, in creating an ever closer union among them, are resolved to share a peaceful future based on common values.
>
> Conscious of its spiritual and moral heritage, the Union is founded on the indivisible, universal values of human dignity, freedom, equality and solidarity; it is based on the principles of democracy and the rule of law. It places the individual at the heart of its activities, by establishing the citizenship of the Union and by creating an area of freedom, security and justice.
>
> (European Union 2010)

Like the constitutional preamble, the Charter skirts the issue of organized religion by intoning a vague "spiritual and moral heritage." The rest of the text in the paragraph that follows highlights the usual Enlightenment tropes. A nod to a shared but undefined spiritual heritage is made, but with the human being, not God, as the moral foundation of Europe.

The debates about the relationship between Europe's identity and its values force us to consider the more fundamental concepts that are central to any discussion about Europe. The question "What is Europe?" is one way of stating a more complex question, namely "What quality, feature, or structure defines Europe, both for its own citizens and for the rest of the world?"[1] Discussing that question informs any constitutional debate, especially those surrounding the codification of "European" values, the rights and freedoms of its citizens. What authority or ideal legitimizes those values?

Two Germans, Jürgen Habermas and Benedict XVI (formerly Joseph Ratzinger), have been part of this larger public dialogue about Europe and its values for most of the 2000s. Each man has written or spoken about "what binds Europe" or "what holds the world together," and each has enunciated a relatively clear position on the type of Europe he wishes to see. Both born in the late 1920s, they experienced Germany's darkest hour during the Third Reich, and although they both became academics, their responses to Nazism were decidedly different: Habermas became associated with the Frankfurt School and its Marxist leanings; Ratzinger entered the church and rejected the turbulence of the student revolts of the 1960s by leaving the school of theology at Tübingen for the more conservative climate at Regensburg. In 2004, they met face-to-face in Munich for a public discussion of the topic "Vorpolitische moralische Grundlagen eines freiheitlichen Staates" (Pre-political Moral Foundations of a Free State). Each read from a prepared text and then answered questions from a select audience of about 30 listeners.

Habermas, as the guest of the Catholic Academy of Bavaria that hosted the event, spoke first. Although Habermas and Ratzinger were each asked to speak on the "pre-political moral foundations of a free state," Habermas altered the title of his contribution in the published volume to "pre-political foundations of the democratic constitutional state." In so doing he marks his intention to make two things clear from the outset: that states do not have or require moral foundations, and that the democratic constitutional state is the ideal expression of state organization.

Habermas centers his talk on the Böckenförde dilemma. The German jurist Ernst Wolfgang Böckenförde was skeptical of the ability of liberal democratic states to generate the necessary moral conditions for their existence. In the first part of his essay, Habermas argues forcefully that "the liberal state can satisfy its own need for legitimacy in a self-sufficient manner" (Habermas 2006: 29). By relying on the philosophical advances of the Enlightenment period, states can establish "legal procedures born of democratic procedures" (ibid.: 27). Citizens are motivated to respect and uphold these laws because they are the co-legislators who developed them in the first place.

But in his talk Habermas does express some concern about external threats, namely a slackening of the democratic bonds that promote solidarity of the citizenry over individual self-interest. In Habermas' view, the fear that society could end up at the end of a "blind alley" out of which there is no escape except "by means of the religious orientation to a transcendent point of reference" is a more recent development (ibid.: 37). Habermas does not mention the events of September 11, 2001, though the fervent religious beliefs of the 9/11 revolutionaries can be considered an example of the transcendent point of reference. Religious fanatics cannot modify or amend their beliefs, and so they end up in the blind alley of religious extremism.

Some observers of the debate were taken aback by the last section of Habermas' remarks which, as Edward Skidelsky put it in *Prospect Magazine*, took a "surprising turn" (Skidelsky 2005). Habermas states that "philosophy has good reasons to be willing to learn from religious traditions" (Habermas 2006: 42). In the dialogue Habermas argues that a liberal state "finds a self-satisfying legitimation ... independent of religious and metaphysical traditions" (Nemoianu 2006). Habermas also acknowledges, however, the existence of a "post-secular age" and cautions that a complete banishment of religion from human affairs—a project for which Charles Taylor (2009) coined the term "exclusive humanism"—would rob society of insights offered by religious traditions. For example, the insight afforded by the belief that human beings are created in the likeness of God can encourage respect for human life.

Fearing the erosion of solidarity in a society dominated by the free market and a complicit bureaucracy that enables the market's unfettered exploitation of human capital, Habermas warns that "it is in the interest of the constitutional state to deal carefully with all the cultural sources that nourish its citizens' consciousness of norms and their solidarity" (Habermas 2006: 46). Religious traditions and beliefs may have some value in a post-secular society if they can be translated "from the religious language into a language that is accessible to the public as a whole" (ibid.: 51–52). At the same time, if secular society can learn from religious heritage, believers must revise their expectations that their beliefs and practices should go unchallenged in society.

Habermas' friendly nod towards religion's role as an ally in the democratic state's "own struggle against the alienating forces of the modern world" (Skidelsky 2005) seemed to be a departure for one of Germany's most outspoken secularists. But as Philippe Portier (2011) has so concisely and convincingly shown, Habermas has undergone a three-stage development in his understanding of religion's position in society and the public discourses needed to sustain democracy. In his early thought, Habermas argued for the disappearance of religion from the public sphere, then for its limitation to the private sphere, and finally for its "publicization": "religion ... should intervene in the public sphere and use its founding documents and traditions to refine 'moral intuitions'" (Portier 2011: 425). According to Portier, Habermas' change of heart was a realization that in secular society religion was not disappearing and that values require sources. The "forceful theological-political criticism" (ibid.: 427) that his work underwent convinced Habermas that even though belief in God could limit a human being's potential, religion itself did have some salutary elements that enabled it to play a civilizing role in the development of human society. Portier maintains that Habermas rejected any role for religious language or thinking in political decision-making. At the same time, "drawing from their rhetorical wells of meaning, [Habermas allows that] religions can further enhance the civilizing impact of their proposals, helping the 'civic dialogue' to achieve 'rationally acceptable results'" (ibid.: 431). Faith can be a complement to reason, not its basis (ibid.). In this scenario, faith acts as a rhetorical device that can facilitate the communication of reason in the public realm. "The alliance of agnostic reason (provided it espouses solidarity)," Portier concludes, "and reason animated by belief (provided it does justice to reason) must be combined to re-civilize the world" (ibid.: 432). In other words, Habermas allows religion a limited role in helping society develop its morality so long as there is no attempt to make religious faith the wellspring of that morality.[2]

The difficulty here, however, is that religious zealots, convinced of the truth that what they believe has been revealed to them, will want that truth to form the basis of civil society. Believers orient themselves to a transcendent point of reference. This is not what Habermas wants, and on at least one occasion he discusses the matter at greater length. His celebrated acceptance speech of the Friedenspreis des Deutschen Buchhandels (Peace Prize of the German Book Trade) in 2001, just a month after the attacks on the World Trade Center and the Pentagon by members of al-Qaeda, outlines his basic conception of the "post-secular society" and how adherents to a religion are to function within it (Habermas 2001b). Speaking as the shock of the attack had yet to wear off, and only a week after American aerial bombardment of Afghanistan had begun, Habermas set out some conditions for the participation of the faithful in society: a cognitive (as opposed to emotional) approach, acceptance of the supremacy of science, and acceptance of the constitutional state.

Of note is that only two weeks earlier Habermas' (2001a) essay "Why Europe Needs a Constitution" had appeared in the *New Left Review*. In the early days of the euro he argued that "as a political collectivity, Europe cannot take hold in the consciousness of its citizens simply in the shape of a common currency" (ibid.: 6). While arguing that post-war Europe had moved towards a common constitution in order to end warfare and contain possible German expansion, Habermas devotes most of his remarks to the "third strand in European integration—the straightforward economic argument" (ibid.: 7).

Perhaps of greater importance for our present purposes, however, would be Habermas' thoughts on European identity and their relationship to the constitutional question. In the *New Left Review* article Habermas explains that Europe's history is a chronicle of nationalism, warfare, and the neglect of human rights (Habermas 2001a). Present-day Europe is relatively better off in this regard, but its identity is wrapped up in the knowledge that it must overcome its troubling past. This historical context, in Habermas' rosy view, makes it easier for Europe to "transition to a post-national democracy based on the mutual recognition of the differences between strong and proud national cultures" (ibid.: 21). He stresses what has become a cornerstone of his conception of Europe, namely that a civic nation can be a voluntary association, one that is not bound by "fate shaped by common descent, language and history" (ibid.: 15). The civic nation, unlike the ethnic one, while incorporating historical developments, relies heavily on a public sphere that mediates the solidarity of citizens. Citizenship in such an entity would require "a European-wide public sphere—a network that gives citizens of all member states an equal opportunity to take part in an encompassing process of focused political communication" (ibid.: 17). This communication will inform the common will that must drive the common European project, as opposed to the common market.

In 2003, on the occasion of worldwide protests against American action in Iraq, Habermas wrote an essay jointly with the French literary theorist Jacques Derrida (though Derrida was too ill at the time to contribute much more than his name). Here Habermas elaborates the ideas of the 2001 essay. In contemplating a shared purpose for European citizenry, Habermas and Derrida argue that "only the consciousness of a shared political fate, and the prospect of a common future, can halt outvoted minorities from the obstruction of a majority will" (Habermas and Derrida 2003: 293). A shared political fate, however, depends on member states feeling as if they belonged together. In spite of a past continental history in which dialogue has given way to armed conflict, Habermas claims that Europe has also had to learn "how differences can be communicated, contradictions institutionalized, and tensions stabilized" (ibid.: 294). Habermas claims that Europe's violent past has taught it to acknowledge "the Other in his otherness" (ibid.), but this abstract affirmation of identity based on civic communication lacks concrete proof that it will stand the test of time.

In reviewing Habermas' most recent contribution to the Europe question, *The Crisis of the European Union: A Response*, Erik O. Eriksen (2012) notes that the English edition has reversed the order of the essays. In the German original edition, "The Concept of Human Dignity and the Realistic Utopia of Human Rights" came before the essay section "The Crisis of the European Union in Light of a Constitutionalization of International Law—An Essay on the Constitution of Europe." Eriksen argues that the essay on dignity and rights should have been the first essay in the book because it lays the groundwork for the longer essay on how the current crises are threatening the union's ongoing process of state-building. Eriksen's argument has merit. For Habermas, human dignity "forms the 'portal' through which the egalitarian and universalistic substance of morality is imported into law" (Habermas 2012). Habermas is relying on Kant when referring to the idea of human dignity, namely the notion that the human being possesses qualities that are ends in themselves, not of relative value but of absolute value. Free will, for example, is closely connected to human dignity; the ability of the human being to act freely is a mark of the human being's dignity.

The concept of human dignity is enshrined and protected in many legal codifications of human rights. It is these rights that form the framework of participation that is essential for the realization of Habermas' democratic public sphere. But "the classical human rights declarations, when they speak of 'inborn' or 'inalienable' human rights, of 'inherent' or 'natural' rights, or of '*droits inaliénables et sacrés*', betray their religious and metaphysical origins" (Habermas 2012: 81). Habermas nevertheless discounts the need for such justification in the modern age: "In a secular state, however, such predicates function primarily as placeholders; they remind us of the mode of a *generally acceptable justification* of the exacting moral content of these rights whose epistemic dimension is *beyond state control*" (ibid.). These rights must be declared and made public in order to become part of a community's legal operating framework, but their justification does not rely on religious morality or church doctrine. Moreover, when Habermas writes in the main essay of the book that "citizens of Europe have good reasons for wanting their respective nation states to *continue to perform their constitutional role* as guarantors of law and freedom" (ibid.: 13), he has the state's role of fostering the protection of fundamental human rights in mind. His civic conception of the nation, as opposed to the ethnic one that has played such a large part in European history, requires a foundational ethic based on human dignity. The ethic is its own justification and requires no outside force for legitimization, merely a legal encoding to protect and ensconce it within the state.

In their meeting in 2004 in Munich, Joseph Ratzinger discussed with Habermas at length the general notion of a secular society based on rationality that is so integral to Habermas' worldview. Ratzinger (2006) suggested that "secular culture is largely dominated by the strict rationality ... that understands itself to be the element that binds people together," a simplistic but essentially accurate summary of the secularist position. But at the same time he wonders whether "Europeans have grown weary of rationality" (Ratzinger 2006: 46), an idea that occurred to him when considering the mood that permeates the writing of twentieth-century European intellectuals such as Carl Schmitt, Martin Heidegger, and Claude Lévi-Strauss.

Ratzinger's contribution to the debate consists of both a critique of reason and an acceptance, indeed an endorsement, of its indispensability. He argues for example that one could well "doubt the reliability of reason" (Ratzinger 2006: 65), citing the atomic bomb and the "breeding and selection of human beings" (ibid.: 66) as misguided products of human science and ultimately, therefore, of reason. Ratzinger (2006) goes on to argue that "the intercultural dimension" of the discussion cannot be ignored: there are parts of the world that do not accept European or Western notions of rationality, and even within cultural traditions tensions exist that undermine any notion that uniformity is possible. Ratzinger's criticisms of rationality do not prevent him from acknowledging its importance to human existence, however. Reason and faith, according to Ratzinger, are "called to purify and help one another. They need each other, and they must accept this mutual need" (ibid.: 78).

The influence of culture on reason is only discussed by Ratzinger in broad strokes. But by raising the issue he highlights one of the main critiques of the secular, or non-transcendent, approach to human affairs, namely the absence of fixed points of reference in an age of relativism. Although he asserts that Western rationality is as culturally dependent as other worldviews, he accepts the basic utilitarian value of reason to safeguard against excesses carried out in the name of religion. In effect he is arguing for the mutual interdependence of reason and faith: "Religion must continually allow itself to be purified and structured by reason" (Ratzinger 2006: 77). At the same time, in order to protect against the "hubris of reason," reason "must learn a willingness to listen to the great religious traditions of mankind" (ibid.: 78). While similar to Habermas' notion that religious tradition can inform the creation of a value system in post-secular society, Ratzinger unsurprisingly advocates a more substantial role for religious faith. With regard to the intercultural issue, however, Ratzinger argues that:

> It is important to include the other cultures in the attempt at a polyphonic relatedness, in which they themselves are receptive to the essential complementarity of reason and faith, so that a universal process of purifications (in the plural!) can proceed.
>
> (Ratzinger 2006: 79)[3]

While the tone here is moderate and tolerant, the underlying basis of the approach to other cultures is "the complementarity of reason and faith," a notion that Ratzinger claims has been part of the European philosophical tradition since the time of the ancient Greeks.

Ratzinger, both before and after being elevated to the chair of St. Peter in 2005, had discussed Europe and its relationship to reason and Christian evangelization in numerous speeches and interviews. Whereas Habermas' view of Europe might be characterized as a legal or constitutional concept, as early as 2000 Ratzinger was arguing that Europe is a "cultural and historical concept" not to be ignored (Ratzinger 2007: 11). The problem, however, is that the "world of European values ... has arrived at its end, and has already left the scene" (ibid.: 23), leaving Europe "hollowed out" and lacking "will for the future" (ibid.: 24). He criticizes the renunciation of any religious basis for the state that began with the French Revolution and the subsequent slavish devotion to reason alone: "When confronted with the frailty of reason, these systems have proved to be fragile and have easily fallen victim to dictatorships" (ibid.: 26). For Ratzinger, "the state cannot create moral force but rather must presuppose it and build upon it" (ibid.: 27), and he goes on to enunciate a constitutional view that could well be shared by Habermas:

> To establish in writing the value and dignity of man, of liberty, equality, and solidarity, along with the fundamental declaration of democracy and of a state governed by law, implies an image of man, a moral option, and a concept of law that are by no means obvious but that are fundamental factors in the identity of Europe.
>
> (Ratzinger 2007: 30)

Where Habermas and Ratzinger would necessarily have to part ways, however, is in ascertaining the source of those values. Ratzinger argues that when it comes to determining the pre-eminence of values such as human dignity, "only God can establish values that are based on the nature of man and are inviolable" (ibid.).

Of note here is that Ratzinger is not saying that values that could inform a constitution come from God alone, but that the values established by God are based on the "nature of man." Setting aside the awkwardness of gender-specific language for the time being, the implication of this statement is fully understood when one comprehends what Ratzinger means by the "nature of man." When discussing Europe, Ratzinger has returned repeatedly to the human being's capacity for reason, though he has often described this as being a European trait, or at least described it as one of Europe's distinguishing features, "an essential hallmark of European culture" that "can become devastating if it becomes detached from its roots and exalts technological feasibility as the sole criterion" (Ratzinger 2007: 43). And in a speech upon receiving the St. Benedict award for the promotion of life and the family in Europe, given to Ratzinger the day before his predecessor as Pope, John Paul II, died, Ratzinger stated that European rational technical culture has done the most to unite the world. Yet he also claimed that a distressing result of this evolution is that "the splendor of being an image of God no longer shines over man, which is what confers on him his dignity and inviolability, and he is left only to the power of his own human capacities" (Ratzinger 2005). In this worldview, the nature of the human being is very much connected to God's nature, and it is the connection that is at the root of human dignity.

Inasmuch as Ratzinger views rationality as a European trait, he is particularly interested in its impact on Christianity, which received in Europe "its most effective cultural and intellectual imprint" (ibid.). That reason and faith can complement each other, as Ratzinger argued in the 2004 debate, is central to his understanding of Christianity and its role in the public sphere. The relation of faith and reason can be largely credited for the affinities found in Habermas' and Ratzinger's conception of the moral foundations of a free state.

A little over a year after assuming the papacy, Benedict XVI gave a speech in Regensburg that infuriated many. After opening reminiscences about his time in Regensburg as a Professor of Theology, he referred to a dialogue from 1391 between the Byzantine emperor Manuel II Paleologus and an unnamed but learned Persian. The Pope was roundly criticized for his remarks. Many felt that the dialogue's description of the work of the Prophet Muhammad as "evil and inhuman" was derogatory, and that the Pope was making a veiled but not very subtle attack on Islam. Benedict quoted from this dialogue because it dealt with the issues surrounding faith and reason and demonstrated, as he put it, that not acting

> in accordance with reason is contrary to God's nature.... For the emperor, as a Byzantine shaped by Greek philosophy, this statement is self-evident. But for Muslim teaching, God is absolutely transcendent. His will is not bound up with any of our categories, even that of rationality.
>
> (Benedict XVI 2006)

Benedict used the rest of the lecture to develop the point that Christianity, thanks to the influence of Greek philosophy starting with the writing of the Gospels, was a Hellenized or Greek religion and ipso facto a European religion. Thus Benedict not only stamps Europe with a Christian heritage, but Christianity with a European heritage. We can extrapolate from Benedict's speech that Islam's disinterest in human rationality makes it non-European.

The clumsiness of the Holy See's response to the criticism that followed the lecture exacerbated the outrage felt by many Islamic cultures.[4] Worth noting, however, is Benedict's attempt to address the intercultural issues he had identified in his debate with Habermas. He unwittingly provided a very tangible example of the need for—and the difficulties of—engaging with other cultures. Such engagement is crucial for developing a codex of common values that can form the basis of a freely governed society. Without saying it explicitly, Benedict, by claiming for Christianity the mantle of a faith infused by reason, reinforced the (Western) conception of Islam as a fundamentalist faith that is immoderate in its zeal. The word Islam means submission or surrender, and the word's definition sums up for the followers of Islam the attitude that human beings should have toward the divine. In the Islamic worldview, God is not relegated to specific spheres of human or societal life. God's place is everywhere. In his speech on Europe's spiritual foundations, given while still a cardinal, Benedict had expressed admiration for Islamic traditions, especially the ideal of utter devotion to God's will. He saw Islam as having a challenge similar to that of Christianity: how to instill spiritual values in a secular world. In fact, Benedict almost appeared jealous of Islam:

> Islam is capable of offering a valid spiritual basis for the life of the peoples, a basis that seems to have slipped out of the hands of old Europe, which ... is increasingly viewed as a declining culture condemned to fade away.
>
> (Ratzinger 2007: 22)

It is difficult to establish, on the basis of two texts, a full understanding of Ratzinger/Benedict's attitude towards Islam. He notes a more complete unity between the religion and the societies that host it than is the case with Christianity and the secular West. Yet he also criticizes the negation of reason that makes possible the unity between religion and society in Islamic cultures. This rejection of Western-style reason that many in the West think of as a hallmark of Islamic fundamentalism also has implications for Habermas' style of deliberative democracy. As Vivienne Boon points out, "the question of how to communicate to those who refuse to communicate puts us right at the very limits of what Habermas' discourse ethics can accommodate" (Boon 2010: 163). Boon goes on to say that "the problems posed by fundamentalism to discourse ethics are far greater than realized by Habermas—as it entails not only a rejection of Western modernity, but also of deliberation, human sovereignty and rationalist epistemology" (ibid.). For many Europeans, the fear that their continent is being "Islamized" stems from the notion that Islam is unable to compromise and to integrate into the secular order of present-day Europe, that its goal is to assimilate other faiths and peoples. Islam has not experienced what Mark Lilla (2007) refers to as the "Great Separation," the wedge that divides religion from politics as understood by Thomas Hobbes. According to Lilla, Hobbes reckoned that "in order to escape the destructive passions of messianic faith, political theology centered on God [should be] replaced by political philosophy centered on man. This was the Great Separation" (Lilla 2007). One should note here that not all Muslims are fundamentalists; Muslim thinkers such as Tariq Ramadan (2005) would argue that Islam can successfully exist in a Western context. If nothing else, the very presence of Islamic culture in Europe forces Europeans to reflect on their understanding of the relationship between reason and faith, and the implications of that relationship for the European project.

And Europe is the point. Benedict and Habermas are both intimately involved with—and concerned about—Europe. Boon, in her critique of Habermas' reflections on Europe, wonders whether Habermas should have avoided the question of European identity in the classic sense and instead relied solely on his "thin proceduralist model" to promote the cause of European integration (Boon 2007). Perhaps Habermas heeded her call; *The Crisis of the European Union. A Response* relies very heavily on what Boon would call the "thin prescriptive model of constitutional patriotism" (Boon 2007). Boon's criticism of Habermas' writings up to 2006 is that the "model of a postnational Europe appeals to a thicker description of Europe that remains more firmly rooted in some particular (namely West-German) political and cultural traditions than others" (Boon 2007: 287–288). According to Boon, this approach "threatens to silence the voices of others (or Otherness) which have alternative claims to Europe and Europeanness" (ibid.: 88). In this regard she is especially critical of Habermas' ignorance of central and eastern European experience. Benedict, for his part, appeals unabashedly to that "thicker description of Europe," though it may surprise some the extent to which Benedict asserts that human reason enjoyed its greatest flowering in the European tradition, and that reason is an essential feature of Christianity's expression and identity. Boon rejects Habermas' intention to ascribe "to Europe an important civilizing role" (Boon 2007: 292), though that is exactly the role Benedict himself sees for Europe.

Boon's disappointment in what could be described as Habermas' softening on secularism still does not adequately explain how one might use a proceduralist approach to gain the endorsement of religious minorities (and in some localities majorities) for a postnational European state. Constitutional patriotism—using a constitution instead of shared history, language, or ethnicity to define a national identity—might be enough to form an entity like the European Union, a united but not unified collection of states that is neither nation nor international association, neither fish nor fowl. But is it enough to keep that state functioning in the manner desired, where human dignity is preserved and fostered, even as it faces fiscal emergencies of the kind that the eurozone is currently experiencing?

Even though Benedict's discussion of Europe pre-dates the current financial and immigration crises, his approach can still be criticized for its tacit nostalgia for a chimera: the idea of a Europe with a more homogenous religious-cultural identity. Even so, neither Benedict's search for answers in Europe's traditions, nor Habermas' quest to postulate a future order based on his principles of collective democratic participation, seem adequate to the task at hand. Neither approach is well versed in the quotidian realities that can bog down any political effort, nor has either adequately addressed the changing makeup of European cultural identity. At any rate Benedict seems willing to raise the issue, something missing from Habermas' reflections (at least in explicit terms).

Since vacating St. Peter's throne in 2013, Benedict has fallen largely silent on the issues confronting Europe. His successor, Pope Francis, has criticized in no uncertain terms the "culture of comfort" that has fostered a "globalized indifference" to the suffering of refugees (Francis 2013), a stance notably more forceful and direct than Benedict's. Francis's various comments on "rampant capitalism" and its effect on the dignity of the human being, most notably in his address to the European Parliament in which he lamented that "men and women risk being reduced to mere cogs in a machine that treats them as items of consumption to be exploited" (Francis 2014) can be seen as a continuation of papal pronouncements on labor and capitalism dating back to Pope Leo XIII's 1891 encyclical *Rerum novarum* and even Benedict's 2009 encyclical *Caritas in veritate*.

In contrast to Benedict, Habermas has continued his running commentary on the failings of the European Union to practice a more inclusive and deliberative form of democracy. *The Crisis of the European Union* (first published in German in 2011) has been followed by *The Lure of Technocracy* (Habermas 2015). This set of essays is not as focused on the European crisis (for example there is a section on German Jewish thinkers), but in the title essay—"The Lure of Technocracy: A Plea for European Solidarity"—Habermas returns to familiar territory by looking at the impact on European unity of the financial crisis of 2008 and the subsequent sovereign debt crises of the 2010s, especially the increasing influence of Euroskepticism among large swathes of the national electorates (ibid.). Habermas would argue that only greater political integration can stem the tides of xenophobic nationalism and crass capitalism that threaten to undo the gains made by the European unification process. In an interview with the *Guardian* after the July 13, 2015 Greek debt accord, Habermas turned his sights towards the governing institutions of the EU as well as national governments such as Germany, arguing that their authoritarian treatment of Greece and intransigence with regard to a restructuring of Greek debt had no democratic legitimacy. Moreover, when asked if the European problem was financial, political, or moral, he ignored the moral aspect altogether, arguing that the economic problems had been exacerbated by the political failings of nationally-oriented leaders:

> We are in a political trap ... this technocratic hollowing out of democracy is the result of a neoliberal pattern of market-deregulation policies. The balance between politics and the market has come out of sync, at the cost of the welfare state.
>
> (Oltermann 2015)

Habermas' hopes for European integration are great, but the inability of Europe's political and administrative leadership to overcome nationalizing tendencies and globalizing economies leave him irritated.

Both Habermas and Benedict have, over the course of the past two decades, articulated visions for Europe that address a central question, namely the question that opened this chapter: What is Europe? Each has tackled this question by posing related questions: What binds Europe? What holds the (European) world together? Habermas and Benedict belong to the same generation, but their understanding of what makes Europe special is not that similar, though they both greatly respect the Enlightenment regard for human reason and the role Europe has played in establishing the Western mode of reasoning throughout the world. They also both use their experience of death and destruction in Germany in the twentieth century to imagine a polity that embeds Germany within a larger system. Such a system, it is hoped, will prevent the repetition of the crimes and horrors of the German past. Human society must respect and safeguard human dignity. Where Habermas and Benedict differ is in determining the (legitimizing) source of that dignity, and their difference in this regard reflects their general worldview and their years of espousing secular versus religious concepts of the world. Whereas Habermas advocates a state-like formation for Europe in which the law legitimizes democratic participation, Benedict relies on shared tradition to (re-)instill in Europe a national consciousness. What remains to be seen is whether either perspective can prove to be enough of a foundation on which to build a federated Europe that can safeguard human dignity in the midst of large financial and immigration crises. Habermas and Benedict could respond to the question "What is Europe?" by claiming that it is an association of states that safeguards and fosters human dignity. But they would not be able to agree on the ultimate source of that dignity.

Notes

1 For a useful introduction to the history of the idea of Europe, see Pagden (2002).
2 Closer examination of Habermas' chief contention that religious and secular worldviews need translation into a common discourse that allows religious and secular discourses to inform each other can be found in Craig Calhoun et al. (2013).
3 Emphasis is Ratzinger's.
4 For example see Ian Fisher (2006).

Works Cited

Benedict XVI (2006) "Faith, Reason and the University. Memories and Reflections," Lecture, Aula Magna of the University of RegensburgTuesday, September 12, 2006. The Holy See. www.vatican.va/holy_father/benedict_xvi/speeches/2006/september/documents/hf_ben-xvi_spe_20060912_university-regensburg_en.html (last accessed: March 2, 2016).

Boon, Vivienne (2007) "Jürgen Habermas' Writings on Europe: Not Habermasian Enough?" *Ethical Perspectives*, 14(3), pp. 287–310.

Boon, Vivienne (2010) "Jürgen Habermas and Islamic Fundamentalism: On the Limits of Discourse Ethics," *Journal of Global Ethics*, 6(2), pp. 153–166.

Calhoun, Craig, Eduardo Mendieta, and Jonathan VanAntwerpen (eds.) (2013) *Habermas and Religion*. Cambridge: Polity Press.

Eriksen, Erik O. (2012) "Review of *The Crisis of the European Union: A Response*, by Jürgen Habermas," in *Notre Dame Philosophical Reviews*, September 18, 2012. http://ndpr.nd.edu/news/33467-the-crisis-of-the-european-union-a-response/ (last accessed: March 2, 2016).

European Union (2010) "Charter of Fundamental Rights of the European Union," *Official Journal of the European Union*, 2010/C 83/02, March 30, 2010. http://eur-lex.europa.eu/LexUriServ/LexUriServ.do?uri=OJ:C:2010:083:0389:0403:en:PDF (last accessed: March 2, 2016).

Fisher, Ian (2006) "Pope's Regrets over Statement Fail to Quiet a Storm of Protest," in *New York Times*, September 19, 2006. www.nytimes.com/2006/09/19/world/europe/19pope.html (last accessed: March 2, 2016).

Francis (2013) "Homily," July 8, 2013, Libreria Editrice Vaticana. http://w2.vatican.va/content/francesco/en/homilies/2013/documents/papa-francesco_20130708_omelia-lampedusa.html (last accessed: March 2, 2016).

Francis (2014) "Address of Pope Francis to the European Parliament," November 25, 2014, Libreria Editrice Vaticana. https://w2.vatican.va/content/francesco/en/speeches/2014/november/documents/papa-francesco_20141125_strasburgo-parlamento-europeo.html (last accessed: March 2, 2016).

Habermas, Jürgen (2001a) "Why Europe Needs a Constitution," *New Left Review*, 11, pp. 5–26.

Habermas, Jürgen (2001b) *Glauben und Wissen: Friedenspreis des Deutschen Buchhandels 2001*. Frankfurt a. M.: Suhrkamp

Habermas, Jürgen (2006) "Pre-political Foundations of the Democratic Constitutional State?" in Florian Schuller (ed.) *Dialectics of Secularization. On Reason and Religion.* Trans. Brian McNeil. San Francisco: Ignatius Press, pp. 19–52.

Habermas, Jürgen (2012) *The Crisis of the European Union. A Response.* Trans. Ciaran Cronin. Cambridge: Polity Press.

Habermas, Jürgen (2015) *The Lure of Technocracy*. Cambridge: Polity Press.

Habermas, Jürgen and Jacques Derrida (2003) "February 15, Or What Binds Europeans Together: A Plea for a Common European Foreign Policy, Beginning in the Core of Europe." Trans. Max Pensky. *Constellations*, 10(3), pp. 291–297.

Irwin, Neil (2015) "How Germany Prevailed in the Greek Bailout," *New York Times*, July 29, 2015. http://nyti.ms/1JR6hlu (last accessed: March 2, 2016).

John Paul II (2003) "Ecclesia in Europa," The Holy See, June 28, 2003. www.vatican.va/holy_father/john_paul_ii/apost_exhortations/documents/hf_jp-ii_exh_20030628_ecclesia-in-europa_en.html (last accessed: March 2, 2016).

Krugman, Paul (2015) "Killing the European Project," *New York Times*, July 12, 2015. http://nyti.ms/1L0mEBO (last accessed: March 2, 2016).

Lilla, Mark (2007) "The Politics of God," *New York Times Sunday Magazine*, August 19, 2007. www.nytimes.com/2007/08/19/magazine/19Religion-t.html (last accessed: March 2, 2016).

Nemoianu, Virgil (2006) "The Church and the Secular Establishment. A Philosophical Dialog between Joseph Ratzinger and Jürgen Habermas," *Logos*, 9(2), pp. 16–42.

Oltermann, Philip (2015) "Jürgen Habermas' Verdict on the EU/Greece Debt Deal," *Guardian*, July 16, 2015. www.theguardian.com/commentisfree/2015/jul/16/jurgen-habermas-eu-greece-debt-deal (last accessed: March 2, 2016).

Pagden, Anthony (ed.) (2002) *The Idea of Europe: From Antiquity to the European Union*. Washington, DC/Cambridge: Woodrow Wilson Press/Cambridge University Press.

Portier, Philippe (2011) "Religion and Democracy in the Thought of Jürgen Habermas," *Society*, 48(5), pp. 426–432.

Ramadan, Tariq (2005) *Western Muslims and the Future of Islam*. Oxford: Oxford University Press.

Ratzinger, Joseph (2005) "On Europe's Crisis of Culture," *Zenit News*, July 25, 2005. www.zenit.org/en/articles/cardinal-ratzinger-on-europe-s-crisis-of-culture-part-1 (last accessed: March 2, 2016).

Ratzinger, Joseph (2006) "That Which Holds the World Together. The Prepolitical Moral Foundations of a Free State," in Florian Schulle (ed.) *Dialectics of Secularization: On Reason and Religion*. Trans. Brian McNeil. San Francisco: Ignatius Press, pp. 53–80.

Ratzinger, Joseph (2007) *Europe Today and Tomorrow*. Trans. Michael J. Miller. San Francisco: Ignatius Press.

Skidelsky, Edward (2005) "Habermas vs. the Pope," *Prospect Magazine*, November 20, 2005. www.prospectmagazine.co.uk/magazine/jurgen-habermas-pope-benedict-xvi-ratzinger/ (last accessed: March 2, 2016).

Taylor, Charles (2009) *A Secular Age*. Cambridge: Harvard University Press.

The Economist (2015) "Europe's Boat People," in *The Economist*, April 25, 2015. http://econ.st/1OJP1RI (Last accessed: March 2, 2016).

6 Cosmopolitan Reflections
Jürgen Habermas and W. G. Sebald[1]

Ian W. Wilson

> The foundation of the European Union can be conceived retrospectively as though the citizens involved (or their representatives) were split into two *personae* from the beginning; in that case every person as a European citizen in the constitution-founding process encounters herself, as it were, as a citizen of an already constituted national people.
>
> Jürgen Habermas (2012: 38)

Habermas' *Crisis of the European Union* inspires a reconsideration of political-philosophical cosmopolitanism in the light of Europe's recent economic crisis. We must address the importance of culture when reconsidering the essays, too, and the realm of the aesthetic must be considered within this discussion of culture. An examination of an aesthetic presentation of cosmopolitan subjectivity alongside Habermas' political one leads to an enhanced appreciation of the contributions of the cultural realm to discussions about cosmopolitanism in the European Union. To such an end, I compare the development of cosmopolitanism in W. G. Sebald's novel *Austerlitz* (2001) to Habermas' conceptualization of that political attitude, relying on both *The Crisis of the European Union* (2012) and earlier texts.

Habermas (1929–) and Sebald (1944–2001) represent important European voices on significant common topics: primarily the Holocaust, modernity, and cosmopolitanism. Though they have different perspectives and emerged from different academic milieus, the shared heritage of the German language and their international stature further draw them into contact. Out of the comparison comes the suggestion of a possible solution to a conundrum in Habermas' work on cosmopolitanism: how can cosmopolitan culture develop? Sebald's novel provides a gradual, empathetic answer.

The intentional conflation of the author W. G. Sebald with his eponymous protagonist in the novel *Austerlitz* (2001) directs readers to its cosmopolitan core, which—with Habermas' help—can suggest a model for a cosmopolitan literature of the European Union to complement the political and economic structures of the European Union. Habermas' essays on cosmopolitanism focus on the political, but they consistently maintain the importance of the cultural aspects of cosmopolitanism for the political to hold strong and be maintained. It is this realm of cultural cosmopolitanism on which *Austerlitz* depends.

Habermas' discussion of "cosmopolitan community" in the main essay in *Crisis of the European Union* (2012: 58) cites Garrett Wallace Brown and David Held's *Cosmopolitanism Reader*; Brown and Held define cosmopolitanism in the introduction to their collection as follows:

> In its most basic form, cosmopolitanism maintains that there are moral obligations owed to all human beings based solely on our humanity alone, without reference to race, gender, nationality, ethnicity, culture, religion, political affiliation, state citizenship, or other communal particularities.
>
> (Brown and Held 2010: 1)

Brown and Held later outline five "interrelated themes" of cosmopolitanism: "global justice, cultural cosmopolitanism, legal cosmopolitanism, political cosmopolitanism, and civic cosmopolitanism" (ibid.: 9). Cultural cosmopolitanism, the aspect I am most directly concerned with here,

> can be understood as relating to how we might be able to cultivate a sense of global justice in a culturally pluralistic world ... cultural cosmopolitans generally assert that all individuals are made up of multifarious cultural identities and influences and that humans always identify with a multiplicity of cultural obligations.
>
> (Ibid.: 10)

Although Habermas refrains from discussing practical details of the development of cultural cosmopolitanism, his formulation of a cosmopolitan political organization of the European Union depends upon it. After a discussion of the details of Habermas' discussion of cultural cosmopolitanism and the cosmopolitan community, I will turn to Sebald's novel as an illustration or test of Habermas' concepts. Sebald's novel presents an aesthetic meditation on the possibilities and necessities of thinking in cosmopolitan terms in order to work toward a rectification of past crimes. In the case of *Austerlitz*, the crimes are those of the Holocaust, and the challenge is to rebuild a functional and empathetic concept of German–Jewish relations.[2]

I Habermas and Cultural Cosmopolitanism

Habermas' main arguments relate to political cosmopolitanism; indeed, he refrains from reference to cultural figures, developments, or organizations in the highly abstract prose of *Crisis of the European Union*. However, elements of cultural cosmopolitanism lurk within his arguments, undergirding its strength. For instance, Habermas recognizes the limits of the political in reaching the aims of the EU, not just carving out a space for the cultural but recognizing its primacy. He writes:

> To be sure, the expansion of communication networks and horizons of perception, the liberalization of values and attitudes, an increase in the willingness to include strangers, the strengthening of civil society initiatives and a corresponding transformation of strong identities can at best be stimulated through legal-administrative means. There nevertheless exists a circular, either mutually reinforcing or mutually inhibiting, interaction between political processes and constitutional norms, on the one hand, and the network of shared political and cultural attitudes and convictions, on the other.
> (Habermas 2012: 46)

Habermas' topic is, of course, the constitutional and political processes that must transpire for the backbone of the European Union—or another cosmopolitan state—to develop. But his statement underscores the most important role, which is chiefly cultural, on which everything else depends. The elements crucial to a real cosmopolitan society—extended communication, experience, values, opinions, openness, the public sphere, and the development of transnational identity—take place most successfully in the cultural and social realms.

In his discussion of cosmopolitan community mentioned above, Habermas explores the tensions between an EU or world parliament and shared political culture. He recognizes, for instance, the inability of global phenomena to affect public opinion in a significant way (ibid.: 62). He writes, "Any political community, no matter how large and how pluralistic it may be, can differentiate itself from its environments with reference to an intersubjectively shared political culture" (ibid.: 62–63) which depends on "self-demarcation and self-assertion" (ibid.: 63). Global issues—European ones—remain too abstract for many members of a global (or European) citizenry. The continued tension between Germany and Greece during deliberations on the potential "Grexit" and the growing eruption of the issue of immigration into Germany's public sphere illustrate this notion well.

According to Habermas, the crux of the problem is identity: "But world citizens do not form a collective that would be held together by a political interest in the *self-assertion* of a way of life that shapes their identity" (ibid.). He calls for solving the problem by making abstract shared concerns more concrete, thereby giving them a "political character" (ibid.). Earlier in the essay, Habermas recognizes the conflict inherent in the EU's current organization related to culture—the shared nature of power between citizens' status as part of a European people and as an EU citizen hampers the ability of citizens to "recognize a part of their collective identity" in such cosmopolitan citizenship (ibid.: 43). Viewing extra-national (e.g., European or global) concerns as triggering ethical responses versus political ones, Habermas argues for taking steps to increase the value of abstract goods (such as education, transportation, and health systems; natural resources; environmental concerns; issues of nuclear waste; but also preventing war and ensuring human rights [ibid.: 63]) so that they can contribute to a sense of a "way of life" (ibid.; original *Lebensform*, see Habermas 2011: 90). Habermas asserts that certain such abstract goods become politicized in national political campaigns because they become "mingled with an element of self-assertion" (2012: 63). A successful and meaningful cosmopolitan state would encourage such "mingling" for other, broader issues. I would contend with Habermas that such mingling can only take place if citizens of a global or European state develop a sense of a collective political identity, a new form of "civic solidarity" in which German and Greek perspectives are shared that Habermas speaks of earlier in his essay (ibid.: 46). Although he does not explore many specific means for developing this solidarity, the shifts he describes fall largely into the realm of the cultural: only with adjustments to deep senses of one's cultural identity and values can such solidarity be developed and such values become more concrete, and thus political.

Habermas' earlier essays on cosmopolitanism develop the line of thought regarding the importance of its cultural component. In "The Postnational Constellation and the Future of Democracy," Habermas describes the need to decouple majority culture from a notion of "national culture" and to replace it with a kind of "constitutional patriotism" that remains part of the commonality of shared descent. It can therefore serve as a model for postnational intercultural relationships (Habermas 2001a: 74). The imagined nature of all nations (ibid.: 64; see also Habermas 2012: 47) can be overcome if citizens of a united Europe can conceive of commonalities in European experience as important and concrete enough to incorporate them into their own cultural and political sensibilities.

Habermas and Derrida argue somewhat more specifically in "February 15, or What Binds Europeans Together":

> The citizens of one nation must regard the citizens of another nation as fundamentally "one of us." This desideratum leads to the question that so many skeptics have called attention to: are there historical experiences, traditions, and achievements offering European citizens the consciousness of a political fate that has been shared together, and that can be shaped together?
>
> (Habermas and Derrida 2003: 293)

They answer this question in the hopeful affirmative, pointing to the realm of European culture, with its "rich cultural diversity," a feature of which is that "acknowledgement of differences—the reciprocal acknowledgement of the Other in his otherness—can also become a feature of a common identity" (ibid.: 294). This line of thinking remains constant in Habermas' later writing, too, for example in *The Crisis of the European Union* where he briefly discusses Kant: "We are inherently familiar with everyday situations in which we feel obliged to show solidarity with strangers, with everything that shows a human face, without any hint of self-assertion" (Habermas 2012: 64). Discussions of immigration and refugees in Germany at the moment of this writing illustrate the difficulties of such a notion. Invocations of "Zivilcourage" (engaged courage of one's convictions to defend the Other)[3] and attempts to directly engage Germans' sense of the foreign have entered public discourse in significant ways. The six different cover pages of the July 25, 2015 edition of *Der Spiegel* (31/2015), each showing a face of "foreignness" and the general motto "Xenophobia Is Poisoning Germany" under different specific mottos focusing on stereotypical reactions and suggested realities such as "Greedy? Hungry," "Uneducated? Repressed," "Threatening? Threatened," and "Criminal? Persecuted" serve an examples.[4]

Most vital, however, is Habermas' phrasing of the essay "Why Europe Needs a Constitution":

> A European-wide public sphere must not be imagined as the projection of a familiar design from the national onto the European level. It will rather emerge from the mutual opening of existing national universes to one another, yielding to an interpenetration of mutually translated national communications.
>
> (Habermas 2001b: 18)

In such moments, one glimpses a vague conceptualization of opportunities to build toward European culture with concrete political results: though no specific program is developed, Habermas describes the emergent political culture as developing in a similar fashion to national cultures, which by implication will take a long time. Neither French nor German national culture developed overnight, nor did such cultures develop purely as a result of the bureaucrats' demands.[5] Yet one can look around Europe and note significant if subtle issues in a developing European culture, whether those be a kind of increased status for the English language as a *lingua franca* or a devotion to freedom of movement within Europe regardless of income[6] or the development of intercultural, international cultural coproductions and events.

As Craig Calhoun writes: "The cosmopolitan image of multiple, layered citizenship can helpfully challenge the tendency of many communitarians to suggest not only that community is necessary and/or good, but that people normally inhabit one and only one community" (Calhoun 2002: 95). If one presumes membership in multiple communities as the key to European cosmopolitan identity, such identity does not remain purely abstract but can be tested. One may do so with literature. Although but a single mode of cultural expression, literary expression—especially that of the novel—can describe deep structures of thought and convictions. The interpenetration identities and communications can be tested via a cosmopolitan literature, which develops its model thematically and formally—that is, which describes cosmopolitan models through the interactions of characters of different nations via intermediary languages in intermediary spaces as well as through a formal linkage across the boundaries of the real world and the imagined, fictional world of the novel.

II Sebald and His Novel *Austerlitz*

Virtually all of the work of W. G. Sebald could be considered cosmopolitan in a general way, compendia as they are of images, memories, photographs, legends, building plans, and quotations from across Europe and beyond. Sebald's final completed extended fictional work, the novel *Austerlitz*, published in the year of his death, is his post-Holocaust novel and his most ghostly, suggesting that its unnamed German narrator, a gentile, has a spiritual twin, a Prague Jewish Holocaust escapee (Furst 2005: xv) and the novel's protagonist, Austerlitz. The novel's plot describes Austerlitz's attempts to understand his own past and to discover the fate of his parents. Austerlitz describes his childhood in 1930's Prague, his departure for the United Kingdom on a *Kindertransport* to live with a family in Wales, his school years, and later his research trips back to the Czech Republic in the 1990s. The novel ends as Austerlitz unsatisfactorily concludes the search for details regarding his mother's death and begins working on a search for the same about his father. Though the novel ends with Austerlitz's search unconcluded, it offers a successful, long-term model for German-Jewish reconciliation, which models other intercultural relationships necessary in a cosmopolitan Europe.

The two figures' friendship, an intriguing photograph of the author within the novel, the narrative relationship between the narrator and Austerlitz for much of the book (Austerlitz as narrator within the novel and the narrator turned into a narratee), and a variety of telling details referring to twins within the text and from Sebald's source material lead one to the conclusion that Sebald, raised after World War II, gestured toward his own imagined twinship with Austerlitz. The cosmopolitanism implicit in this twinship reorients the discourse of German-Jewish post-Holocaust reconciliation and suggests a model for European cultural integration.

Sebald made it difficult to disentangle his own biography from that of his narrators; in the case of *Austerlitz*—specifically in the case of the intriguing photograph—neither his biography nor his image can be escaped: the narrator's biography resembles Sebald's own, and his slight image appears in the text. Perhaps, though, given my topic, Sebald's own biography cannot but play an important role: he himself led a cosmopolitan life, leaving his native Bavaria in 1963 after his *Abitur* to study *Germanistik* first in Freiburg, then in Switzerland, then in England (Arnold 2003: 118). He taught at the University of East Anglia in Norwich, where he also founded the British Centre for Literary Translation (BCLT 2013).

He began his literary career late in life, publishing a few poems over the years, with his first long works, *Nach der Natur: Ein Elementargedicht* (translated as *After Nature*) published in 1988, and *Schwindel: Gefühle* (*Vertigo*), a long prose work, in 1990. He worked chiefly in German but maintained an uneasy relationship to Germany. His choice of material varied greatly but was rarely set in Germany. In his long literary works, his concerns were broadly European versus particularly German; his geographical scope was diverse and crisscrossed centuries; and he often depicted travelers like Stendhal and Hölderlin or those with complicated national identities such as Franz Kafka, Max Aurach, Michael Hamburger, and Austerlitz. Melancholy dominated his works, many of which focus on loss.

Sebald's work is also remarkable for its insertion of actual photographs and other graphical elements into the prose. Examples of these graphic elements include maps, paintings, stamps, and engravings. In *Austerlitz*, there are 88 images in its 413 pages. Many of the images occupy a full page; indeed, ten of them extend over two pages. Most images play an important role in the novel's plot. Many such images are examples of Holocaust photographs, which Marianne Hirsch describes as,

> uniquely able to bring out this particular capacity of photographs to hover between life and death, to capture only that which no longer exists, to suggest both the desire and necessity and, at the same time, the difficulty, the impossibility, of mourning.
>
> (Hirsch 1997: 20)

Indeed, many of *Austerlitz*'s commentators have linked images of Austerlitz's mother to such a vital psychological need.[7] Austerlitz searches for photographic evidence of his mother's fate, ultimately locating in a theater's archives an image that Věra confirms to be Agáta, his mother (Sebald 2001a: 357). He never locates an image that suggests her ultimate fate after her interment in 1941, her arrival in Theresienstadt in 1942 (ibid.: 285), and her deportation to the east in 1944 (ibid.: 291). Nor is he able to determine the fate of his father, the search for whom he has begun in Paris when the novel ends.

Věra, Austerlitz's maid and nanny in his early life, from whom he learns so much about his past, suggests the importance in Sebald's work generally of such images:

> One got the impression, she said, of something stirring within them, as if one heard no sighs of despair, gémissements de désespoir, so she said, said Austerlitz, as if the pictures themselves had a memory and remembered us, remembered that which we survivors and those who are no longer with us had been in the old days.
>
> (Ibid.: 262)[8]

Such a statement underscores the importance of images throughout the text.[9]

The post-Holocaust nature of the novel suggests both its material—the aftereffects of the Shoah—and some of its themes: searching out origins, returning "home," and the complications of memory. The unnamed German gentile narrator meets Jacques Austerlitz in the main train station in Antwerp in early summer 1967 (ibid.: 10–18); their friendship blossoms during unexpected meetings over the course of about six months in Liège (ibid.: 40–42), Brussels (ibid.: 42–45), and in Zeebrugge (ibid.: 45–46), when they take the ferry together to England. Each time, the narrator notes that they take up their conversations right where they left off. Belgium, so important to the notion of the EU, grants Austerlitz and the narrator neutral ground on which to develop their friendship. For the next eight years, it continues during planned meetings in London, a kind of liminal European space. When the narrator returns to Germany in 1975, their contact breaks off abruptly (ibid.: 49–50). The novel does not explicitly describe it as such, but one might interpret this break as representing the impossibility of German-Jewish reconciliation in the 1970s.

After the long introductory section described above, the novel's plot does not properly begin until Austerlitz and the narrator resume their friendship over 20 years later: the narrator surprisingly encounters Austerlitz in a London bar in December 1996 while waiting for a train. This meeting takes place on page 57 of a novel of over 400 pages. Their friendship recommences just where it had been decades earlier: "Thus Austerlitz took up the conversation, without saying a word about our meeting—which occurred completely accidentally after so long—more or less where it was broken off" (Sebald 2001a: 60). Austerlitz has only recently learned much of the story of his childhood—or as the narrator presents Austerlitz as saying, "who I actually am" (ibid.: 64)—and begins to tell his story.

In March 1997—over the course of a day spent in and around Austerlitz's house in the London East End, which occupies over 185 pages in the novel—Austerlitz tells the narrator the core of his story (ibid: 173–358). After having heard a radio broadcast in the spring of 1993 about the *Kindertransporte*, Austerlitz was spurred on to trace his own journey as part of such an evacuation backwards—from Great Britain back to Prague. He speaks of his trip there to rediscover the origins of his family, of meeting Věra, and of what she tells him of his early years. He describes both his search for the broader truth and for clues hinting at that truth, which include his mother's deportation to the concentration camp of Theresienstadt and his own visit to the (again) Czech town of Terezín to discover signs of her fate.

III Austerlitz and the Narrator

Before describing the complex relationship between the narrator of *Austerlitz* and its protagonist (and subordinate narrator) Austerlitz, I must now turn to a provocation that grants the narrative structure more importance: a photograph of Sebald within his novel that purports to be a photo of

Austerlitz. Because it purports to be of Austerlitz, the character with Jewish heritage who has escaped the Holocaust, but is actually a representation of Sebald himself, the gentile German author, this photo suggests at minimum an affinity between the two. This affinity could be interpreted as tasteless, as an affront to Holocaust survivors or their descendants; I interpret it, however, as a key component of the twinship the novel presents. The twinship represents a model of reconciliation and cosmopolitanism.

The photograph in question illustrates a moment during the protagonist's —Jacques Austerlitz's—visit to Terezín, the former Nazi concentration camp town Theresienstadt, as he attempts to locate signs of his mother, whom, he has learned, was imprisoned there. The prose accompanying the image—in the midst of a meditation on the many strange items available for purchase at a junk shop—is presented as having been spoken by Austerlitz himself.

> What, I asked myself, said Austerlitz, might be the meaningfulness of the river never rising from any source, never flowing out into any sea but always back into itself; of *veverka*, the squirrel forever perched in the same position; of the ivory-colored porcelain group, which represented a riding hero who on his steed, just rearing up on its hindquarters, turns back in order to raise up an innocent feminine creature already bereft of her last hope with his left arm, and to save her from a—without a doubt—cruel fate not revealed to the observer? Just as timeless as this perpetual, always just occurring moment of rescue were all the ornaments, utensils, and mementoes stranded in the Terezín bazaar, which—due to unfathomable connections—had outlived their former owners and survived the process of destruction, so that I could now perceive my own shadow image among them weak and barely recognizable.
>
> (Sebald 2001a: 280–281)

An aesthetic issue emerges when one compares this reflection with the photograph of Sebald: the type that is sometimes seen on a book's dust jacket or accompanying an interview with an author. The photo seems to have been taken by the author himself; the similarity cannot be missed, especially in the hairline. Thus travel, intended to enable a search for items and images of people which have survived the process of destruction, also leads to new connections: that between Sebald and his protagonist.

Under other circumstances, such a photograph could easily be dismissed as inconsequential, as sloppy or coincidental, or even as a touch of humor. Several critics have noted the photo,[10] but Brad Prager (2005) alone among the novel's critics mentions the reflection as "likely Sebald himself," though Prager describes the fact as inconsequential and relegates the revelation to a footnote. Prager argues, "Sebald is not suggesting that he is Austerlitz, only that he is inserting himself into Austerlitz's story" (Prager 2005: 99), though his article, too, emphasizes the importance of the "proximity" (ibid.: 98) of Sebald to the narrator and the narrator to Austerlitz. Prager leaves the implications of such an insertion—of the gentile German author's identification with his own Holocaust escapee of Jewish origin—unexplored in favor of an argument focusing on "whether there are boundaries around the empathy that an author can sensibly display" (ibid.: 76). While Sebald's connection between himself and Austerlitz is subtle, I would go further than Prager and emphasize the extreme danger Sebald suggests through his connection to Austerlitz: not only is his narrator open to critique along these lines, but Sebald as well. Though he had to make his suggestion covertly so as not to sidetrack the main emphasis of the novel—i.e., Austerlitz's search for truths about his past—Sebald opens himself to criticism through this image, but also demands that we consider the subtext of the entwined—the twinned—fates of the Jewish survivor of the Holocaust and the gentile post-war German.

In Sebald's *œuvre* and in *Austerlitz* itself, the conflation of author and character takes on added significance. Given the frequency of Sebald's use of photographs in his work, sloppiness is unlikely. Austerlitz is Jewish, but he escaped Prague and the Holocaust aboard a *Kindertransport* and grew up in Wales in the care of a pastor and his wife. The shadowy conflation of Sebald with Austerlitz is one that poses vital questions: To what extent can a non-Jewish German claim such empathy with a Jewish survivor of the Holocaust? Is such empathy appropriate? Such a connection, combined with the additional conflation of Sebald with the novel's narrator, intensifies the intercultural and cosmopolitan nature of the novel.

Austerlitz uses a careful structure that attempts to walk the very thin line between sensitivity to the German gentile narrator's position vis-à-vis his subject matter on the one hand, and his strong affinity for Austerlitz, a Jewish Holocaust escapee, on the other. The novel is without a single line of quoted dialog and has only very few distinct paragraphs, which can run to 40 pages each. It features a narrator with a dominant voice and difficult style employing exceedingly long sentences, a single footnote, and many images. The narrator's role, however, often seems reduced to that of listener. Not only does the narrator present Austerlitz as a narrator of his own story, but Austerlitz, too, presents additional narrators nested within his narration: the novel's narrator presents Austerlitz as a narrator within his narrative, who in turn presents other characters narrating, too, in a complex structure of multiple narrative levels one might liken to the structure of a Chinese box or a Russian nesting doll. Narrative theory often likens such multiple levels to the frame of a painting, referring to the initial level as the frame narrative and the interior one as the main narrative. Examples include great early collections of stories such as *The Arabian Nights*, *The Decameron*, and *The Canterbury Tales* (See M. H. Abrams 1993: 195). Traditional frame narratives feature only one frame, but others—including *Austerlitz*—can get much more complex, featuring frames within frames. For example, within the greater frame of the narrator's presentation, Austerlitz himself becomes a narrator, who in turn presents a tour guide's comments on the Freemason Temple attached to the Great Eastern Hotel (Sebald 2001a: 61–63), Hilary's lectures on the Battle of Austerlitz (ibid.: 103–106), Evan the cobbler's tales of Welsh myth (ibid.: 116), and—most prominently—Věra's stories of Austerlitz's childhood (ibid.: 221–262). At the novel's most narratively complex point, the narrator presents Austerlitz's tale of his visit to Věra. During the visit, Věra reports Austerlitz's father's recounting a story: "Maximilian occasionally told—so Věra remembered, said Austerlitz—how he once..." (ibid.: 241). One begins to get lost in the structure of the novel: who originally told the stories we read, and by how many levels of mediation have the stories been filtered?

A dominant feature of the novel is its insistence on carefully noting who is speaking. Although the general form seems to urge one not to differentiate between speakers, readers are frequently reminded that Austerlitz is speaking: a constant refrain of "Austerlitz said" ("sagte Austerlitz") runs throughout the text. The story of Austerlitz's return to Prague and his visit to Terezín occupies just short of 200 pages of the novel. Rather than presenting Austerlitz's very long descriptions of his past and his travels in the form of a frame story, however, which would allow Austerlitz to become a stronger, more independent narrator on his own account, the book's actual narrator frequently reminds the reader that Austerlitz's story does not reach its audience directly but rather via the mediation of the narrator. In addition to phrases like "sagte Austerlitz," breaks to make the setting of Austerlitz's narration clear are common. For example, at one point, Austerlitz and the narrator move from Austerlitz's London sitting room to a nearby cemetery on the way to the train station (ibid.: 324–358); Austerlitz continues to tell his story, but the narrator breaks in just often enough to disrupt any sense that Austerlitz has displaced him as narrator. The narrator insists on his own presence in the novel, though he barely participates in its events at all. This insistence has the effect of foregrounding the narrator's character, the unusual quality of the friendship between him and Austerlitz, and the historical valences of such a friendship.[11]

The novel powerfully insists on an affinity between Austerlitz and the German narrator who is so like Sebald himself. He too is a writer, an émigré from a small town in Bavaria to the east of England. Most prominent among these instances are several mentions of twins or doubles in the book. Describing his childhood in Wales early in the novel, Austerlitz tells us via the narrator, "Sometimes it was as if I were trying to recognize reality from within a dream; then, I felt as if an invisible twin brother were walking next to me, the opposite of a shadow, so to speak" (Sebald 2001a: 80). Such a statement, coupled with frequent comments in the book that the narrator encounters Austerlitz unexpectedly, by chance, in unusual places in Belgium and London, strongly suggests that the friendship has a peculiar, perhaps symbolic or even spiritual bond.

The spiritual kinship suggested between Austerlitz and the narrator seems to have come from one of Sebald's inspirations for the novel, the true story of Susi Bechhöfer, a German Jewish girl, who left Munich with her twin sister Lotte aboard a *Kindertransport*. Raised in Wales by a preacher and his wife and renamed Grace Mann, Bechhöfer eventually discovered the truth of her identity and then searched to uncover the fate of her Jewish mother, Rosa. Her story was first told on a BBC program and later appeared in the 1996 book *Rosa's Child*. Sebald acknowledged his debt to this material in at least one interview in 2001, though he got a number of details of her story wrong. While Sebald claimed that he had come across the story on television—"You know how ephemeral these appearances are on television—you see a film or you don't see it, and then it vanishes forever and you can't get a copy of it despite your best efforts" (Cuomo 2007: 111–112)—one can read this dismissal as fitting into the novel's spirit of only alluding to a connection between Sebald and Austerlitz; the transitory quality of the television broadcast Sebald mentioned in the interview suggests the gentile German Sebald's desire to identify with another, but only indirectly, and not just any other but rather a Jewish Holocaust escapee. Had such a gesture been more obvious than the novel so enigmatically presents it, it would certainly have been more open to the criticism that Sebald was exploiting the Holocaust.[12]

Sebald recognized the difficulties of a non-Jewish German writing a Holocaust-themed novel with a Jewish protagonist, stating in a 2001 interview:

> I think certainly for a German gentile to write about Jewish lives is not unproblematic. There are examples of that, writers attempting this in Germany in the 1960s and 70s, and many of those attempts are—one can't say it really otherwise—shameful. In a sense they usurp the lives of these people.... It's very, very difficult terrain.... Yet at the same time ... the likes of us ought to try to say how they receive these stories.... It's a more acute version of a problem that all writers have.
>
> (Cuomo 2007: 111–112)

What makes Sebald feel that he can successfully negotiate such "difficult terrain"? The narrator's—and Sebald's—position, living outside of Germany and viewing it from afar, having been born, in a way, too late, at the end of the war, suggests that both narrator and author require a kind of salvation, or perhaps better, a kind of redemption. The spatial and temporal exile in which the narrator and Sebald live enables a heightened awareness of the need to point to the historical crisis of the Holocaust while reminding the historian of the unresolvable nature of the search (See Elsaghe 2007). As numerous critics have noted, *Austerlitz* and its narrator pose significant challenges in the realm of psychoanalysis and trauma studies.[13] My reading of the novel, including its photographs, suggests a way a non-Jewish German can approach a Holocaust narrative and even find elements of common experience. Sebald's novel gently suggests an empathetic model for post-Holocaust reconciliation, based on what

Andreas Huyssen has called "transgenerational traumatization" (Huyssen 2003: 151).

IV *Austerlitz* as Cosmopolitan Novel, Sebald as Cosmopolitan

Returning to the quotation with which I began my essay, I choose to emphasize Habermas' statement of the two legal personae composing each citizen of the European Union for its provocative and evocative formulation (Habermas 2012: 38). It is as if the twinned pair of Austerlitz and the narrator/Sebald have also been split into two personae, but two different national personae, Czech-British Jew and German gentile. The novel's form suggests that the two belong together and can be merged into one through the medium of shared experience, shared storytelling, and shared listening.

Sebald carefully notes the dates in which the events in his novel take place: though "almost baroque" in form (Furst 2005: xviii), the novel carefully locates its characters in time and place. The novel never directly mentions the EU or many other political entities after the Nazi era, but its characters—and Sebald, too—would clearly be considered citizens of this super-state, each divided into the "personae" of a European citizen and a member of "an already constituted national people" (Habermas 2012: 38). The duality of these two personae, cosmopolitan and national, accounts for the very delicate nature of the spiritual kinship of Austerlitz and his narrator, who is a stand-in for Sebald himself. For while theoretically fraught with dangerous implications of exploitation and poor taste, the identification between a gentile German and a Holocaust escapee of Jewish origin carries with it less significant problems if we consider these two men as citizens of the European Union. They may retain their various national connections, however tenuous, and also find common ground on the basis of EU citizenship.

Such a dream of a cosmopolitan society (ibid.: 58), a Europe—and ultimately a world—in which strangers locate a common ground in the cultural, social, and political realms, depends to a large extent on communication. The linguistic complications of *Austerlitz* reflect this reality well: the narrator and Austerlitz, having first met in Belgium, have initially used one of its languages, French, to communicate with each other. Only on the ferry from Zeebrugge do they realize that they share another language—English—and shift into it (Sebald 2001a: 46). Neither man speaks either language as a native, though the novel is of course written in German and Czech appears in the novel as well, especially in Austerlitz's discussions with Věra. European realities mandate such linguistic stretches, which become mediated by the narrator to such an extent that they barely register to the reader. Like so much in the novel, its small but significant linguistic details pass by unremarked upon by the casual reader.

To return to the German side of things, Habermas—himself German—identifies the changes that transpired in citizens of the Federal Republic as mandatory for a successful cosmopolitan European Union: "What ultimately won over our European neighbors were, first and foremost, the changed normative convictions and the liberal-minded attitudes of the younger generations who had grown up in the Federal Republic" (Habermas 2012: 123). Like the friendship between Austerlitz and the narrator, representatives for European Jews and gentile Germans, which is successful in spite of the narrator's Germanness. Both Austerlitz (a Czech Jew fluent in French, raised as an English speaker in Wales, and employed as a professor in London) and the narrator (a German native living in a kind of self-imposed exile in England) exemplify the kind of citizens Habermas finds indispensable for a cosmopolitan version of the European Union: those able to "find their bearings more rapidly in the postnational constellation" (ibid.: 124). Instead of "withdrawing into an egocentric blend of aestheticization and utility maximization" (ibid.: 124), the two figures epitomize what Europe (and Germany within it) most need: strangers who learn from each other, seeing in the other a kind of spiritual twin of the self.

VI Conclusion

Though much of Habermas' work on cosmopolitanism focuses on the political changes necessary to make it work within Europe, he also insists on the importance of cultural cosmopolitanism, too. Within the framework of German culture, the greatest challenge to a model of cultural cosmopolitanism is the German–Jewish relationship and the possibilities of reconciliation. W. G. Sebald's *Austerlitz* describes such reconciliation between a Holocaust escapee and a gentile German, both living in exile in England. An additional level of cosmopolitanism, though, comes from the profound formal experimentation of a photograph purportedly of Austerlitz but in fact reflecting W. G. Sebald himself, the novel's author. This covert violation of textual levels suggests an additional mode of cosmopolitan empathetic relationships: a spiritual twinning of the Jewish protagonist and the gentile author. Though not as provocative, trite, or direct as a handshake between a former concentration camp inmate and a former guard, Sebald's model more gently and profoundly uses the background of the Holocaust but focuses largely on post-war dislocations and reconfigurations that enable a cosmopolitan vision of German-Jewish reconciliation and European citizenship.

About the midpoint of the novel, the narrator waits in Austerlitz's house, transfixed by the reflection in the glass door of the veranda of the fire in the fireplace. When Austerlitz returns, the narrator remarks on the "incomprehensibility of mirror images" (Sebald 2001a: 173). Austerlitz responds with a story of his fascination with a small detail, that of a tiny flame, in a Rembrandt painting, something minor that has endured for centuries. Such are the reflections of the other in *Austerlitz*: though such images frequently provide examples of the absent other in photographs or objects representing a lost time— such as those in the window of the bazaar—the most important ones remain the impressions of the other within oneself. *Austerlitz* achieves myriad ends. Among these ends is a model of interaction between gentile Germans and Jews. Through strong bonds of friendship that border on twinship, the mediating languages of French and English, and the mediating spaces of Belgium, England, and France, the novel offers models of interactions of citizens of the European Union. The novel thus provides a version of the vital cultural element of the project of developing a cosmopolitan Europe.

Notes

1 I would like to acknowledge several groups of students with whom I have read Sebald's *Austerlitz* for class as well as the comments of colleagues at Centre College during an informal presentation of an early draft of this paper. Centre College Faculty Development Committee grants supported its completion.
2 Here I am heavily indebted to Brad Prager (2005), as well as Lewis Ward (2012).
3 For example, see: "Feuer in Tröglitzer Flüchtlingsheim," *Die Zeit Online*, 4 April, 2015: www.zeit.de/gesellschaft/zeitgeschehen/2015-04/troeglitz-asylbewerberheim-feuer-sachsen-anhalt.
4 See www.spiegel.de/spiegel/print/index-2015-31.html for images of all six covers.
5 However, as Michel Foucault has argued in *Discipline and Punish*, rules for standing at attention, handwriting, and the like powerfully inform the development of a national culture.
6 See for example Christian Jakob (2015), the story of "Marta Álvaro," who moved to Germany from Spain to work and study, only to find her residency permit revoked when she sought temporary relief from the social safety net. She said that she found the behavior of the German authorities "anti-European," arguing that for the German authorities, "whoever has an income is a European. And whoever has none is a Spaniard and has to return home. They may as well reestablish the [national] borders."
7 See for example Carolin Duttlinger, "Traumatic Photographs: Remembrance and the Technical Media in W. G. Sebald's *Austerlitz*" (155–71) and Russell J. A. Kilbourn, "Architecture and Cinema: The Representations of Memory in W. G. Sebald's *Austerlitz*" (140–54), both in *W. G. Sebald: A Critical Companion*, ed. J. J. Long and Anne Whitehead (Seattle: U of Washington P, 2004); and, less directly, J. J. Long, *W. G. Sebald: Image, Archive, Modernity* (Seattle, U of Washington P, 2007).
8 Translations into English mine.
9 See also George Kouvaros (2009).
10 For example, John Sears (2007) and Bettina Mosbach (2007).
11 In this vein, see Katja Garloff (2006: 157–169).
12 Sebald's exploitation of Bechhöfer's story, and the attention brough to it through the interview alluded to—as well as a deeper discussion of Sebald's source materials for Austerlitz's story—lie outside the scope of this chapter.
13 See for example Dora Osborne (2007); many of the essays in Scott Denham and Mark McCulloh (2006); and Dominick LaCapra (2013).

References

Abrams, M. H. (1993) "Short Story," in *A Glossary of Literary Terms*. 6th edn. Fort Worth, Tex.: Harcourt, pp. 193–195.

Arnold, Heinz Ludwig (ed.) (2003) *W. G. Sebald*. Text + Kritik, 158: Munich.

Atze, Marcel (2005) "Casanova vor der Schwarzen Wald: Ein Beispiel intertextueller Repräsentanz des Holocaust in W. G. Sebalds *Austerlitz*," in Marcel Atze and Franz Loquai (eds.) *Sebald: Lektüren*. Eggingen, Germany: Isele, pp. 228–243.

British Centre for Literary Translation (BCLT) (2013) "About us," *British Centre for Literary Translation*. Accessed: September 10, 2013: www.bclt.org.uk/about-us/.

Brown, Garrett Wallace, and David Held (eds.) (2010) *The Cosmopolitan Reader*. Madlen, Mass.: Polity.

Calhoun, Craig (2002) "The Class Consciousness of Frequent Travellers: Towards a Critique of Actually Existing Cosmopolitanism," in Steven Vertovec and Robin Cohen (eds.) *Conceiving Cosmopolitanism: Theory, Context, and Practice*. Oxford: Oxford University Press, pp. 86–109.

Cuomo, Joseph (2007) "A Conversation with W. G. Sebald," in Lynne Sharon Schwartz (ed.) *The Emergence of Memory: Conversations with W. G. Sebald*. New York: Seven Stories, pp. 93–117.

Denham, Scott, and Mark McCulloh (eds.) (2006) *W. G. Sebald: History-Memory-Trauma*. Berlin: de Gruyter.

Duttlinger, Carolin (2004) "Traumatic Photographs: Remembrance and the Technical Media in W. G. Sebald's *Austerlitz*," in J. J. Long and Anne Whitehead (eds.) *W. G. Sebald: A Critical Companion*. Seattle: University of Washington Press, pp. 155–171.

Elsaghe, Yahya (2007) "W. G. Sebalds *Austerlitz* als Beitrag zum deutsch-jüdischen Kulturdialog," in Jean-Marie Valentin (ed.) *Germanistik im Konflikt der Kulturen: Akten des XI. Internationalen Germanistenkongresses*. New York: Lang, pp. 245–250.

Furst, Lilian (2005) *Random Destinations: Escaping the Holocaust and Starting Life Anew*. New York: Palgrave.

Garloff, Katja (2006) "The Task of the Narrator: Moments of Symbolic Investiture in W. G. Sebald's *Austerlitz*," in Denham and McColloh (eds.), *W. G. Sebald: History-Memory-Trauma*. Berlin: de Gruyter, pp. 157–169.

Habermas, Jürgen (2001a) "The Postnational Constellation and the Future of Democracy," in Max Pensky (ed. and trans.) *The Postnational Constellation: Political Essays*. Cambridge, Mass.: MIT Press, pp. 58–112.

Habermas, Jürgen (2001b) "Why Europe Needs a Constitution," *New Left Review*, 11, pp. 5–26.

Habermas, Jürgen (2011) *Zur Verfassung Europas: Ein Essay*. Berlin: Suhrkamp.

Habermas, Jürgen (2012) *The Crisis of the European Union: A Response*. Trans. Ciaran Cronin. Malden, Mass.: Polity Press.

Habermas, Jürgen and Jacques Derrida (2003) "February 15, Or What Binds Europeans Together: A Plea for a Common European Foreign Policy, Beginning in the Core of Europe." Trans. Max Pensky. *Constellations*, 10(3), pp. 291–297.

Hirsch, Marianne (1997) *Family Frames: Photography, Narrative, and Postmemory*. Cambridge, Mass.: Harvard University Press.

Huyssen, Andreas (2003) *Present Pasts: Urban Palimpsests and the Politics of Memory*. Stanford: Stanford University Press.

Jacob, Christian (2015) "Keine neue Heimat für Marta," *Taz.de*, August 11, 2015. www.taz.de/!5218958/ (last accessed: March 2, 2016).
Jacobson, Dan (1998) *Heschel's Kingdom*. Evanston, Illinois: Northwestern UP.
Josephs, Jeremy, and Susi Bechhöfer. (1996) *Rosa's Child: The True Story of One Woman's Quest for a Lost Mother and a Vanished Past*. London: Tauris.
Kilbourn, Russell J. A. (2004) "Architecture and Cinema: The Representations of Memory in W. G. Sebald's *Austerlitz*," in J. J. Long and Anne Whitehead (eds.) *W. G. Sebald: A Critical Companion*. Seattle: University of Washington Press, pp. 140–154.
Kilbourn, Russell J. A. (2006) "Kafka, Nabokov … Sebald: Intertextuality and Narratives of Redemption in *Vertigo* and *The Emigrants*," in Denham and McColloh (eds.) *W. G. Sebald: History–Memory–Trauma*. Berlin: de Gruyter, pp. 35–63.
Kouvaros, George (2009) "Images that Remember Us: Photography and Memory in *Austerlitz*," in Gerhard Fischer (ed.) *W. G. Sebald: Schreiben ex patria/ Expatriate Writing*. New York: Rodopi, pp. 389–412.
LaCapra, Dominick (2013) *History, Literature, Critical Theory*. Ithaca, N.Y.: Cornell University Press.
Long, J. J. (2007) *W. G. Sebald: Image, Archive, Modernity*. New York: Columbia UP.
Mosbach, Bettina (2007) "Superimposition as a Narrative Strategy in *Austerlitz*," in Lise Patt (ed.) *Searching for Sebald*. Los Angeles: Institute for Critical Inquiry, pp. 390–411.
Osborne, Dora (2007) "Blind Spots: Viewing Trauma in W. G. Sebald's *Austerlitz*," *Seminar*, 43(4), pp. 517–533.
Prager, Brad (2005) "The Good German as Narrator: On W. G. Sebald and the Risks of Holocaust Writing," *New German Critique*, 96, pp. 75–102.
Sears, John (2007) "Photographs, Images, and the Space of Literature in Sebald's Prose," in Lise Patt (ed.) *Searching for Sebald*. Los Angeles: Institute for Critical Inquiry, pp. 204–225.
Sebald, W. G. (1999) *Luftkrieg und Literatur*. Munich: Hanser.
Sebald, W. G. (2001a) *Austerlitz*. Munich: Hanser.
Sebald, W. G. (2001b) "Ich fürchte das Melodramatische," *Der Spiegel*, 11, pp. 228–234.
Ward, Lewis (2012) "A Simultaneous Gesture of Proximity and Distance: W. G. Sebald's Empathic Narrative Persona," *Journal of Modern Literature* 36(1), pp. 1–16.

Part IV
Institutions

7 Educating the European Union
Internationalization through Integration[1]

Thomas O. Haakenson

In his various publications related to the challenges facing the European Union, most recently the challenges that have resulted from the financial crises infecting member states' economies and threatening the long-term viability of the euro itself, Jürgen Habermas repeatedly has emphasized the need for a robust European public sphere as a forum for the legitimation of the political structures needed to stabilize the EU project. In "Why Europe Needs a Constitution," published in *New Left Review*, Habermas argues that European political identity needs "symbolic crystallization" through an act of foundation such as the adoption of a constitution (Habermas 2011). Such "crystallization" is needed, he argues, because as a "political collectivity, Europe cannot take hold in the consciousness of its citizens simply in the shape of a common currency" (ibid.). In *Zur Verfassung Europas: Ein Essay*, published in English as *The Crisis of the European Union: A Response*, Habermas makes clear his allegiance to a model of worldly cosmopolitanism articulated by Enlightenment philosopher Immanuel Kant, suggesting what Habermas hopes is "a convincing new narrative from the perspective of a constitutionalization of international law which follows Kant in pointing far beyond the status quo to a future cosmopolitan rule of law" (Habermas 2012: 1–2). Habermas notes, in particular, that "the enduring political fragmentation of the world and in Europe is at variance with the system integration of a multicultural world society and is blocking progress towards civilizing relations of violence within societies and between states through constitutional law" (ibid.: 7). For Habermas, taking a cue from his earlier work on the public sphere, the legitimation of the EU and key to its—and the euro's—long-term stability is the recognition and development of a European public sphere devoted to "the persuasive power of good arguments" as the true means for democratic consensus-formation and governmental stability (ibid.: 6). Integral to both of the above texts, and to Habermas' philosophical debt to Kant, is the idea of education as a mechanism to ensure individual self-determination, to demonstrate, as Kant claimed, that individuals are free from "self-incurred tutelage" to another (Kant 1784).[2]

In the following essay, I focus on one aspect of Habermas' vision for a "European public sphere": namely, higher education. Key to the creation of the type of engaged "European citizen" envisioned by Habermas is an educational system that is devoted to the principles of democratic participation as well as invested in the development of educational processes, structures, and institutions that allow for such education. While EU higher educational reform efforts have sought to standardize transfer and degree requirements to afford ease of mobility of student members of the EU nations, the decreasing emphasis on access to education versus a focus on the outcomes of education have created an imbalance in EU higher educational reform, embodied in both the 2010 and the 2020 initiatives. Recognizing the influence, and the instability, of near simultaneous higher educational reform measures in China and the United States of America reveals that, in order to stay true to the admittedly problematic and Eurocentric educational tradition which Habermas supports, the member states of the EU must increase their focus on access to educational opportunity as a form of individual self-determination, rather than continue to overemphasize the standardization of transfer credit or degree requirements as a means of ensuring educational quality. It is my central concern that an overemphasis on transfer credit or degree standardization biases educational reform toward outcomes-focused, rather than access-focused, measures of success.

The Context: Habermas and Educational Reform

This chapter is part of a larger project that focuses on the internationalization of education as a key component in European as well as global integration. More specifically, my book-length study, tentatively titled *Internationalization Through Integration: Higher Educational Reform in International Context*, is a comparative analysis of official educational policy in the creative fields, in communist and former communist countries, in relation to the development of global capitalism, most often associated with the United States. The intent of my research study is twofold: First, I analyze the implications of educational policy and its reform on cultural expression as manifest in the creative professions. Second, I provide a detailed study of local, national, and transnational educational reforms in relation to classroom and quotidian interactions that employ, subvert, or directly challenge official policies. In my study, I utilize the "culture industry thesis" developed by Max Horkheimer and Theodor W. Adorno. I find in its synthesis of the psychological, material, and ideological aspects of cultural expression key ways in which to explain the opportunities as well as the challenges of educational reform in the creative fields in the communist and post-communist context.

Given his philosophical, professional, and personal connections to the Frankfurt School, and to Adorno in particular, Habermas' biases toward Europe as the harbinger of world civilization are to be expected. I want to invoke this aspect of Habermas' thinking critically. On the one hand, I concur with Habermas in broad, historical strokes that the effort to create

Educating the European Union 143

a "cosmopolitan world civilization" finds advocates in Kant's philosophy and the European Enlightenment project in general. On the other hand, what Horkheimer and Adorno make clear in, among other publications, their book-length study *The Dialectic of Enlightenment* (Adorno and Horkheimer 1997[1944]) in which the "culture industry thesis" first appears, is that the European Enlightenment project exposed the opposite of the idealized, civilizing aspirations to which Habermas often pays homage. Colonialism is, of course, one expression of European Enlightenment, both colonialism's more positive efforts to improve quality of life as well as colonialism's more insidious effects: torture, genocide, exploitation, enslavement. Horkheimer and Adorno reveal the destructive side of Enlightenment through their juxtaposition of a Marxist recognition of the insatiable appetite of capitalism and a Freudian/Sadian understanding of the destructive—but occasionally and violently erupting—animalistic human nature suppressed by the supposedly civilizing forces of the European Enlightenment project. Habermas emphasizes, I would suggest, modern efforts to guarantee human rights as a democratic response to European Enlightenment failures to these ends. What the juxtaposition of Habermas with Horkheimer and Adorno reveals, for the purposes of the present study, is that a much more critical perspective on the supposedly inherently positive European Enlightenment model of democracy is needed, a critical perspective that takes into account much more robustly the destructive economic forces that Habermas is all too often willing to minimize or to ignore completely.[3]

While neither the space of this chapter nor the scope of the present anthology is sufficient to explore Habermas' philosophical framework beyond the comparatively narrow frame of the aesthetic and what I suggest is the relationship of the aesthetic to higher educational reform in the creative professions, a brief nod to the breadth and scope of Habermas' project is in order. One of his most ambitious and philosophically significant publications—the two-volume *Theorie des Kommunikativen Handels* ("Theory of Communicative Action") from 1981—reveals Habermas' poststructuralist grounding with respect to the philosophy of reason, the aesthetic, and social transformation. In the English translation of volume one, *Handlungsrationalität und gesellscahftliche Rationalisierung* ("Reason and the Rationalization of Society"), Habermas is clear to note that reasonable understanding is the result of a process of deliberation, as opposed to the a priori category of social engagement:

> With the concept of communicative action there comes into play the additional presupposition of a *linguistic medium* that reflects the actor-world relations as such. At this level of concept formation, the rationality problematic, which until now has arisen only for the social scientist, moves into the perspective of the agent himself. We have to make clear in what sense achieving understanding in language is thereby introduced as a mechanism for coordinating action ... we even

have to presuppose a consensus formation among participants that is in principle of a linguistic nature.

(Habermas 1984: 94)

Habermas' focus on "communicative action," while not exclusive to the realm of the aesthetic, finds its most succinct framing in his explanation of the impact of the aesthetic experience on individual, and collective, understandings of the world. In "Modernity—an Incomplete Project," Habermas argues that the separation of science, morality, and art, associated with the advent of cultural modernity, itself an outgrowth of the Enlightenment, paradoxically renders the aesthetic experience an even more vital way in which to reflect on and potentially to change the social world. Habermas (1983) describes the aesthetic encounter as a "critical mirror" in this sense, yet a mirror with a very active function:

An aesthetic experience, which is not framed around the experts' critical judgments of taste can have its significance altered: as soon as such an experience is used to illuminate a life-historical situation and is related to life problems, it enters into a language game which is no longer that of the aesthetic critic. The aesthetic experience then not only renews the interpretation of our needs in whose light we perceive the world. It permeates as well our cognitive significations and our normative expectations and changes the matter in which all these moments refer to one another.

(Habermas 1983: 13)

Habermas, rather than suggesting that the realm of aesthetic experience is ancillary to political or social processes, demonstrates that the realm of the aesthetic encounter is in fact the place and space in which radical rethinking about the world beyond the gallery, outside the exhibition hall, other than the artist's atelier takes place.

Despite the above, significant concern with the limited, and limiting, framing of the challenges confronting European identity as well as the EU, Habermas thus does provide an avenue through which to discuss the role of education as an integral part in creating and maintaining democracy. To these ends, Habermas' current thinking about European identity and the crises affecting the EU is heavily indebted to his own, earlier work on the emergence of the European Enlightenment "public sphere" as a (non-egalitarian) forum for the quotidian interaction of individuals in debates, discussions, and exchanges as integral parts of democratic consensus formation. Habermas repeatedly emphasizes in both "Why Europe Needs a Constitution" as well as in *The European Union in Crisis: A Response* that public debate is essential to the continued, positive development of European identity specifically, and to the EU project in general: "Differences that are coming more in to the open in environmental, military, and juridical fields contribute to a soundless strengthening of European identity" (Habermas 2011: 25). Further, he suggests that Europe already provides by example the basic framework for the creation of a robust "cosmopolitan community of states and world citizens" (Habermas 2012: xi).

Nowhere is the role of Europe in creating the structures for collective, democratic consensus formation more pronounced than in its educational system. Yet efforts to standardize and to reform European higher educational institutions by focusing on outcomes rather than access threaten one of the basic tenets of Habermas' intervention. As he notes, efforts to conserve "the great democratic achievements of the European nation state" must recognize among these achievements "not only formal guarantees of civil rights, but levels of social welfare, education, and leisure that are the precondition of both an effective private autonomy and of democratic citizenship" (Habermas 2011: 6). Furthermore, Habermas suggests that the European Union Charter of Basic Rights articulates "a social vision of the European Project" (Habermas 2011: 21). Key among the Charter's provisions, of course, is Article 14:

Article 14—Right to education
1. Everyone has the right to education and to have access to vocational and continuing training.
2. This right includes the possibility to receive free compulsory education.
3. The freedom to found educational establishments with due respect for democratic principles and the right of parents to ensure the education and teaching of their children in conformity with their religious, philosophical and pedagogical convictions shall be respected, in accordance with the national laws governing the exercise of such freedom and right.

The challenges currently confronting European Union higher educational reform involve most directly the first component of Article 14 of the European Union Charter of Basic Rights: access to education, as well as to vocational and technical training.

Despite Habermas' interventions, and the Charter of Basic Human Rights' emphasis on educational access, the forces of economic and political pressure associated with what Habermas calls "economic globalization" have resulted in demands that higher educational institutions "conform through reform" to still-emerging global standards concerning credit-hours, curricular content, learning outcomes, and course transferability across geopolitical borders (Habermas 2011: 9). The focus on the creative professions in my forthcoming book is meant to highlight the myriad effects of—and possibilities operative against—the pressure to standardize. The challenge for all educators in higher education, and especially for those in the geopolitical regions with a tradition dedicated to the so-called liberal arts, is to retain the often non-teleological aspects of higher education associated with exploration, experimentation, and failure, in light of the demands for standardized measures to indicate students' successful achievement of pre-defined objectives. The creative professions, which often emphasize non-teleological aspects of creativity and creative exploration, are situated ideally to expose the limits of standardization in higher education, challenge the related global universalisms, and introduce—most explicitly at the level of implementation, but perhaps also elsewhere—alternative methods for assessing student learning. Such a confrontation with processes of standardization may benefit public debate in so far as it reorients those conversations to a greater focus on access over-and-above outcomes.

The European Union

The primary objective of the Bologna Declaration of 1999 was to establish a so-called European Higher Education Area (EHEA) by 2010. The goal of the EHEA is to make higher education in Europe "more compatible and comparable, more competitive and more attractive" (Vasilliou 2010: 3). The development of the EHEA can be seen as an outgrowth of the Erasmus student mobility program, established in 1987, as well as the European Credit Accumulation and Transfer System (ECTS). European Commissioners in support of the EHEA initiative, confronted by economic crisis in the late 2010s, proposed that "public and private investment in modernised [sic] higher education should reach at least 2 percent of GDP" (European Union 2010: 4). Most countries have yet to respond to the increased funding imperative.

The Bologna Declaration's implementation established a three-cycle system approach to higher education, with cycles corresponding roughly to the bachelors, the masters, and the doctorate levels. Universities continued to monitor inputs, but were encouraged increasingly to shift to a focus on outputs, such as "learning outcomes" and "competencies." The university-led Tuning Project, launched in 2000, contributed to the definitions of these concepts, and was financially supported by the European Commission (González and Wagenaar 2008: 9).[4] The National Qualifications Frameworks established as a result of Bologna indicate learning outcomes expected at each level. At the follow-up Berlin Bologna conference in September 2003, degree programs were identified as having a central role in the Bologna Process (ibid.: 10). The resultant National Qualifications Frameworks are in turn connected to two frameworks that operate at a more abstract level: the Framework for Qualifications in the European Higher Educational Area of Bologna (EQF for HE), and the EU European Qualifications Framework for lifelong learning. The EQF for HE was adopted at the Bergen Bologna conference in May 2005 (ibid.: 11). The Tuning Commission developed specific competencies for nine subject areas, none of which engages the fields of production in the creative arts (ibid.: 18).[5] There is also indication in the Tuning Commission's published report that alternatives to the traditional semester system are warranted, as "other options are possible" (ibid.: 23).

One of the continued goals of the EU's efforts to develop the EHEA is the establishment of "measurable targets" in each country to increase the number of students in higher education and widen participation of underrepresented groups. As of 2007, only 30 percent of 30–34 year olds in Europe had any level of higher education. The target set in 2009 at the meeting of commissioners at Leuven/Louvain-la-Neuve, is that 40 percent of the same age group have higher educational experience by 2020. These targets included measures for non-formal and informal learning as part of a higher educational experience, what in the US is known as competency-based credits or degree programs. Competency-based credits were developed in opposition to the credit hour established by the Carnegie Foundation, which focuses on "contact hours." A related result is the European Universities' "Charter on Lifelong Learning" developed by the European University Association (EUA). The EU thus has mechanisms for addressing the issue of access to higher education, yet the focus in higher educational reform, in Germany and beyond, has been largely on developing clear outcomes-based, rather than access-based, determinants of educational reform success.

One of the key contributions of Erasmus to the implementation of the Bologna Declaration is the development of outcomes and competencies at all levels for various disciplines, oftentimes called Sectoral Qualifications Frameworks. The publication *Tuning Educational Structures in Europe* provides the details of the Erasmus contribution (González and Wagenaar 2008). Notably absent from this publication and others like it, however, are the less quantifiable forms of knowledge and knowledge production, including those associated with the creative professions. Indeed, to these ends, access to education is rendered less important than the outcomes from particular fields. As González and Wagenaar have noted, however: "If we want to maintain and improve our standard of living we need to find ways to widen access to initial studies and learning at all ages" (ibid.: 4).

In its 2010 and 2020 educational reform initiatives, the European Union has demonstrated an increasing focus on connecting higher education to outcomes-based measures, notably in the areas of economic growth and the employability of graduates (i.e., "gainful employment" in US Department of Education terminology). In 2000, members of the Lisbon European Council defined a clear mission for educational reform in its member countries: to enable the European Union "to become the most competitive and dynamic knowledge-based economy in the world, capable of sustainable economic growth with more and better jobs and greater social cohesion" (European Commission 2006: 208). As part of what became known as the "Lisbon strategy," the Lisbon European Council asked the ministers for education to look to the future and to "undertake a general reflection on the concrete future objectives of education systems, focusing on common concerns and priorities while respecting national diversity" (ibid.: 209). The development of the Lisbon strategy demonstrated the significant role education in general, and higher education in particular, was envisioned to play in "the economic and social development of the Union." A key policy outline for making the European Union the "most competitive and dynamic knowledge-based economy in the world," the Lisbon strategy focused on the aggressive adaptation of education and training systems to the "knowledge society" through "improving the existing processes and by a new open method of coordination as the means of spreading best practice and achieving greater convergence towards the main EU goal" (ibid.: 208). Three strategic goals, and thirteen "common concrete" objectives, were established for educational reform as part of the Lisbon strategy. The three strategic goals focused on (1) making educational systems more effective and improving their quality; (2) making them more accessible; and (3) making them more open (ibid.: 210). Activities in various member states, including in Germany, have suggested that the three strategic goals, despite their apparent emphasis on access, have been subsumed to outcomes-based measures, given the Lisbon strategy's overarching economic motivation in seeking EU-wide convergence of educational systems and the use of employment-related measures to determine the strategy's success. The EU has not kept these motivations secret:

> While the setting of quantified targets is not unusual in areas such as employment or the economy, it was a very new and bold step at European level in a field like education. Targets have the merit of being explicit and making it easier to assess the progress made.
> (European Communities 2006: 208)

Goals for the 2020 initiative reflect a further convergence of outcomes-focused measures related to economic growth, increasing educational access (i.e., "at least 40 percent of 30–34-year-olds completing third-level education") only insofar as the increase corresponds to employment (i.e., "75 percent of the 20–64-year-olds to be employed") (European Commission 2013).

Higher Educational Reform in China

Key to understanding both the external factors influencing higher educational reform in Europe, as well as the role of economic forces to which Habermas gives little credence, is an awareness of significant higher educational reforms underway in China. Policymakers and educational officials in the EU have recently acknowledged more explicitly the role that Chinese higher educational activities play as both explicit and implicit catalyst for educational reform in Europe. To these ends, presidents from both Chinese and European universities met for the first time on April 25, 2013 at the EU–China University Presidents' Dialogue, organized as part of the

EU–China Higher Education Platform for Cooperation and Exchange (HEPCE) in Brussels, Belgium. The meeting was in part a commemoration of 10 years of cooperation between China and members of the EU as part of the China–EU comprehensive strategic partnership; a partnership which, since 2003, has sought to foster increasingly close exchanges and substantial cooperation in such areas as trade and investment, foreign affairs and global issues, and culture and education (Hui 2013). The unique structure of China's higher educational system was evident at this first meeting of the HEPCE in Brussels. The meeting demonstrated that the challenges of integrating higher educational systems internationally are not simply policy and structural ones. The concern with such integration is cultural, and these cultural challenges are manifest in the privilege given to outcomes-based measures.

The modern Chinese university itself has a fairly recent history, often associated with China's defeat during the Sino-Japanese War of 1894–1895 and a general sense that modernization, specifically the role of education and technology, had contributed to Japanese success during the war (Brandenburg and Zhu 2007: 11). As a result, Emperor Guangxu (1871–1908) established Peiyang (or Beiyan) University (now Tianjin University), the first modern Chinese university, on October 2, 1895. Qiushi Academy (currently Zhejiang University) quickly followed in 1897, as did Jingshi University (now Beijing University) in 1898. By 1931, there were 39 universities in China, and by 1947, some 207 higher educational institutions, including 55 comprehensive institutions (ibid.). In 1949, significant reform measures in China restructured the higher educational system along Soviet lines. Private higher educational institutions were brought under state control, and an emphasis was placed on "specialization rather than comprehensiveness." The 1949 reforms, as Guo-huo Wang notes, "reflected the new political ideology and desire for economic development" (Wang 2010).

The period between 1949 and 1990 reflects dramatic shifts in Chinese higher educational reform. The so-called Great Leap Forward from 1958 to 1963 witnessed an explosion in the number of higher educational institutions in China, from 229 in 1957, to 841 in 1959, to 1,289 in 1960. The following decade, however, witnessed a restrictive government backlash, and the number of higher educational institutions was reduced to 407 in 1963. The so-called Cultural Revolution, begun in 1966, resulted in stagnation in higher education in China. In 1977, however, Deng Xiaoping gained political power and reintroduced a national examination system for college admissions. Of those who had gained eligibility between 1966 and 1977, approximately 18 million completed the national exam between 1977 and 1979. Of those who completed the exam, roughly 880,000 were admitted into higher educational institutions in China (Wang 2010). The national exam system was formalized further in the 1980s.

As a result of economic challenges, the Central Committee of the Chinese Communist Party and the State Council jointly issued a Program for Education Reform in 1993. The reform again allowed the establishment of private universities and colleges. The (re)introduction of privatized higher educational opportunities led to exceptional short-term growth. As Guo-hua Wang (2010) notes, citing a 2007 report from the Chinese Ministry of Education, "in 1990, less than 4 percent of the 18–22 age group was enrolled as students in higher education institutions compared to 22 percent in 2005."

In addition to reintroducing private higher educational opportunities, the Program for Education Reform also proposed criteria and standards for assessing educational quality. As mechanisms to advance the quality of higher education in China, the Chinese government introduced Project 211 in 1995, to grant special funding to 100 universities, and Project 985 in 1998, to fund a further 10, as catalysts for development. In 1999, the Higher Education Law sought to increase quality in education by giving more control of higher educational institutions to administrators and faculty, or what the law called "democratic management" (Wang 2010). China's entry into the World Trade Organization in 2001, as well as a series of reforms in the early 2000s that sought to transform Soviet-style subject colleges into comprehensive universities, have meant that conversations about Chinese higher educational reforms are increasingly with a comparative global perspective in mind.

Current efforts at educational reform in China are motivated by several factors. As Eric Abrahamsen (2012) notes in the *New York Times*, "Nearly everyone agrees on the problems: overemphasis on rote memorization, a top-down instructional style that crushes individuality and a near-total reliance on exams to evaluate progress." Chinese Premier Wen Jiabao chaired an Executive Committee that was formed to draft an education development plan in 2008. Similar to the European Union, these efforts in China to reform education have focused on a 10-year plan, adopted in 2010 and set for completion in 2020. Reform goals are outlined in the published report, "State Guidelines for Medium-to-Long-Term Education Reform and Development Plan between 2010 and 2020," also known as the "Development Plan" (Wang 2010).

The "Development Plan" in China focuses generally on the loosening of state controls on education and the development of private entities to lead reform efforts. The specific goals of the Development Plan are to improve the overall quality of education in China, while simultaneously advancing science, technologies and culture, and accelerating China's modernization process. The Development Plan focuses on goals such as the advancement of teaching and scientific research, as well as the promotion of collaboration between universities and research institutions. In addition, the Development Plan seeks to encourage what it calls "knowledge consultation" and the transfer of technologies and research results into products. Finally, a corollary to the ambitious scale of the Development Plan is the goal of nurturing talent and cultivating a group of internationally recognized, globally ranked universities in China by 2020 (Wang 2010).

Guo-hua Wang (2010) of the China Research Center suggests that there are two key ramifications of the Development Plan for higher education in China: "a relaxation of central control; and opening up of the college admission process."[6] The call for the government to distance itself from educational institutions would require Chinese officials to allow autonomy of educational institutions and to allow university and college administrators and faculty to oversee campus operations. The primary roles of the government would continue to include funding and establishing general educational policies.

Students in China complete a National College Entrance Exam (NCEE), or Gao Kao (or "gaokao"), in order to be offered a place at a Chinese university (Brandenburg and Zhu 2007). The call for a transition from the "one-exam-decides-all" method to an evaluation of prospective students using a multitude of tests and other criteria—such as teacher recommendations and extracurricular activities—poses additional sets of possibilities and challenges for Chinese educational officials.

In terms of private entities working on educational reform, examples such as Xing Wei College near Shanghai, founded by Harvard-educated investor Chen Weiming, have sought to introduce relatively affordable private models. Tuition at Xing Wei is $1,575 per year, an amount considered "within financial reach" of prospective students (Abrahamsen 2012). Yet, Abrahamsen suggests in his brief text, the continuity of the Soviet-borrowed approach to education as a means to train workers, and China's effort to encourage creativity and individuality to produce more efficient workers, is palpable—and limiting. Another obstacle is the potential threat that an emphasis on too much individuality would play in China, potentially weakening social control in a country whose government retains control over many aspects of daily life. Invoking what might be considered more overtly Western concepts of self and self-betterment, while Xin Wei's stated aim is to create a globally competitive workforce, Abrahamsen (2012) concludes: "it would be nicer to think that students might someday be nurtured for their own sake, rather than as a means to achieving some social goal." Put another way, Guo-hua Wang (2010) suggests that, while China's current higher educational Development Plan "encourages nurturing students' creativity and independent thinking to foster scientific innovation, it certainly collides with cultural values that cherish obedience as a virtue."

Higher Educational Reform in the USA

China is, of course, not the only global economic powerhouse influencing current higher educational reforms in Europe. The US continues to play a key role as well. To these ends, understanding current debates in the US about federal (and state) support of higher education further explains the increasing emphasis on outcomes-based measures in Europe.

The initial authorization of the Higher Education Act in 1965 was, and continues to be, seen as a significant effort to democratize access to a college or university education in the United States. The Act proved successful in many respects: 70 percent of US high school graduates enrolled in college in 2009, compared with 45 percent in 1960, according to the Bureau of Labor Statistics. To these ends, the Act authorizes the disbursement of approximately $150 billion per year to colleges and universities in the US, based primarily on how many students these institutions enroll. The anticipated reauthorization of the Higher Education Act in 2013 and 2014, however, has focused great attention on several controversial aspects and unexpected outgrowths of the Act, most notably the issues of student debt, of institutional accountability for student learning, and the ethics of higher education as business.

In light of the above concerns, recent debates over the reauthorization of the Higher Education Act have focused on developing mechanisms for higher educational institutional accountability; accountability in terms of both student debt loads as well as student employability after graduation, known as "gainful employment." President Barack Obama announced in late August of 2013 a series of proposals that, according to Tamar Lewin (2013) of the *New York Times*, seek to make "colleges more accountable and affordable by rating them and ultimately linking those ratings to financial aid." Obama's plan seeks to connect the amount of federal aid US colleges and universities would receive to those institutions' rankings in areas such as tuition, graduation rates, debt and earning of graduates, and the percentage of lower-income students who attend. By 2018, Obama's proposals suggest, colleges and universities who rate highly using these criteria would be eligible for more federal grants and their students would be eligible for more affordable loans.

Key to Obama's initiative is the linking of federal aid to educational outcomes, and among the measures used to calculate that relationship is a new criterion: graduates' earnings. The linking of federal aid to educational outcomes is especially troubling for public universities that have seen their federal and state support decrease significantly. Twenty-five years ago, tuition made up about 25 percent of public university revenues; today these same institutions receive about 50 percent of their revenue from student tuition. The decreased state support of public universities suggests that federal aid has taken on an increasingly significant role in funding higher education. To offset potentially decreased federal and state support, for public as well as private higher educational institutions, Obama calls for low-cost innovations such as competency-based degrees and massive open online courses, or MOOCs. The focus on competency-based degrees and MOOCs shifts the focus of higher educational reform from one of access, to one of outcomes.

While Obama's proposals as part of the reauthorization of the Higher Education Act suggest that federal funding would be tied in some degree to the percentage of lower-income students who attend, several dozen higher-education leaders at a policy "lab" hosted by Minnesota's state Office of Higher Education and the Lumina Foundation in late September 2013 highlighted a significant problem with Obama's outcomes-based approach to rethinking higher educational funding: the lack of focus on student access. The policy lab featured former Macalester College President Michael McPherson, now president of the Chicago-based Spencer Foundation and an expert on US student financial aid (*Star Tribune* 2013). McPherson and other members of the policy lab noted that federal aid for higher education in the US currently functions as a voucher system, and aid is allocated to qualifying students rather than to any particular institution. Given the demographic shifts in the higher education population in the US, "the students who most need those vouchers are place-bound adults with little or no opportunity to 'spend' them anywhere but at their nearest public college or university." As such, McPherson and his fellow presenters suggest that the impact of Obama's proposed institutionally focused, outcomes-based federal aid model would be antithetical to the idea of access to the democratization of higher education. Not only would students be given less choice and less access to higher education, but colleges and universities would be encouraged to become more, rather than less, selective in order to guarantee an overall higher graduation rate among its students. While tying institutional financial rewards to the graduation rates of select cohorts, such as minority or low-income students, may appear to be one possible solution, such outcomes-focused methods of accountability fail to resolve the issue of broad, student-focused access to colleges and universities that best serve these students' professional needs and life constraints.

Enter Habermas

In focusing on the role of education in Habermas' vision for a "worldly cosmopolitanism," following the model of European Enlightenment philosopher Immanuel Kant, I have tried to map out the explicit factors influencing higher educational reform in the European Union, as well as those forces which Habermas does not fully take into account, namely implicit and explicit economic challenges posed by China and the US. I hope to show, in this assemblage of texts and policy developments, that an emphasis on outcomes versus access in higher educational reform in the European Union does disservice to the vision Habermas articulates. Clearly, economic pressures, whose increasing speed Habermas rightly notes, are the key forces behind the outcomes-based focus of much of European higher educational reform. It remains to be seen, however, if such outcomes-based approaches can ever lead to the kind of robust, open exchange of ideas envisioned in Habermas' Europe, and even beyond it.

In focusing on the education of creative professionals in my forthcoming book, *Internationalization Through Integration: Higher Educational Reform in International Context*, I identify a discreet set of disciplines and areas of study that have proven challenging to standardize across cultures as well as practices that in many ways are directly antithetical to the neoliberal processes currently dominating higher educational reform efforts in the EU, China, and the US. In addition to the anti-capitalist tactics embraced by avant-garde artists in Europe and the US in the late nineteenth and early twentieth centuries, these creative fields' most successful and most vocal figures have themselves embodied life philosophies that directly challenge what Habermas describes as "economic globalization." As such, the figures associated with, and the educational strategies employed by, the creative professions may provide the most salient counter-logic to the implicit and explicit neoliberal dimensions of higher educational reform, in Europe and beyond. Put in other words, the current demands that education be subsumed to economic motives finds its avant-garde counterpart in figures such as the designer, architect, and futurist (Richard) Buckminster Fuller, whose anti-capitalist, anti-neoliberal logic deserves the final say and is worth quoting at length:

> We should do away with the absolutely specious notion that everybody has to earn a living. It is a fact today that one in ten thousand of us can make a technological breakthrough capable of supporting all the rest. The youth of today are absolutely right in recognizing this nonsense of earning a living. We keep inventing jobs because of this false idea that everybody has to be employed at some kind of drudgery because, according to Malthusian Darwinian theory he must justify his right to exist. So we have inspectors of inspectors and people making instruments for inspectors to inspect inspectors. The true business of people should be to go back to school and think about whatever it was they were thinking about before somebody came along and told them they had to earn a living
>
> (Fuller, in Barlow 1970: 30)

Notes

1 Research for this essay, as well as the related book project *Internationalization through Integration: Higher Educational Reform in International Context*, was made possible thanks to the generous support in summer 2012 of the Fulbright German Studies Seminar and in summer of 2013 of the Deutscher Akademischer Austauschdienst (DAAD).
2 Kant notes in the essay, a foundational text of European Enlightenment, that "Enlightenment is man's release from his self-incurred tutelage. Tutelage is man's inability to make use of his understanding without direction from another."
3 Habermas oddly downplays the economic dimensions of the crisis to these ends: "Reasons of space prevent me from commenting on the legitimate empirical question of an economic dynamic within world society which has for decades been exacerbating a long-standing democratic deficit" (Habermas 2012: 12).
4 According to the authors, the concept of "learning outcomes" identifies what a learner is expected to know, understand, and be able to demonstrate, expressed in terms of "levels of competence." In comparison, "competencies" are developed in all course units and assessed at different stages of the program.
5 The subject areas identified in the 2010 publication of the project Tuning

Educational Structures in Europe are Business Administration, Chemistry, Education Sciences, European Studies, History, Earth Sciences, Mathematics, Nursing, and Physics.

6 The author also provides in her reading a concise description of the "Development Plan":

> The plan is divided into four sections. Each section covers several chapters and each chapter includes numerous issues. Section One describes the plan's overall strategy. Section Two lays out missions to accomplish and goals to achieve. Section Three outlines the reform of the educational infrastructure. Section Four provides measurements to ensure implementation. Six chapters are devoted to specific measures, which include the following: strengthening the quality of teaching faculty; increasing the government funding of education to 4 percent of GDP by 2012; completing education laws and regulations; and ensuring every step of the reform meets the laws and regulations. In order to accomplish these missions and goals, the Development Plan encourages educational institutions to design their own reform programs and policies.

References

Abrahamsen, Eric (2012) "A Liberal Arts Education, Made in China," *New York Times*, July 3, 2012.

Adorno, Theodor W., and Max Horkheimer (1997 [1944]) *Dialectic of Enlightenment*. London / New York: Verso.

Barlow, Elizabeth (1970) "The New York Magazine Environmental Teach-In," *New York Magazine*, March 30 1970.

Brandenburg, Uwe, and Jian Zhu (2007) *Higher Education in China in Light of Massification and Demographic Change: Lessons to be Learned for Germany* (Arbeitspapier nr. 97). Gütersloh: Center for Higher Education (CHE).

European Commission (2006) *The History of European Cooperation in Education and Training*. Luxembourg: European Commission.

European Commission (2009) *Charter of the Fundamental Rights of the European Union*. http://ec.europa.eu/justice/fundamental-rights/charter/.

European Commission (2010) *The EU Contribution to the European Higher Education Area*. Luxembourg: Publications Office of the European Union.

European Commission (2013) *Europe 2020 Targets*. http://ec.europa.eu/europe2020/europe-2020-in-a-nutshell/targets/index_en.htm.

González, Julia, and Robert Wagenaar (eds.) (2008) *Tuning Educational Structures in Europe: Universities' Contribution to the Bologna Process*, 2nd edn. Bilbao, Spain: Pubicaciones de la Universidad de Deusto.

Habermas, Jürgen (1983) "Modernity—An Incomplete Project," in Hal Foster (ed.) *The Anti-Aesthetic: Essays on Postmodern Culture*. New York: The New Press. Reprint 1988.

Habermas, Jürgen (1984) *Theory of Communicative Action. Volume 1: Reason and the Rationalization of Society*. trans. Thomas McCarthy. Boston: Beacon Press.

Habermas, Jürgen (2001) "Why Europe Needs a Constitution," *New Left Review*, 11, pp. 5–26.

Habermas, Jürgen (2012) *The Crisis of the European Union: A Response*. London: Polity Press.

Hui, Lu (2013) "China, EU Hold First-ever Dialogue on Higher Education," *English.news.cn*. http://news.xinhuanet.com/english/culture/2013-04/26/c_124633047.htm (last accessed: March 2, 2016).

Kant, Immanuel (1784) "What is Enlightenment?" *Modern History Sourcebook.* www.fordham.edu/halsall/mod/kant-whatis.asp (last accessed: March 2, 2016).
Lewin, Tamar (2013) "Obama's Plan Aims to Lower Cost of College," *New York Times*, August 22, 2013.
Star Tribune (2013) "Your Attention Please, on Higher Ed," *Star Tribune*, Editorial Board, October 2, 2013. www.startribune.com/opinion/editorials/226221171.html (last accessed: March 2, 2016).
Vasilliou, Androulla (2010) "Foreword," in *The EU Contribution to the European Higher Education Area*. Luxembourg: Publications Office of the European Union.
Wang, Guo-hua (2010) "China's Higher Education Reform," *China Currents*, 9(1). Available from China Research Center: www.chinacenter.net/2010/china_currents/9-1/chinas-higher-education-reform/ (last accessed: March 2, 2016).

8 European Integration and Economic Interests

Marcella Myers

European integration has been essentially an economic pursuit. The European Coal and Steel Community, European Atomic Energy Community, and European Economic Community created common policies in agriculture, transportation and pooled resources for research and development. The necessity of administering these European institutions and policies has led to the establishment of an extensive bureaucratic structure leading some to argue that the EU has a democratic deficit. The EU democratic deficit combined with processes of globalization have left member states relatively helpless to control their national economies. However, this may not be an accurate picture of the helplessness of national governments. Rather, the EU bureaucratic structures leave enough flexibility for member states to make decisions in policy implementation, heavily influencing national economies. Furthermore, national governments have made political choices that contribute to the acceleration of globalization. Not only are member states not helpless victims, they are willing participants in the processes of economic and financial globalization. Furthermore, institutional structures of member states influence implementation of EU policy directives that have resulted in serious consequences for the future of the Lisbon Strategy and EU citizens.

In the 1990s, Tony Blair and Gerhard Schroeder adopted neoliberal economic policies, also known as Third Way, meant to reduce government spending and reform social programs. The neoliberal policies adopted by center-left politicians led to an increase in contracting private companies to carry out public services. This chapter discusses how nation states have been less victims, and more active participants in the processes of globalization, through the adoption of neoliberal policies resulting in privatization of public goods, exposing citizens to market discipline, and undermining the social contract.

Globalization and Privatization

Globalization and its effect on national governments is an ongoing debate and identified as one of the causes of national governments' inability to control capital flows into and out of their borders (Strange 1996). Habermas has argued that in the process of neoliberal economic globalization, the idea of a social Europe "has perceptibly failed" (Habermas 2014). As Evelyne Huber and John D. Stephens (2001) have observed, it is hard to resist the impression that trans-border economic activity has changed the environment in which welfare states operate, making it impossible for them to perform the distributive functions they performed in the early post-Second World War era. According to Habermas (2001), democratic governments should have the opportunity to counter the "undesired social consequences of globalization by complementary social and infrastructural policies." However, the problem may not be an inability for national governments to control national budgets and regulate financial markets but a lack of political will.

The discussion regarding globalization and its relationship with national governments is an important one to the integration debate, because globalization is part of the rationale for further integration and for the portrayal of national governments as its victims. However, there is some evidence to suggest national governments are willing participants in globalization (see Scholte 1997). The creative destruction—the process through which technological advances replace previous forms of production—accelerated by globalization furthers the self-interest of politically influential economic elites. Habermas (2012) argues that "globalized markets have been outstripping politics" and OECD countries are finding it hard to "stimulate economic growth while at the same time ensuring social security and tolerably just distribution of income for the mass population" (Habermas 2012: 4).

The first EU institutions, specifically the European Coal and Steel Community and the European Economic Community, were economic pursuits. Economic concerns have continued to dominate; European member states have adopted closer economic ties and turned to austerity measures emphasizing budgetary restraint. Many of the policies that are now associated with neoliberalism are rooted in political choices made in the late 1970s and following decades. These political choices coincided with an increase in corporate incomes. Corporate incomes between 1979 and 1989 rose faster than GDP, while "there was an increase in the proportion of corporate income distributed as dividends, resulting in an increase in real dividends of 65 percent" (Atkinson 1996: 39). These rises in corporate income are not attributable only to profits from new goods and services or an increase in the consumption of those goods and services. These increases are the result of political choices made by governments.

In the early 1980s, as governments adopted monetarist economic policies, capital owners realized the attractiveness of government bonds. Monetarist policies mean that governments seek to influence the economy through interest rates and sale of government bonds. According to Scharpf (2000), prior to the early 1980s even a minimal return on an investment had been attractive; this began to change with the adoption of monetarist policies. Risk-free government bonds and the expected return from those investments "rose to high positive levels"; and because of the safe, high return on bonds, only other investment projects with "expected profits significantly above that level would still have a chance to be financed" (Scharpf 2000: 30). As a result, "business employment would fall unless there was significant increase of business profits—which could be achieved only through a redistribution from labor to capital incomes" (ibid.). With this redistribution, profits began to flow from labor and investment in workers (i.e., healthcare, pensions, and wages), to capital and corporate profits represented by increasing attention to shareholders and dividends. As firms looked for higher profits in "banking, telecommunications, transportation, and retailing, they provoked successive waves of deregulation" most notably in the United States in the late 1970s and 1980s (Schwartz 2001). Deregulation further enabled corporations to concentrate profits and assets.

The political choice to deregulate financial markets increasingly constrained policy options for governments (Huber and Stephens 2001). Deregulation and a reluctance for governments to intervene in markets is indicative of the adoption of neoliberal policy goals that seek to limit the size and scope of government, accomplished in part through the restructuring of pension, healthcare, and unemployment benefits. Furthermore, "whatever social policies they [national governments] choose, they may adapt to constraints imposed by deregulated markets—in particular global financial markets" (Habermas 2011: 11). Many EU member states have adopted various aspects of these goals. "If pressures exerted by globalization had anything to do with those changes [in welfare states], it is only through the political choices made in response to the pressures" (Martin 1997: 2): political choices that go beyond deregulation, to include the privatization of public goods and services.

Rationale of Privatization

Shifts in investments and deregulation in banking and other protected industries coincided with moves to privatize government functions. The theory behind privatization is that a market solution will be more efficient, providing services at lower cost, thus saving taxpayers' money. Pressures to deregulate and adopt market solutions to problems of public service delivery generated discussions regarding distribution of services and resources and are key to discussions regarding distributive justice, social justice and a "social Europe."

Neoliberal agendas have placed public services under scrutiny; often this scrutiny results in cutting or reducing public services. The cutting of public services increases risk to individual citizens. Governments have introduced market mechanisms to the provision of public goods. These mechanisms include privatization of publicly held entities (e.g., public housing, utilities, and telecommunications); maintaining ownership, but contracting services through private providers (e.g., road construction); public-private partnerships in which private capital is used to fund public services (e.g., schools);

and publicly funded initiatives. Many of these solutions put citizens in the position of purchasing services previously provided by the state while private companies reap the profits. These policy choices, made by the same political actors who are lacking the will to impose regulatory norms on financial, labor, and trade markets, result in "the emergence of an underclass," child poverty, and a low wage, flexible labor market (Habermas 2012: 105).

Beneficiaries of privatization are often firms, as a result of the provision of public goods by private providers.

> This agenda [privatization] hollows out the core functions of the state, it sells off the remnants of a deliberative public sphere to profit-maximizing financial investors, and it subordinates culture and education to the interests and moods of sponsors who are dependent on market cycles.
>
> (Habermas 2012: 105)

Through government contracts, public/private partnerships (PPPs), and publicly funded initiatives (PFIs), firms are able to generate profits from investments with relatively low risk. Firms are "increasingly exercising a parallel authority alongside governments in matters of economic management affecting the location of industry and investment, the direction of technological innovation, the management of labor relations and the fiscal extraction of surplus value" (Strange 1996). Firms that are able to take advantage of tax havens and offshore financial institutions to concentrate profits in the corporation and, in the end, through bonuses and stock options, in the hands of corporate managers. Corporate diversification has occurred to such an extent that parent companies may have multiple subsidiary holding companies and limited liability companies.

Many firms that have profited from government contracts in the form of public-private partnerships (PPP) and privately funded initiatives (PFI) are large, with multiple subsidiaries that operate in the financial, social services, and construction industries. In part, this is the result of contracting out construction and maintenance of public buildings: for example, schools and hospitals. Services provided by government have traditionally not been subject to market pressures, and therefore may be considered sheltered. Introduction of PPPs and PFIs into the provision of public services moves these services into competitive markets to some degree, removing their sheltered status. On the other hand, provision of public services also means that those firms contracting with the government through PPPs/PFIs gain some protection in the sense that services are necessities, thereby guaranteeing the payment of the contract by governments to the firm.

Subsidiary companies allow large transnational corporations to engage in rent-seeking by pursing government contracts, public-private partnerships (PPPs), and privately funded initiatives (PFIs). Rent-seeking takes place when transfers of money occur, not related to production; and commonly occurs through subsidies or tax cuts granted to specific groups. In this case, rent-seeking takes place when corporations seek government contracts. Government contracts are attractive because governments guarantee payment to the corporation, sometimes regardless of corporate performance. Furthermore, corporations earn profits from government contracts and receive tax advantages through offshore or European corporate registrations.

As firms adopted the provision of public services, new opportunities for business emerged through market-based social policy (Klenk and Nullmeier 2012). For example, the trend through the last 20 to 30 years has been for employers to shift from defined benefit pension plans to defined contribution plans, 401(k), or other investment funds to which employers may contribute, so the risk is now individualized (Orszag and Stiglitz 1999). The process of individualization puts employees into private markets to purchase services. For financial services, the process of privatization of pensions in the form of defined contribution plans coincides with increased investment in personal retirement accounts, and a plethora of other financial instruments designed to maximize individual retirement investment. Raffer (2003) has argued that abolishing public (and defined) pension schemes opens an enormous market for private finance firms.

One of the primary reasons governments make use of PPP/PFI contracts is that privately financed capital spending is off budget (Spackman 2003), so that social problems are not tackled using public capital resources or in response to political pressure (Flinders 2005). Private companies are attractive for welfare state reformers because firms have easier access to capital markets (Klenk and Nullmeier 2012). Advocates of PPP/PFIs argue the contracts provide additional benefits of "quality improvement, innovation, management efficiency and effectiveness" (Bovis 2010: 381).

PPP/PFI contracts are long, often 30 years or more, allowing the cost of the capital investment made by the private sector to be recovered over a long time period through a unitary charge. Unitary charges are a combined payment for assets (buildings and equipment) and services paid to the special vehicle companies (SPV) for availability of facilities and performance-related service provision. Unitary charges reflect the cost of using the building, plus the cost of facilities management (Whitfield 2011). The government pays unitary charges to the private contractor on a monthly basis or in a single annual payment.

Ultimately, the adoption of PFI contracts leads to the creation of public limited holding companies and SPV companies to administer and oversee the contracts. Many of the same management companies and individuals employed as managers and directors sit as directors on multiple subsidiary companies, and shareholder interest is primarily limited to parent companies. The use of public limited holding companies and SPVs has the effect of concentrating not only assets, but also stockholder interest, salaries, and bonuses paid to executives and management companies in the hands of a few. There has been a "marked rise in the rewards to managers, both in terms of salaries and severance" and stock options (Strange 1996: 64).

In the UK, this concentration is part of the picture of rising income and wealth inequality, with individuals at the top of the distribution experiencing above average, rapid increases in income (Hills 1996). At the top of the distribution, the top decile has increased from 167 percent of the median in 1977 to 191 percent in 1999 (Atkinson 1999). These inequalities exist across OECD countries. In 2011, the OECD reported that increases in household income inequality are largely due to "changes in the distribution of wages and salaries which account for 75 percent of household incomes of working-age adults" (OECD 2011: 6).

The introduction of competition into the provision of public goods creates welfare markets; these markets support employer interests and open new business opportunities (Klenk and Nullmeier 2012: 33). The welfare market is problematic for several reasons; as Strange points out, market economies—welfare or otherwise—multiply risks, the more developed, complex and large the market, the larger the risks (Strange 1996: 91). Emphasis on private answers to public goods has resulted in governments seeking to privatize and contract out a growing number of previously public services. The beneficiaries of privatization and public-private partnerships and contracts have been corporations. Growing inequality has coincided with the increasing use of offshore financial centers and tax havens that have allowed firm ownership and firms to "internally allocate resources through transfer pricing" and the increasingly opaque national tax and regulatory authorities (Cerny 1995: 609).

Economic Interests, Income, and Social Benefits

The success of economic interests in the process of EU integration is, in many ways, not surprising. Economic interests are well funded and organized; access to resources enables them to apply pressure more effectively than more poorly funded and organized citizen interest groups. Political choices often reflect preferences associated with well-organized interests (Nooruddin and Simmons 2006; Hacker and Pierson 2011). Citizens most in need of public services are not well organized, and "the probability and efficacy of political participation is not equally distributed throughout the population" (Nooruddin and Simmons 2006: 1022). Social inequalities that developed with the liberalization of markets,

> do not constitute a concern for everyone, and have been even less of a domain of intervention for public powers: neoliberals consider that the redistribution operated by social states is not only detrimental in terms of economic effectiveness but also incites individuals to rely on others.
> (Maltone et al. 2012)

Habermas identifies the global liberalized markets as a process of accelerated modernization, which creates both winners and losers. He argues that short- and long-term losers in a globalized, liberalized modernization process are not in a strong veto position and therefore have little influence on the policymaking process. Appropriate levels of "general social welfare largely depends on the degree of support for notions of distributive justice" (Habermas 2011: 10). Under conditions of accelerated modernization, Habermas (2012) argues that individuals no longer perceive responsibility for those around them. This has the effect of reducing support for the notions of distributive justice Habermas identifies as necessary for the continuation of appropriate levels of general social welfare across the eurozone and EU. The EU has pursued goals that are at odds with each other: the pursuit of economic integration along with the adoption of neoliberal policy goals; and the adoption of the Lisbon Strategy to pursue a social Europe.

Implications for Workers

While firms and some individuals benefit from privatization, the system of PPP/PFI and private contracts contributes to the formation of flexible labor markets. The benefit to firms is through short-term contracts, self-employment and part-time employment, which relieve firms from the responsibilities of providing benefits, payment of payroll taxes and contributions to employee pension, health, and unemployment compensation funds. Firms that are able to avoid the payment of these benefits contribute to pressures on national governments.

When a multinational registers outside the country in which it has operations, the corporation gains more than a tax advantage. The corporation employing contract employees may also avoid employers' association membership, and contracted employees are less likely to have union membership or affiliation. Thus, the employer and employee may not pay into all, or any, of the insurance-based social programs, for example pension schemes. While the firm may avoid payment of some benefits, national governments of most EU member states remain responsible for basic social benefits, paying the costs of maintaining social programs and paying benefits without contributions.

Neoliberal or Third Way policies of the 1990s—policies identified with the administrations of Tony Blair, Bill Clinton, and Gerhard Schroeder—led to some negative consequences for workers. Third Way policies contributed to the growth of flexible labor markets and low paid jobs that increased dependency on income supports. At the same time, reductions in protection in terms of pensions, long-term employment contracts, unemployment insurance and workers' compensation for employees have occurred (Deakin et al. 1995).

Since 2008, many countries have experienced changes in the structure of their labor market; changes that typically "include the extension of maximum lengths of fixed term work, the extension of the number of permissible renewals, and the creation of 'new' types of less protective contracts for target groups" (Clauwaert et al. 2013: 90). New contracts frequently offer less protection and target "specific groups of workers, such as young people, who are already among the most vulnerable as regards labor market entry, progress and retention" (ibid.). Flexible jobs with employment offering below the threshold for social insurance create problems for future entitlements (Mangen 2000). In the case of German workers, the amount paid to them in unemployment insurance and pensions is determined by the number of years the individual has worked and the amount of money paid into the insurance scheme. For example, *Le Monde* reported changes in German slaughterhouse employment in which employees moved from an hourly wage to piece work, paying employees according to the number of units produced (Gattinois 2013). This change in pay structure has the effect of reducing wages; lower wages mean smaller contributions to unemployment insurance and pensions. Smaller contributions to unemployment mean that workers, should they become unemployed, will have smaller unemployment compensation. Less contribution to a pension means that, on retirement, workers will receive smaller pensions. Finally, lower wages result in less tax revenue for governments at all levels.

The Social Contract

What have emerged in the last 30 years throughout advanced industrialized countries are governments that pursue neoliberal policies, undermining social democracies, and in the end the social contract: the idea that individuals as members of societies agree to carry some (limited) responsibility for each other. An emphasis on neoliberal policies has implications for workers, but the effect of these policies have social consequences with potential negative effects for social democracies and the EU commitment to the Lisbon Strategy.

According to Habermas (2012), liberal rights regarding the inviolability and security of the person, free commerce, and free exercise of religion—combined with democratic rights for participation—constitute classical civil rights. Classical civil rights are citizen rights that restrain government interference with the everyday lives of citizens. Classical civil rights do not include or constitute social rights. However, according to Habermas, citizens have equal opportunities to make use of these classical rights only "when they simultaneously enjoy a sufficient level of independence in their private and economic lives" (2012: 79). In other words, for citizens to have the capability to "deliberate and act for the general good, they must be certain that the satisfaction of basic material needs is guaranteed" (Ryner 2010: 557). Ryner argues that in addition to this guarantee of material needs, "requisite amounts of leisure are required for the nurturing of cognitive capabilities and the capacity to affiliate with fellow citizens" (ibid.)

One theme of the Third Way is "no rights without responsibilities," but "by guaranteeing no rights without responsibilities, Third Way welfare and economic policy exposes individuals to market discipline" (Ryner

2010: 556). This, combined with a modern legal construct encouraging subjective rights without duties, leads to societies in which citizens feel little responsibility for each other. "People who stand in a legal relation to each other are concerned about potential claims they expect others to make on them" (Habermas 2012: 84). This preoccupation with individual rights serves to undermine the social contract, because obligations to fellow citizens are only a result of the claims on one person that a second person can make (Habermas 2012). The undermining of the social contract occurs because of the emphasis on legal claims; the framework does away with moral and social obligations that lie outside legal frameworks. Legal responsibility replaces social responsibility, how legal responsibility is defined and codified depends in part on representation and access to resources that enable individuals and groups to defend their social rights within legal frameworks.

As a result, as Habermas observes, the less well-organized, most vulnerable social groups lose access to resources and representation in a neoliberal society. The system results in favorable policies for those who can organize most effectively on behalf of their interests, while those who "cannot overcome the problems of collective action or mobilize sufficient influence fail to get their preferred resource allocation" (Nooruddin and Simmons 2006: 1009). This means that economic interest groups, well organized and funded, will most often win the battle for resources. The neoliberal agenda "sells off the remnants of a deliberating public sphere to profit-maximizing financial investors, and it subordinates culture and education to the interests and moods of sponsors who are dependent on market cycles" (Habermas 2012: 105).

Neoliberal pursuit of market mechanisms takes multiple forms. Privatization is one of those forms and pursued through multiple methods. One of those methods is through public-private partnerships and initiatives. The cases of the United Kingdom and Germany illustrate first how such arrangements benefit private interests; second, how the structures of national governments and economies influence EU policy implementation; third, how the outcomes of policy implementation differ, due in part to those structural differences.

Case Studies

Pursued aggressively in Great Britain, the adoption of neoliberal policies resulting in privatization of public goods is the logical outcome of a liberal market economy. In the UK, PPPs and PFIs are used for construction and maintenance of infrastructure, as well as the provision of healthcare and education. A very interesting case of the use of PFI contracts is the National Health Service in the UK. It is of interest for several reasons. First, it is a good example of the mixed results that occur with the use of PFI contracts. Second, the NHS, and the PFI contracts associated with it, are an example of how corporate interests benefit, sometimes at the expense of taxpayers. Third, the NHS was one of the many examples of the British government embracing privatization first under Margaret Thatcher and continuing under Tony Blair.

In contrast, Germany is a coordinated market economy and the adoption of market mechanisms has occurred at a more limited pace. The use of PPPs and PFIs is primarily limited to construction and maintenance of infrastructure, while the provision of public services has remained under control of the Federal and *Länder* governments through social partners. Though one could argue privatization has occurred because the social partners provide healthcare and health insurance, the structure is very different in Germany. Social partners operate under heavy government oversight as do health insurance providers. Furthermore, the adoption of PPPs and PFIs adhere to EU policy regarding their use.

The Logic of Corporate Organization

Many parent companies hold multiple PPP/PFI contracts for construction, maintenance, and disposal services, alongside the provision of medical services and educational services. Limited holding companies are useful because they offer limited liability to shareholders and protection from hostile takeovers. Ownership restrictions include shareholders being unable to sell or transfer their shares without offering them first to other shareholders for purchase. Shareholders cannot offer their shares to the public over a stock exchange and the number of shareholders cannot exceed a fixed figure. In addition, the private limited company is subject to lower tax rates (UK Companies Limited 2013). The holding company does not run operations; it simply holds enough of majority stock to control the subsidiary or subsidiaries. In the case of Barclays Plc., the parent company holds a controlling interest in Kintra Ltd., just one PFI contractor. Between Kintra Ltd. and Barclays Plc. there are 11 companies, the majority are private limited companies, several incorporated specifically to attract and operate PFI contracts.

The logic in the parent company creating subsidiaries is twofold. First, the larger the firms and partnerships, the larger comparative advantage in the market (Strange 1996: 137). Comparative advantage means that when the gaps in efficiency between two firms are greater for some products rather than others, the firm has a comparative advantage in the product with the greatest gap in efficiency. Second, by controlling the subsidiaries, the parent company controls the stocks and ultimately the money, concentrating assets from multiple contracts in the hands of a few large parent companies. The return on the investment accrues to the parent companies, "shareholders in private finance initiative schemes can expect real returns of 1,525 percent a year" (Gaffney et al. 1999: 116). In the case of Kintra Ltd., two of three listed directors are corporate management companies, Infrastructure Managers Ltd. and Biif Corporate Service. Infrastructure Managers Ltd. is a management company created specifically to operate and manage assets delivered under the government's PFI scheme (Companies House Direct 2013). The company is a subsidiary of Biif Bidco Ltd., a holding company and subsidiary of Barclays. Infrastructure Managers Ltd. and Biif Corporate Service manage seven holding companies and private limited companies designed specifically as special vehicle companies (SPV) for PFI contracts. Lanterndew Ltd. is the parent company of five of these private limited companies. Lanterndew's director is also the director of Biif Parentco Ltd., Biif Inssureco Ltd., Biif Holdco Ltd., Biif Gp. Ltd., and is a private equity investor in Barclays Infrastructure Funds. These companies are all subsidiaries of Barclays Bank Plc. Barclays and its subsidiaries hold equity shares in PFI contracts in medical facilities that paid a total of £166.5 million in unitary charges (HM Treasury 2012); Barclays Plc. reported a post-tax profit in 2011 of £3,951 million (Annual Report 2012). In 2013, profits fell to £2,945 million, rising to £3,798 million in 2014 (Annual Report 2014).

Hochtief, Germany's largest construction company, operates a division devoted to the acquisition of PPP contracts. In 2012, Hochtief and its subsidiaries had acquired eight PPP/PFI 25- and 30-year contracts worth an estimated £1.8 billion (HM Treasury 2012). These contracts are exclusively for education facilities. As with the corporations identified above, Hochtief has many subsidiaries operating under three divisions: North America, Southeast Asia, and Europe. Hochtief, like Barclays, is a global corporation, generating €114.3 billion in net income and €286.4 million post-tax profits in the first half of 2013 (Hochtief 2013). Since 2013, Hochtief has shifted focus away from contracting services back to construction and engineering projects. The rationale for such a shift is that although the service contracts are long term and profitable, they require more capital investment (Webb and Fahmy 2015).

The UK and the use of PFIs

The South London Trust is one example of the provision of public services using PFIs, in this case health care. The South London Trust ran deficits for five years and was dissolved in October 2013, after which new organizations took over management of its services (South London Healthcare 2013). By the end of 2013, the South London Trust accumulated debt of £200 million, and the Department of Health paid the excess costs of PFI buildings at two hospitals and wrote off the accumulated debt of the Trust (Department of Health 2013). In effect, the failure of the South London Trust leaves taxpayers paying off corporate managers. Following its dissolution on October 1, 2013, the NHS South London Trust—which ran the Queen Elizabeth, Queen Mary and Princess Royal hospitals—transferred responsibilities to The Kings College Hospital NHS Trust, which went on to acquire the Princess Royal University Hospital, and took over operation of services at Orpington Hospital. A new NHS Trust, Lewisham and Greenwich, now runs the Queen Elizabeth Hospital. Finally, Oxleas

NHS Foundation Trust acquired Queen Mary's Hospital (South London Healthcare 2015). As part of the agreement to dissolve the South London Trust, the Queen Elizabeth, Queen Mary and Princess Royal hospitals were required to make the full £74.9 million of efficiencies identified by the Trust Special Administrator; the Department of Health agreed that, where possible, it would sell vacant or underused facilities. Perhaps more significant, the Department agreed to pay the excess costs of the PFI buildings at the Queen Elizabeth and Princess Royal Hospitals and write off the accumulated debt of the Trust so that the "new organizations are not saddled with historic debts" (Department of Health 2013). This is of particular interest because the "new organizations" are not new at all.

Under the previous South London Trust, Innisfree Group Ltd., one of the three shareholders in the South London Trust, had equity share in 17 PFI contracts in medical services totaling £590.1 million (HM Treasury 2012). Innisfree Group Ltd. has three shareholders and 24 employees and in the 2012 fiscal year paid £6,801,000 in salaries and wages, £2,862,000 in directors' emoluments, and £4,229,000 in dividends (Duedil 2013). SPV Meridian Hospital, under the new agreement, owns the Queen Elizabeth Hospital. The Meridian Hospital SPV consists of two equity holders; Innisfree holds a total of 72.5 percent equity shares, while John Laing is a 27.5 percent equity holder, the SPV has a total capital value of £96.1 million (HM Treasury 2012). The unitary charges are collected by SPV Meridian Hospital. SPV United Healthcare administers the Princess Royal University Hospital. SPV United Healthcare has two equity holders, Innisfree and Semperian, both holding 50 percent equity.

Ultimately, even when the PPP/PFI contracts fail, as in the case of the South London Trust, taxpayer money accrues to privately contracted corporations. Strange has argued that increased market volatility, the variation of market values over time, has added to banks' income from management fees of various kinds. However, the "amount of tax paid over to the state has not increased accordingly" (Strange 1996: 64). For example, the Queen Elizabeth PFI project, part of the South London NHS Trust, is now owned by Semperian PPP Investment Partners, Innisfree and John Laing Infrastructure Fund (Cooper and Ungoed-Thomas 2012); the unitary charge for the Queen Elizabeth PFI contract in 2011–12 amounted to £26.6 million, while in 2010–11 it was £25.4 million (HM Treasury 2012). The John Laing Infrastructure Fund (JLIF) holds equity share in 10 PFI contracts, with 100 percent equity share in nine, totaling £251.5 million in unitary charges in the 2011–2012 fiscal year (HM Treasury 2012). JLIF is a limited company with a single shareholder, John Laing Investments Ltd., the shareholder value in 2011 was £136.2 million, with a post-tax profit of £30.04 million. In 2014, shareholder value was £686.9 million with a post-tax profit of £147.5 million (Duedil 2013). According to JLIF, the company expects to increase its contracts through PPPs in countries abroad as they pursue further public-private ventures (Laing 2012). John Laing Investments is the single shareholder of JLIF, with a shareholder value of £47.1 million (Duedil 2013).

PFI contracts are in some way similar to the purchase of government bonds. The investment on the part of the private companies is relatively safe, as the unitary charges ensure that the contracted corporation will recover some of the costs. The incentive for the contractor is not necessarily to provide a service, but to make profit. As in the case of the South London Trust, the PFI contractors will recover some of the loss, and because the companies administering the PFI contracts are registered public limited companies, the parent companies are protected from financial losses.

Germany's PPPs

A European Commission green paper outlining the legal aspects of PPPs in the EU guides public-private partnerships in Germany. There is not explicit general PPP law; however, procurement law and monitoring mechanisms provide powerful oversight. In Germany PPP/PFI contracts are largely absent in the provision of healthcare. Statutory Health Insurance Association and the National Hospital Federation make healthcare policy, while the Federal Joint Committee issues directives for the provision of healthcare. However, similar to the UK, the German healthcare system has come under pressure to be more efficient and accountable. In Germany, the non-profit and for-profit sectors have coexisted for decades. The German Ministry of Health is responsible for crucial elements of healthcare policy and imposes administrative regulations that states and communities are required to adhere to (Mattei el al. 2013). In 1972, the government passed a hospital financing law to ensure population needs in terms of hospital access. Initially, the federal government made investments to establish hospitals through tax revenues allocated through state parliaments, with subsequent running costs carried by the health insurance providers (ibid.). This structure created a dual system where individual states have considerable financial decision-making power. However, the statutory health insurance companies, medical practitioners' associations and hospital associations also exert considerable pressure on the relevant decision-making processes (ibid.).

Statutory health insurance provides coverage for approximately 90 percent of the German population. Health insurance financing is through health insurance funds, which are financially and organizationally independent (Statutory Health Insurance 2013). Employer and employee contributions provide funding for health insurance funds, the insurance funds in turn contract health care providers. The National Association of Statutory Health Insurance Funds acts as the central lobby for the statutory health insurance funds and creates binding collective regulations. Together with the National Association of Statutory Health Insurance Physicians, the National Association of Statutory Health Insurance Dentists and the German Hospital Federation, the National Association of Statutory Health Insurance Funds forms the Federal Joint Committee, "which decides on the specific benefits to be included in the statutory health insurance catalogue" (Statutory Health Insurance 2013). Strictly speaking, this dual health provision of health insurance and funding makes the use of PPP/PFI contracts unnecessary. However, contracting health care providers is an example of the adoption of private contracting to fulfill provision of a public good. The framework for healthcare provision, as outlined above, reflects the neo-corporatist, coordinated market structures that influence public policy-making in Germany.

If Germany does not employ PPP/PFIs in the provision of health care, the use of these instruments is primarily in the construction of municipal buildings, hospitals, and schools. Because of the structure of government in Germany, municipalities implement roughly 75 percent of federal and state legislation. Municipalities earn most of their revenues from taxes, government grants for delegated services, and from fees and charges for their own services; the local and independently generated revenues total 44 percent of municipal revenue (Grossi and Reichard 2008). Municipalities turn to PPP contracts primarily for construction and transportation needs. By using PPP contracts, local governments "escape the rigid and bureaucratic legal framework of public administration into the relative freedom of the business sector" (ibid.: 607). Furthermore, the expectation on the part of municipal governments is that the managers of the corporations will be independent from political party influence. The turn to private solutions has also come due to EU pressure to increase competitiveness in the public sector through deregulation of public services (ibid.).

It would be easy to suggest that PPP/PFIs and private contracts should be avoided, and that privatization is a poor substitute for public provision of public goods and services. However, not all PPP/PFI contracts have negative consequences. In some cases, these are the best options for both government and citizens. The positive outcomes are that contracts can provide services efficiently at lower cost without putting citizens at risk. Particularly when PPP/PFI contracts involve construction and transportation, the contracts, through the projects corporations manage, create jobs—contributing to economic growth.

Negative consequences emerge when the procurement process structurally favors corporations without proper oversight or review. In addition, governments should recognize that each contract with a new corporation for a different project creates a proxy bureaucracy, making oversight and control difficult. When governments fail in the processes of contract writing, awarding, and review, corporations have the potential to fall short, leaving governments to pay the consequences.

Conclusion

Economic interests have benefited from EU integration in more ways than outlined here. However, the example of contracts, public-private partnerships and privately funded initiatives does indicate how the flow of money in this specific example is bottom up. The adoption of policies that seek to deregulate and privatize are political choices with serious economic consequences.

In addition to the issue of political choices and political will, the structures of national governments are important. The adoption and oversight of public-private partnerships and contracts differs widely between countries. Although the UK and Germany both adhere to EU standards concerning PPPs, the network of oversight in Germany is arguably more rigorous than in the UK. This is in part due to national governing frameworks. Not only is Germany a federal system, it is neo-corporatist. This means that public policy is not only made in parliamentary committees and government ministries: employer associations, industry representatives, and union associations also participate in the policymaking process. A single body does not have the sole responsibility for oversight. Not only is the configuration of policymaking in the UK more centralized in the House of Commons and government ministries, the body governing oversight of PPP and PFI contracts is itself a PFI operated by a special vehicle company. Although the UK has the most extensive system of economic regulation, and regulators are technically accountable to Parliament "there is very little structural supervision" (Majone 1999: 11). The embedded differences in the political and economic systems of these countries explain in part the implementation of policy made by the EU. Consequences for citizens include an expanding flexible labor market and a reduction in social protections. This in spite of continued public support for the Lisbon Strategy. The structural differences will persist regardless of the development of a common identity between EU citizens. Although the EU has made a public commitment to a social Europe, the goals of the Lisbon Strategy may be difficult to achieve. As Majone (1999) has observed, the Single Act, Maastricht, and Amsterdam Treaties explicitly exclude the harmonization of social legislation.

Globalization may not be the great threat to national governments. The process of globalization may pose challenges to governments, but national governments suffer from self-inflicted wounds in the form of deregulation and privatization. Self-inflicted wounds are the result of political choices that benefit economic interests. EU citizens have benefited from integration in some smaller ways—free movement, right to work in other member states, etc. However, one driving force behind EU integration has been economic. The problem of integration may be less about a common identity, and more about the awkward pivot that institutions formed primarily with economic interests in mind must make if political integration is the desired outcome.

References

Antoniades, Alexander (2008) "Social Europe and/or Global Europe? Globalization and Flexicurity as Debates on the Future of Europe," *Cambridge Review of International Affairs*, 21(3), pp. 327–346.

Atkinson, A. B. (1996) "Seeking to explain the distribution of income," in John Hills (ed.) *New Inequalities: The Changing Distribution of Income and Wealth in the UK*. New York: Cambridge University Press.

Atkinson, A. B. (1999) "The Distribution of Income in the UK and OECD Countries in the Twentieth Century," *Oxford Review of Economic Policy*, 15(4), pp. 56–75.

Bovis, Christopher (2010) "Public-private Partnerships in the Twenty-First Century," *ERA Forum*, 11, pp. 379–398.

Broadbent, Jane, and Richard Laughlin (2010) "The Role of PFI in UK Government's Modernization Agenda," *Financial Accountability and Management*, 21(1), pp. 75–97.

Cerny, Philip G. (1995) "Globalization and the Changing Logic of Collective Action," *International Organization*, 49(4), pp. 595–625.

Clauwaert, Stefan, Aline Hoffmann, Romuald Jagodzinski, Isabelle Schömann, Michael Stollt, and Kurt Vandaele (2013) "Workers' Rights, Worker Mobilization and Workers' Voice," in Romuald Jgodzinski (ed.) *Benchmarking Working Europe 2013*. Brussels: ETUI.

Companies House Direct (2013) "Infrastructure Management Ltd." Accessed March 23, 2013: http://wck2.companieshouse.gov.uk/.

Company Check (2013) Accessed March 23, 2013: http://companycheck.co.uk

Cooper, Kathryn, and John Ungoed-Thomas (2012) "Finance firms get tax bypass on NHS; as hospitals lay off staff and shut wards to help pay their private finance initiative fees, the money is going straight into tax havens," *Sunday Times* September 2, 2012.

Deakin, Nicholas, Ann Davis, and Neil Thomas (1995) *Public Welfare Services and Social Exclusion: the development of consumer-oriented initiatives in the European Union* Ireland: European Foundation for the Improvement of Living and Working Conditions.

Department of Health (2013) "South London Healthcare NHS Trust to be dissolved by 1 October 2013." Accessed March 24, 2013: http://mediacentre.dh.gov.uk/2013/01/31/south-london-healthcare-nhs-trust-to-be-dissolved-by-1-october-2013/.

Duedil (2013a) "John Laing Infrastructure Financials," Accessed March 21, 2013: www.duedil.com/company/04401816/john-laing-infrastructure-limited/financials.

Duedil (2013b) Accessed September 2013: www.duedil.com/.

Duedil (2013c) "Innisfree Limited," Accessed March 29, 2013: www.duedil.com/company/03039792/innisfree-limited.

Erie, Steven P., Vladimir Kogan, and Scott A. MacKenzie (2010) "Redevelopment, San Diego Style: The Limits of Public–Private Partnerships," *Urban Affairs Review*, 45(5), pp. 644–678.

Flinders, Matthew (2005) "The Politics of Public-private Partnerships," *BJPIR*, 7(2), pp. 215–239.

Gaffney, Declan, Allyson M. Pollack, David Price, and Jean Shaoul (1999) "The Private Finance Initiative: PFI in the NHS—Is there an Economic Case?" *British Medical Journal*, 319, pp. 116–119.

Gattinois, Claire (2013) "En Basse-Saxe la "ceinture de graisse" du pays prospère grâce à des salaires de misère," *Le Monde*, September 16, 2013. Accessed September 20, 2013: www.lemonde.fr/economie/article/2013/09/16/en-basse-saxe-la-ceinture-de-graisse-du-pays-prospere-grace-a-des-salaires-de-misere_3478114_3234.html.

Goetz, Klaus (1999) "Senior Officials in the German Federal Administration: Institutional Change and Positional Differentiation," in Edward C. Page and Vincent

Wright (eds.) *Bureaucratic Elites in Western European States.* Oxford: Oxford University Press.

Grossi, Giuseppe, and Christoph Reichard (2008) "Municipal Corporatization in Germany and Italy," *Public Management Review*, 10(5), pp. 597–617.

Habermas, Jürgen (2011) "Why Europe Needs a Constitution," *New Left Review*, 11, pp. 5–26.

Habermas, Jürgen (2012) *The Crisis of the European Union: A Response.* Translated Ciaran Cronin. Cambridge: Polity Press.

Habermas, Jürgen (2014) "Democracy in Europe: Why the Development of the European Union into a Transnational Democracy is Necessary and How it is Possible." Lecture delivered in September 2014 at the University of Oslo ARENA Centre for European Studies. ARENA Working Paper 13/2014. www.sv.uio.no/arena/english/research/publications/arena-publications/workingpapers/working-papers2014/wp13-14.pdf (last accessed: March 2, 2016).

Hacker, Jacob S. (2004) "Dismantling the Health Care State? Political Institutions, Public Policies and the Comparative Politics of Health Reform," *British Journal of Political Science*, 34(4), pp. 693–724.

Hacker, Jacob S., and Paul Pierson (2011) *Winner-Take-All Politics: How Washington Made the Rich Richer—and Turned its Back on the Middle Class.* New York: Simon & Schuster.

Hills, John (1996) "Introduction: After the Turning Point," in John Hills (ed.) *New Inequalities: the changing distribution of income and wealth in the UK.* New York: Cambridge University Press.

HM Treasury (2012) "PFI Current Projects List," *HM Treasury*. Accessed September 5, 2012: www.hm-treasury.gov.uk/ppp_pfi_stats.htm.

Hochtief (2013) *Hochtief Half-Year Report: January to June 2013.* Essen, Germany: HOCHTIEF Aktiengesellschaft.

Huber, Evelyne, and John D. Stephens (2001) *Development and Crisis of the Welfare State.* Chicago: University of Chicago Press.

International Monetary Fund (2012) *World economic outlook: a survey by the staff of the International Monetary Fund 2012.* Washington D.C.: International Monetary Fund.

John Laing (2012) *Interim Report.* John Laing Infrastructure Fund Limited.

Jones, Nick M., and Anita Charlesworth (2012) *The Anatomy of Health Spending 2011–12.* Nuffield Trust. Accessed March 21, 2013: www.nuffieldtrust.org.uk.

Kappeler, Andreas, and Mathieu Nemoz (2010) "Public-private Partnerships in Europe—Before and During the Recent Financial Crisis," *Economic Financial Report.* European Investment Bank.

Klenk, Tanja, and Frank Nullmeier (2012) "Welfare Industries: Enterprises as Providers of Public Goods," *Zeitschrift für Vergleichende Politikwissenschaft*, 4, pp. 29–52.

Majone, Giandomenico (1999) "The Regulatory State and its Legitimacy Problems," *West European Politics*, 22, pp. 1–24.

Maltone, Carmela, Bernard Yvars, and Hannah Brady (2012) "Globalization and Social Inequalities in Europe: Assessment and Outlook," *Eastern Journal of European Studies*, 3(1), pp. 5–30.

Martin, Andrew (1997) "What Does Globalization Have to Do with the Erosion of Welfare States? Sorting out the issues," *Program for the Study of Germany and Europe Working Paper Series #7.5.* Harvard University, Center for European Studies.

Mattei, Paola, Mahima Mitra, Karsten Vrangbæk, Simon Neby, and Haldor Byrkjeflot (2013) "Reshaping Public Accountability: hospital reforms in Germany, Norway and Denmark," *International Review of Administrative Sciences*, 79(2), pp. 249–270.

Nooruddin, Irfan, and Joel W. Simmons (2006) "The Politics of Hard Choices: IMF Programs and Government Spending," *International Organization* 60(4), pp. 1001–1033.

OECD (2011) "Growing Income Inequality in OECD Countries: What Drives it and How can Policy Tackle it?" *OECD Forum on Tackling Inequality*, Paris, May 2, 2011.

Orszag, Peter R., and Joseph E. Stiglitz (1999) "Rethinking Pension Reform: Ten Myths about Social Security Systems." Paper presented at the *New Ideas about Old Age Security* conference, The World Bank, Washington D.C., September 14–15.

Raffer, Kunibert (2003) "Social Expenditure, Pension Systems, and Neoliberalism." Paper presented at the *Conference on the Privatization of Public Pension Systems: Forces, Experiences, Prospects*. Vienna, Austria, June 19–21.

Reuters (2013) "People: John Laing Infrastructure Fund Ltd." Accessed March 22, 2013: www.reuters.com/finance/stocks/companyOfficers?symbol=JLIF.L.

Ross, Alice, and Chris Bryant (2013) "German Business Seeks Angela Merkel's Return in Election," *Financial Times* September 20, 2013. Accessed September 20, 2013: www.ft.com/intl/cms/s/0/4b97e212-2118-11e3-a92a-00144feab7de.html#axzz2fTEtzxf9.

Ryner, Magnus (2010) "An Obituary for the Third Way: The Financial Crises and Social Democracy," *The Political Quarterly*, 81(4), pp. 554–563.

Scharpf, Fritz W. (2000) "Economic Changes, Vulnerabilities, and Institutional Capabilities." in Fritz W. Scharpf and Vivien A. Schmidt (eds.) *Welfare and Work in the Open Economy Vol. I: From Vulnerability to Competitiveness*. New York: Oxford University Press.

Scholte, Jan Aart (1997) "Global Capitalism and the State," *International Affairs*, 73(3), pp. 427–452.

Schwartz, Herman (2001) "Round Up the Usual Suspects! Globalization, Domestic Politics, and Welfare State Change," in Paul Pierson (ed.) *The New Politics of the Welfare State*. New York: Oxford University Press.

Spackman, Michael (2003) "Public-private Partnerships: Lessons from the British Approach," *Economic Systems*, 26(3), pp. 283–301.

Statutory Health Insurance (2013) Accessed December 15, 2013: www.gkv-spitzenverband.de/english/statutory_health_insurance/statutory_health_insurance.jsp.

Strange, Susan (1996) *Retreat of the State: The Diffusion of Power in the World Economy*. Cambridge: Cambridge University Press.

UK Companies Limited (2013) "UK Private Limited Company." Accessed March 22, 2013: www.ltdcompany.co.uk/company-formation/private-limited-company/.

Webb, Alex, and Dahlia Fahmy (2015) "Balfinger Turns to Industrial Deals after UK Takeovers," *Bloomberg Business*, June 26, 2015. Accessed July 30, 2015: www.bloomberg.com/news/articles/2014-06-25/bilfinger-turns-to-industrial-deals-after-sealing-u-k-takeovers.

Whitfield, Dexter (2011) *The £10bn Sale of Shares in PPP Companies: New Source of Profits for Builders and Banks*, ESSU Research Report 4. Ireland: European Services Strategy Unit.

9 Does German Austerity Travel?
The Baltic States' Reactions to the Euro Crisis

David Rossbach

Germany's conservative approach to fiscal policy has been at the heart of the efforts to address the European financial crisis. There has been a range of reactions to the German insistence on austerity measures from recipients of European Union (EU) and International Monetary Fund (IMF) aid packages. This begs the question of just how well the German austerity model can be applied to other economic and political-cultural settings. The Baltic States were among the first to experience the financial crisis in late 2007 and were among the hardest hit economies in relative terms. Latvia, in particular, would have its economy contract at a steep rate while Estonia and Lithuania would face relatively less severe difficulty. Latvia would be one of the first recipients of aid from the IMF and as such served as an early test case for the austerity approach to the crisis.

The political reaction to austerity in the Baltic States was far less turbulent than would later be seen in Ireland, Portugal, Spain and, most notably, Greece. In economic terms, early indications would suggest that the economies of the Baltic States have weathered the storm and are back to experiencing modest levels of growth. During the first quarter of 2013, only two states in the eurozone cut their overall public debt levels: Germany and Estonia. Germany's debt fell from 81.9 percent of GDP to 81.2 percent, while Estonia's fell modestly from 10.1 percent to 10.0 percent of GDP—the lowest rate in the eurozone (Reuters 2013).

This leads us to consider the question of why the German government's insistence on short-term austerity and structural reforms has seemingly worked in some states while it has been met with significant political resistance in others. The preeminent German philosopher Jürgen Habermas (2012) has argued there must be a broadening of competencies at the European level, rooted in and legitimized by the supremacy of European law, in conjunction with a readjustment of the public attitude from strictly national to a "cosmopolitan" European mindset. In other words, a shift from separate "European peoples" to "European citizens" of a collective political entity. His suggestion is rooted in what he considers to be the fundamental building blocks of a democratic polity: equal rights among citizens and the equal protection of these rights by the rule of law, political institutions conducive to democratic decision-making, and the development of a civic mindset of solidarity. This chapter argues that the formal accession process applicant states must undergo, supervised by the EU, attempts to create a "cosmopolitan" political space and that due to the active leverage exerted by the EU during the accession processes, the Baltic States were better equipped to implement economic reforms in response to the European financial crisis. The EU application process required the Baltic States to consciously address the very elements Habermas suggests are essential to a cosmopolitan democracy.

Habermas' Critique of the Euro Crisis

Jürgen Habermas has argued broadly and consistently against the European Union's response to the financial crisis and German Chancellor Angela Merkel's approach in particular. In his 2012 work *The Crisis of the European Union: A Response*, Habermas argues that a revision to the Lisbon Treaty is necessary to coordinate policy sufficiently among the eurozone states, but that a strictly federal model is inappropriate for a transnational democracy such as the EU. Instead, he focuses on the need for the extension of the legitimacy of state-level institutions to the existing European institutions. The primary vehicle for the extension of legitimacy has been the development of European law over the past half-century.

The question of legitimacy lies at the heart of Habermas' argument and requires elaboration. Democratic laws are legitimate because of the democratic process that produces these laws. An effective organization of civil society communicates public wishes into policy. The state must then have the ability to implement these laws or as Habermas (2012) says, to produce "the political shaping of living conditions." Yet the increasing interconnectedness of countries today means that there are "increasingly narrow systemic restrictions" on what the nation state can actually do about shaping these living conditions (ibid.). There must be a corresponding ability to extend decision-making above the nation state to international organizations. However, the extension of decision-making processes beyond the nation state runs the risk of lessening the legitimacy of domestic decision-making processes, despite the fact that it is a natural extension of the principle of democracy (ibid.).

The sovereignty of the state is based on the "freedom of choice," not "legal freedom." The latter refers to the equality of each citizen. The transference of powers from the nation state to the supranational authorities does not undermine the equality of citizens so long as the democratic process within the nation state is intact: i.e., the process of widespread deliberation and inclusion of social and political groups.

For Habermas (2012), the long-term stability for the EU can only come through policy coordination via a sufficiently democratic legal implementation of policy across member states. The process of decision-making is of central importance in this conception. Habermas (ibid.) states his three building blocks of a democratic community:

a The democratic association of free and equal persons,
b The organization of collective decision-making powers, and
c The medium of integration of civic solidarity among strangers.

These building blocks will form the basis of analyzing the Baltic States' democratic orientation and their political responses to the euro crisis later in this chapter.

At the nation state level, all of these components are established legally, but need to be incorporated and embraced politically. The components established legally are accepted by the public because the laws were passed through the democratic process; the executive is also subject to these laws (Habermas 2012). This amounts to the effect of civilizing potential violence. The same democratic process also empowers the state to have the sole responsibility to enforce law.

Within the European Union, laws are made and enforced at different levels. At first glance the EU legislative process might resemble federalism: constituent member states yielding some sovereignty to central European institutions. Yet as Habermas notes, in a purely federal system the federal government retains the right to change the constitution. The EU lacks a central constitution and the member-states must unanimously agree to change treaties. The EU as an entity lacks final decision-making authority over its own makeup and processes (Habermas 2012). All the while, European law is supposed to supersede national law.

The building blocks Habermas identifies provide the foundational legitimacy for any international agreements these states may make in the future. A polity with internal legitimacy transfers that legitimacy, provided that the decision-making at the supranational level also exhibits its own democratic legitimacy for its constituent members. It is on this last point that Habermas reserves his strongest criticisms: the decision-making bodies of the EU have a 'democratic deficit' because of the imbalance towards the power of national governments. Habermas suggests:

> This reconfiguration of the components of a democratic community into the shape of a federation beyond the nation state does not imply a loss of legitimacy because the citizens of Europe have good reasons for wanting their respective nation states to *continue to perform their constitutional role* as guarantors of law and freedom. In that case, however, the sharing of sovereignty between the citizens of the European Union and the peoples of Europe would also have to be transformed into a consistently implemented co-legislation and into the symmetrical accountability of the Commission to the Council and the Parliament.
>
> (Habermas 2012: 13)

The German Experience with Austerity

Throughout the twentieth century, Germany's economic policy has centered on the role of institutions as the regulators and facilitators of competition in the economy (Bulmer 2014). The philosophical underpinnings of German economic policy have been "a strong commitment to monetary stability, fiscal conservatism and maintaining international competitiveness" (ibid.: 1246). Due to Germany's position as the largest economy within the eurozone, German economic preferences have become Europe's preferences when it comes to the management of the financial crisis. Germany's focus on tightening public spending as a solution to economic crisis further evolved coming out of the 1990s unification experience. While much of the rest of Europe was experiencing an economic resurgence during the 1990s and early 2000s, Germany began to lag behind. Reunification with East Germany increased the total German labor force by roughly one-third, with many of these workers having inadequate training for a competitive and open labor market (Jacobi and Kluve 2006). The effect was a rising unemployment rate for both parts of the country; the east consistently nearly double that of the west. The growing unemployment situation interacted with Germany's long-standing generous unemployment insurance policy to balloon the public budget deficit. At the same time, Germany was bound by the Maastricht criteria for euro adoption that limited the government's ability to respond through relaxing monetary policy discipline. The Maastricht criteria set limits on inflation at 2 percent, an overall debt to GDP ratio at 60 percent and on annual budget deficits at 3 percent (Dinan 2010). As a result of these converging forces, Germany was the first country to violate the Maastricht criteria that it had most strenuously argued in favor of during the treaty negotiations.

The controversial policy responses the German government took came to be known as the Hartz reforms, and were implemented in waves from 2002–2005. The fundamental aspects of the Hartz reforms focused on labor market deregulation, substantial revision of unemployment payment schemes, and increasing employment agencies' effectiveness and efficiency (Jacobi and Kluve 2006). The fact that the reforms were instituted by the Social Democrat–Green Party government led by Chancellor Gerhard Schroeder made the reform proposals all the more audacious. Controversial at the time, the interpretation of the impact of the Hartz reforms on the German economy has proven no less idiosyncratic in the decade since adoption.

Krebs and Scheffel (2013) provide an overview of the winners and losers created by the Hartz reforms. Supporters of the Hartz reforms point to the dramatic reduction in the unemployment rate following implementation of the reform packages. Between 2005 and the end of 2012, unemployment fell from nearly 11 percent to 5.5 percent (Krebs and Scheffel 2013). Krebs and Scheffel (2013) suggest that the Hartz reforms as a whole account for a permanent, non-cyclical reduction in the unemployment rate of nearly 3 percent.

Also among the economic winners were median income households who saw their tax burden reduce as spending on unemployment reduced.

Yet despite many of the quantitative benefits of the Hartz reforms, the legacy of the reforms is still contested. The Hartz reforms had the effect of creating losers in the system from among the still-unemployed and low-skill workers. Among the long-term unemployed, the Hartz reforms cut the period of time one was able to receive aid in the hopes of "encouraging" the pursuit of work. The short-term unemployed also opposed the reforms as fears of benefit cuts and future job prospects unnerved many workers. Finally, the reforms in length of time one could receive aid drove many workers into low-wage positions just above levels of subsistence. As real wages have stagnated during the Eurocrisis, these workers still find themselves in need of assistance (Dempsey 2011).

The electoral impact of the Hartz reforms was considerable. Divisions over the Hartz reforms within the governing Social Democratic Party contributed to the decision of the far-left element of the party to splinter and form The Left Party, *Die Linke*. Following the split, the Social Democrat–Green government was voted out of office in 2005 and Angela Merkel's Christian Democrats began their tenure in government. The issue of the Hartz reforms and evaluations of the resulting successes and failures continue to be an issue in domestic politics and the party landscape has been affected by these evaluations.

The relevant question we are left to ask in the context of Habermas' concept of cosmopolitanism is: just how cosmopolitan was the Hartz reforms process (and by extension the focus on austerity as a means to address economic crisis)? To answer this question, we must return to the building blocks of a democratic polity that Habermas argues are the foundations upon which a cosmopolitan citizenry may come about. Germany undoubtedly meets the first two building blocks without great difficulty. The German Constitution clearly establishes the freedoms and legal equality of its citizens. The Bundestag and mixed-member electoral system are archetypes of parliamentary representation and meet the expectations of "collective decision-making powers" described by Habermas. Where the Hartz reform process runs into conceptual problems is in meeting Habermas' third criteria: the civic solidarity of its citizens. As noted above, the effects of the Hartz reforms have not been felt equally across German society. The Hartz reforms created clear "winners and losers" and as such there has been a lack of public consensus regarding the effectiveness and advisability of the reforms. The end product of this lack of consensus was the electoral punishment of the governing parties responsible for the reforms and the continued politicization of interpreting the historical legacy of the reforms.

The Copenhagen Criteria and the Baltic EU Accession Process

Having described the German experience with economic reforms rooted in principles of austerity we now shift our attention to the Baltic States and the establishment of their democratic systems as guided by the application process to the EU. Following the end of the Cold War and collapse of the Soviet Union, the EU was flooded with applications for membership from 10 states of Central Europe and the formerly Soviet Baltic republics. The potential for rapid expansion posed numerous technical and existential questions to the existing EU-15. The applicant states were all significantly poorer than the existing EU states and had experienced varying degrees of cultural and economic isolation from Western Europe. Where the initial response to these applications was to form ad hoc trade liberalization and aid agreements (Dinan 2010), the need for a more formalized, orderly and controlled process was clear to the existing Western member states.

In 1993, as a reaction to the new reality of increased applications to the EU, the European Council agreed to the so-called "Copenhagen Criteria" future applicants would have to satisfy. The criteria would fall into three categories:

- "Stability of institutions guaranteeing democracy, rule of law, human rights, and respect for and protection of minorities.
- Existence of a functioning market economy and the capacity to cope with competitive pressure and market forces within the EU.
- Ability to take on the obligations of membership, including adherence to the aims of political, economic, and monetary union" (Dinan 2010: 137)

Among the Baltic applicants, Estonia opened formal negotiations along with the first wave of post-communist states in 1998, while Latvia and Lithuania were part of a second group of applicants in 2000, engaging in a more aggressive reform timeline to catch up to the first cohort (Dinan 2010). These applications met with a mixed response by the existing EU-15. Germany advocated for early admission for Poland and the Czech Republic, while proving less enthusiastic about the rest of the post-communist applicants (Dinan 2010). The strongest opposition to the new applicants came from states such as Spain, Ireland, Portugal, and Greece, which had been the main benefactors of EU regional development funding (Dinan 2010). The influx of poorer post-communist states meant unwelcome competition for such funding.

With the elevation of the Baltic States to candidate status, their internal formal reform process began in earnest. It is at this stage of formalized candidacy that the EU is able to extract the most substantive reforms out of applicant states. As Grabbe notes, the reform process "can have both minimalist and maximalist interpretations, and these in turn affect the demands made on CEE applicants. So far, the EU has generally presented a maximalist interpretation to the applicants" (2007: 115). Thus individual opt-outs of specific policy areas such as euro adoption or Schengen participation are no longer available to candidate states as was the case for states such as the United Kingdom, Denmark, or Sweden in earlier waves of expansion.

The EU is able to exert what Vachudova (2005) refers to as "active and passive leverage" on applicant states to force the requisite reforms. Active leverage refers to the conditional nature of EU membership and the EU's administration of the Copenhagen process of supervision. Active leverage is a powerful tool the EU has at its disposal because of the asymmetrical relationship between applicant states and the EU: i.e., the applicant state arguably needs the EU more than the EU needs the applicant state (Vachudova 2005). This process is also aided by the meritorious nature of the Copenhagen Criteria, that merit alone—i.e., sufficient progress meeting the criteria—will determine the invitation to join the EU and not simply time spent on the candidate list. The ongoing application of Turkey is a fine example of this concept.

Passive leverage refers to the attraction of membership in the EU notwithstanding any specific policy benefits. Passive leverage implicitly speaks to nationalist notions of the candidate country taking its rightful seat at the table of European states and the increased clout a candidate country would enjoy on the international stage based on membership in the EU. The effectiveness of passive leverage depends largely on the credibility of the candidate country as a democratic state. In the case of the Baltic States, the fact that Estonia was among the first wave of post-communist applicants, and that Latvia and Lithuania were fast-tracked into this first cohort of new members despite their late applications demonstrates their credibility in the eyes of the EU at the time. However, the effectiveness of passive leverage depends more importantly on the extent to which the support-base of the ruling parties in government expects reforms (Vachudova 2005). The distinction between reformers and the old regime served as a defining cleavage of the post-communist party systems in the 1990s and in the Baltics the governments were consistently formed by those in the reformist camp (Kitschelt 1995).

Yet as Grabbe (2007) notes, the EU accession process is limited as to how far it can push domestic reform in applicant states on issues existing member states themselves find domestically divisive. Grabbe also suggests that there is a baseline of economic development necessary for EU conditionality to take root, forming a "virtuous circle working between reforms, economic reforms and EU accession prospects" (2007: 120). The Baltic States were among the most attractive destinations for foreign direct investment (FDI) capital throughout the 1990s and 2000s and the influx of capital was among the causes of their particular financial crisis in 2007–2009 (Deroose et al. 2010).

The key to the concept of active and passive leverage is the finite nature of its impact. Once a candidate state is admitted to the union and takes its seat at the decision-making table, the opportunity to exact meaningful reforms has passed. Throughout the history of European integration, we have repeatedly seen individual states frustrate the decision-making process from within. The internal compliance mechanisms within the EU are weak and national governments display the strongest power in institutional terms.

Habermas' Democratic Building Blocks and the Baltic States

Through adherence to the Copenhagen Criteria, the Baltic States had in the 1990s and early 2000s begun the transformation process on the very building blocks that Habermas points to as essential for European democracy going forward. The Baltic States were forced to address the question of equal citizen rights in the form of their sizable ethnic Russian populations. Administrative organizations were constructed according to the norms of parliamentary democracies. Finally, the debate over reforms brought about the development of civil society and a normalization of democratic values consistent with Habermas' concept of the "cosmopolitan citizen."

Habermas' first democratic building block is the notion of equal rights for individuals upheld by the impartial application of the rule of law. It is perhaps in this area that the citizens of the Baltic States had to face their most difficult challenges during their transition. Ethnic nationals now had to come to political terms with their new ethnic Russian minorities. The treatment of ethnic Russians produced perhaps the strongest political criticism the European Commission would have for the Baltic governments during their accession processes. The Commission would specifically request that the Baltic States speed along their naturalization procedures so as to maximize the legal rights of their Russian minorities (European Commission 1997a).

Evans and Lipsmeyer (2007) examined the subject of ethnic differences in evaluations of the democratic transition in early the 1990s in the Baltic States. Estonia was the standout case where evaluations of the transition differed the greatest across ethnic groups. Lithuania had modest differences that resembled other Central and Eastern European states more closely than their Baltic neighbors. Estonia and Latvia each had a gap in voter turnout rates among the various ethnicities. There was a sizable difference in attitudes in terms of satisfaction with democracy, with the largest gap appearing in Estonia, while in Lithuania the relationship was actually inverted: ethnic Russians had a higher satisfaction rate than ethnic Lithuanians (Ehin 2007). The authors ultimately conclude that the notion of Baltic distinctiveness in terms of ethnic differences was overstated in the early transition period. If anything, there was Estonian distinctiveness.

Over a longer period of examination, Ehin (2007) finds more instances of differences in attitudes across the ethnic groups in areas such as regime support, support for democracy, and institutional trust. Yet Ehin (2007) also ultimately argues that differences across the Baltic States were more important than differences across ethnicities. Again Estonia and Latvia displayed some gap in attitudes across the national and Russian populations, most notably in terms of ethnic Russian support for a return to communist or some other strongman rule. Yet overall support for regime performance across the region resulted in a U-shaped curve over time, indicating that the democratic institutions were improving their performances in a recognizable way.

The political party systems of the Baltic States have also reflected an ethnic divide. Two defining cleavages in Baltic party systems have been (1) ethnicity (Majority National–Russian), and (2) reformers vs. vested interests. Ideologically, center-right parties have tended to dominate, thus the traditional right–left dimension has been less salient (Aslund and Dombrovskis 2011). Ethnic Russian parties have never participated in government and the parties are largely personality driven. Partially due to the focus on personality, the 1990s saw a considerable level of volatility in terms of new party formation, old party dissolution, and ranges in the number of effective parties (Lewis 2000).

Habermas' second building block to a democratic society is an administrative organization that supports democratic standards. The political criterion of the Copenhagen Criteria speaks specifically to the implementation of democratic administrative organizations as Habermas conceives them. Early on in their democratic transitions, the Baltic States implemented free and competitive parliamentary systems that passed inspection by the European Commission, as did the judicial systems erected to indiscriminately apply the rule of law (European Commission 1997a, 1997b, 1997c).

The question of administrative reform may also be examined through the use of quantitative evidence. Among the most widely accepted measures of democracy is the Polity IV dataset (Marshall et al. 2013). The Polity IV dataset is an attractive measure of democracy for a number of reasons. First and foremost among these reasons is the comprehensiveness of countries included and length of time examined. Annualized scores are available for a 200-year period in over 160 polities (Marshall et al. 2013). While the size and scope of the Polity dataset are impressive, the conceptual foundations of the Polity score are particularly appropriate for tapping a dimension of democracy Habermas is implicitly stressing: executive restriction. The Polity score directly measures the openness and competitiveness of executive recruitment and executive constraint in the political system, a key dimension of democracy that Dahl (1971) stressed in his seminal work, *Polyarchy: Participation and Opposition*.[1]

The Baltic States each measure very favorably on the Polity scale of democracy. The Polity IV scale runs from –10 (full autocracy) to 10 (full democracy). Estonia began its rankings in 1991 with a mid-range democracy score of 6 before improving to a score of 7 in 1999 and settling on a score of 9 from 2000 to the present. Latvia has had a score of 8 since 1991 and Lithuania has held the highest score possible—10—since 1991. These rankings are in line with the established democracies of Western Europe.

The third and final criterion that Habermas suggests is essential to democracy is the establishment of a civil society that can create a sense of solidarity and collective stake in the state's future. The Baltic States had a mixed experience with civil society under communist rule. Estonia had the richest tradition of intellectual liberalism, manifest in networks and clubs, while Lithuania had the central importance of the Catholic Church and disconnected networks of college activists (Bennich-Bjorkman and Likic-Brboric 2012). All three states also had the unifying memory of their pre-communist independence in the early twentieth century, and this history played an important role in crafting national identity in the late 1980s as well as early in the transition process (Krickus 1997; Plakans 1997; Raun 1997).

The ethnic division between the majority ethnic communities in the Baltic States and the minority Russian populations has already been addressed in this study. Yet this division notwithstanding, where all three Baltic States displayed national unity during the transition of the 1990s was in their single-minded focus on integration into the EU and NATO. The focus on integration with Europe brought about a broad consensus between national governments and their respective publics on liberal economic policies deemed necessary for EU accession, and eventual euro adoption. Writing on Estonia, Thorhallsson and Kattel suggest that:

> Accession to the EU (and NATO) then to the eurozone became overarching political goals behind which the government could rally support without much actual discussion in society at large. In fact, it can be argued that such large-scale goals were utilized to avoid deeper political conflicts. This has engendered a political culture of conflict avoidance; this, however has not led to a wide-reaching consensus on smaller-scale issues.
>
> (Thorhallsson and Kattel 2013: 90)

These observations can be applied to the other Baltic States as well, and it is this national consensus on macroeconomic policies that would manifest itself through public acceptance of austerity measures during the height of the Baltic crisis.

Economic Transition, Crisis and Recovery in the Baltic States

To understand the nature of the financial crisis in the Baltic States we must first review the nature of policymakers' economic reform approach during the EU accession talks. The focus in early 1990s transition was on establishing a national currency and exchange rate policies. Estonia took the radical lead as usual in 1992. Estonia's policy was:

(1) Set a fixed exchange rate, first to the German deutschmark and then to the euro.

(2) Establish international currency reserves sufficient to cover the entire money supply.
(3) Use current account balance to determine monetary policy (thus there was no independent setting of monetary policy, leading to a situation where capital inflows created inflation).
(4) Institute a balanced budget, leaving no room for bond borrowing (Aslund and Dombrovskis 2011; Thorhallsson and Kattel 2013).

Estonia's policy approach was buttressed by IMF support and considerable Western foreign direct investment. The other Baltic economies had less radical but similarly focused monetary policies, using pegs of some sort to fix exchange rates and tight fiscal policies (Deroose et al. 2010).

The economies of the Baltic region began to be known as the "Baltic Tigers," but EU membership took some of the emerging economies' power away. All three states joined the Exchange Rate Mechanism II (ERM II) so these countries had neither control of their monetary policy, nor any capital controls as members of the single market. The lack of capital controls led to an influx of foreign capital that encouraged a credit bubble, a housing bubble, greater inflation, and a current accounts deficit (Deroose et al. 2010). During this time, public fiscal policy in Latvia also continued to expand and was focused on economic stimulation. In Estonia and Lithuania, fiscal policy was tighter, capital reserves higher, and thus those economies suffered a much milder downturn at the height of the crisis (Deroose et al. 2010).

The 1998 Russian currency crisis meant the consolidation of banking sectors in the region, which in turn were dominated by Swedish banks. For Swedish bank officials, the low-risk–high-reward margins were a financial boon to their safe but slow domestic lending. Thus in the Baltic States, the lending by Swedish banks was expansive and had little qualifications necessary for the individual borrower. From the banks' perspective, the Baltic trade represented a small fraction of their overall business but represented a huge source of profits. In Estonia, foreign ownership in the banking sector represented 97 percent of the market. In Lithuania, foreign ownership made up 85 percent of the market. Latvia saw relatively less foreign ownership in the banking sector, which represented 60 percent of the market thanks to the strong position of Latvian-owned Parex Bank. Thus the Latvian exposure to the domestic lending climate was greater than its neighbors as strong parent banks subsidized its neighbors' lending (Aslund and Dombrovskis 2011).

These uncontrollable capital inflows fueled economic growth until the start of the global financial crisis. This led to a decrease in the savings–GDP ratio and drove inflation beyond the Maastricht convergence criteria for euro adoption. Some of this was natural price inflation, some was driven by rising energy prices, and some was due to labor market tightening as wages rose and worker productivity increased (Aslund and Dombrovskis 2011).

The collapse of Lehman Brothers began a domino effect and froze credit availability around the globe. The Baltic economies began to decline in late 2007 and hit bust in 2008 with the Latvian economy hit the hardest. The second largest bank in their financial sector, the Latvian owned Parex Bank, failed in November 2008. The government would seek emergency funding from the IMF and European Commission to nationalize and recapitalize the bank (Aslund and Dombrovskis 2011). From 2008 to 2009, GDP would contract 18 percent in Latvia, 14.8 percent in Lithuania, and 14.1 percent in Estonia (Aslund and Dombrovskis 2011).

Latvia implemented the most aggressive form of austerity, a form that has now become the standard required by German officials in Berlin for the states of southern Europe. The initial December 2008 stability plan called for reducing public employees by 15 percent, reducing wages by 15 percent, and state procurement of goods and services by 25 percent, as well as a VAT increase of 3 percent. Excise duties were also to be raised on gasoline and on a variety of beverages. In the final estimation, the nominal public wage cut was 25 percent (Aslund and Dombrovskis 2011). Members of the public themselves began to clamor for sharp austerity, aimed specifically at the top levels of government, state employees, local government, and boards of state corporations.

These policy calculations were also taking place in an environment of economic forecasts that were constantly being adjusted downwards as the actual recession became much worse than anticipated. Calculating a budget deficit was therefore practically impossible. The initial GDP contraction for Latvia in 2009 was initially estimated at −5 percent yet was actually −18 percent. Despite the moving target, governments began to implement austerity as an approach to the crisis, with Latvia again being the exemplar.

The new government's primary goal was to reduce budget deficit to 7 percent of GDP and insisted that unpopular measures were unavoidable. Officials' focus was initially on public spending cuts and not new tax revenues. The cuts included an emphasis on structural reforms of the public sector rather than blanket reductions. In particular, public administration, health care, and education were targeted. Justification was given by international comparison, in particular to the other Baltic States. Staff reductions in state bureaucracy were relatively the easiest to make in terms of public opinion as the public was upset with bureaucrats as a segment of society (Aslund and Dombrovskis 2011). Public sector salaries declined by 26 percent from November 2008 to November 2009. By comparison, private sector salaries declined by 10 percent. Both categories remained stagnant in 2010. Unemployment rose from 6.6 percent in the second quarter of 2008 to 20.7 percent in the first quarter of 2010. The further downgrading of Latvian economy forecasts in mid-2009 had the effects of a second cut to pubic salaries of 20 percent and other public spending by 40 percent (ibid.).

The only notable stimulus funding in Latvia came via EU grants from the Structural, Social, and Cohesion Funds. The amount of EU funding

Latvia received grew from 4 percent of GDP to 7.4 percent in 2010 (Aslund and Dombrovskis 2011). The Latvian government did provide some matching funds in order to receive the stimulus money. The focus of this funding was on short-term public works projects, unemployment benefit extensions, and other social safety net programs. In Estonia, EU structural funding increased from 3.75 billion kroons in 2007, to 5.45 billion in 2008, up to 11 billion in 200. Thus in 2009 EU funding represented 12 percent of the entire state budget (Thorhallsson and Kattel 2013).

The Latvian austerity approach would not remain confined to spending cuts and would begin to address new revenues as well. In 2010, the flat income tax increased from 23 percent to 26 percent. Teachers received pay raises but salaries were still 20 percent below 2008 levels. The real estate tax base would broaden as well. One setback for the government program was the Constitutional Court overturning earlier pension cuts and forcing the government to pay back pensioners (Aslund and Dombrovskis 2011).

Outside of the Baltics the debate focused on the possible devaluation of national currencies as a means to spur exports. The devaluation option was unpopular among the Baltic publics but was more widely supported by American economists. The arguments in favor of devaluation pointed to the historic example of Argentina and suggested that the way to increase competitiveness was to devalue the currency. However, the arguments against devaluation ultimately won the day. All three states remained committed to the early adoption of the euro, especially Estonia and Lithuania where it was thought devaluation would have hurt their economies where the crisis was not as deep (Aslund and Dombrovskis 2011). Estonia would be the only country in Europe in 2010 with a budget surplus.

In spring 2010 Estonia announced that it would adopt the euro on January 1, 2011 (BBC 2010). The announcement marked the end of the Baltic Crisis and signaled the willingness for the EU to resume expanding the eurozone. Elsewhere, to the south of Europe, the rest of the European financial crisis was just starting to hit its stride. Baltic States began holding elections in October. Incumbent governments were reelected but with adjusted coalition members, consolidating power for the center-right (Aslund and Dombrovskis 2011; Thorhallsson and Kattel 2013). Even the hardest hit economy, Latvia, received approval from the European Commission to adopt the euro on January 1, 2014 (BBC 2013). Lithuania adopted the euro on January 1, 2015. While Greece remains mired in concerns over a potential Grexit from the euro, the Baltic States all successfully adopted.

Returning again to Habermas' concept of cosmopolitanism, we must ask the same question we asked of the German austerity experience, i.e., how cosmopolitan was the Baltic austerity process? The international dimension present in the Baltic cases that was absent in the German case complicates the answer. Like Germany, the constitutional rights and legislative structures in the Baltic States sufficiently meet democratic expectations. The difficulties involving the equality of the Russian-speaking minority were addressed during the Copenhagen process and remain an ongoing issue. Thus the crucial distinction between the German implementation of the Hartz reforms and the Baltic implementation of austerity packages revolves around the axis of international players in the Baltic case. Where the German austerity process was initiated and executed by a democratically legitimate domestic government, the austerity packages implemented in the Baltic States were done so at the behest of external forces, i.e., the International Monetary Fund, the European Commission and the European Central Bank. This calls the "cosmopolitan" credentials of the Baltic process and the transferability of Habermas' notions of democratic legitimacy to the European level into greater question. According to Habermas' logic, the institutions making up the "Troika" arguably have a degree of transferred legitimacy by virtue of the governments constituting their membership. Yet the charge of a "democratic deficit" in relation to the Commission, in particular, and the non-directly elected nature of the IMF and ECB boards pose a challenge to Habermas' democratic building blocks.

Conclusions

The central question this chapter poses is whether the German austerity model is one that may successfully be imported to troubled European economies? Judging by the case of the Baltic States during the early days of the financial crisis, the answer would seem to be yes, under the proper contextual foundations. While the international dimension to the Baltic austerity process might present problems for Habermas' concept of cosmopolitanism, the concept proves useful at the domestic level. Applying Habermas' building blocks to a democratic society, the experience of the Baltic States shows that these three elements served the economies well during the crisis. Each state had passed the European Commission's early test of equal legal rights for its Russian minority populations despite a divergence of political attitudes between the populations. The Baltic States each reformed their democratic institutions to conform to European norms of decision-making and constraint of executive powers.

Most importantly, the post-communist transition taught the citizens of the Baltics that reform must come swiftly and radically. The transition experience brought about broad consensus across the region on macroeconomic policy and goals. Thorhallsson and Kattel summarize the Baltic experience well in describing Estonia's public reaction:

> There were no strikes and only very minor public mass meetings or protests during the crisis. Any visitor to Estonia would have had virtually no idea during 2009 that this was a country going through the second-deepest economic decline in Europe, and was suffering from mass unemployment.
>
> (Thorhallsson and Kattel 2013: 95)

Conversely to the relative calm in the Baltic States, there was a marked lack of consensus characterizing the public reaction to the euro crisis in Southern Europe. We see the lack of agreement in the form of severe electoral fragmentation, which made coalition government, at best, difficult or, at worst, impossible. We also see it in the form of street protests with varying levels of violence. The countries of Southern Europe, each in their own way, did face a transition to democracy similar to the transition faced in the Baltics. Yet the Baltic States were aided in their transition by a formalized process supervised by an uncompromising EU wielding all the leverage it could muster.

The specifics of the euro crisis have varied a great deal in each of the economies in crisis. A number of factors differentiate the situation that faced the Baltic States from the situations found in Southern Europe, particularly that of Greece. First and arguably foremost was simply the timing of the matter. Latvia was among the first states to seek financial assistance from international bodies such as the IMF and European Commission. Latvia was not burdened by a European Commission and a German government that was long since tired of negotiating aide packages and having to answer for those packages to a domestic political audience.

Second, the governments of the Baltic States had broadly pursued balanced fiscal policies for the decade preceding the crisis. Thus their crisis was not a crisis born of speculation in the international bond markets. As the global crisis expanded, bond investors preemptively limited their exposure. The result was rising interest rates that would push states like Spain, Italy, and Greece either into crisis or to the brink of crisis.

Finally, the Baltic States had a primary focus on euro adoption, while the other states in crisis were already members of the eurozone. The region's goals were to keep the fixed exchange rate to the euro and to keep their budget deficits to 3 percent of GDP. These goals provided clarity to both the Baltic publics and policy makers alike. Because of this focus, Estonia had adopted the euro, Latvia will do so at the start of 2014, and Lithuania is on track to adoption. The primary problem facing the economies prior to the crisis was massive capital inflows, not trade imbalances. It remains to be seen whether the EU fiscal compact or proposed reforms to the banking sector will prove effective in preventing similar imbalances to develop in the future.

Habermas' democratic criteria suggest an important framework for analysis of the strengths of the EU as well as the challenges it faces. Using this framework (while noting some of its similarities with the Copenhagen Criteria), this study identifies some of the reasons that the Baltic States were able to implement austerity measures more successfully than their neighbors in southern Europe. This study also suggests that differences in timing, relative wealth, EU status and national history play an important role in both the ability and utility of states in implementing austerity programs similar to those advanced by Germany in times of economic crisis.

Note

1 Some have criticized the Polity dataset for the secondary attention it pays to participation, another essential component of democracy. See Munck and Verkuilen (2002) for a review of Polity and other comparable measures of democracy.

References

Aslund, Anders, and Valdis Dombrovskis (2011) *How Latvia Came through the Financial Crisis*. Washington, DC: Peterson Institute for International Relations.

Bennich-Bjorkman, Li, and Branka Likic-Brboric (2012) "Successful but Different: Deliberative Identity and the Consensus-Driven Transition to Capitalism in Estonia and Slovenia," *Journal of Baltic Studies*, 43(1), pp. 47–73.

Bulmer, Simon (2014) "Germany and the Eurozone Crisis: Between Hegemony and Domestic Politics," *West European Politics*, 37(6), pp. 1244–1263.

British Broadcasting Corporation (2010) "EU Approves Estonian Entry for 1 January 2011." Accessed September 2013 at: www.bbc.co.uk/news/10611399.

British Broadcasting Corporation (2013) "Latvia to Become 18th Eurozone Member from 2014." Accessed September 2013 at: www.bbc.co.uk/news/business-22781146.

Dahl, Robert (1971) *Polyarchy: Participation and Opposition*. New Haven: Yale University Press.

Deroose, Servaas, Elena Flores, Gabriele Giudice, and Alessandro Turrini (2010) "The Tale of the Baltics: Experiences, Challenges Ahead and Main Lessons," *ECFIN Economic Brief*, Issue 10.

Dinan, Desmond (2010) *Ever Closer Union: An Introduction to European Integration*. 4th ed. Boulder: Lynne Rienner Publishers.

Ehin, Piret (2007) "Political Support in the Baltic States, 1993–2004," *Journal of Baltic Studies*, 38(1), pp. 1–20.

European Commission (1997a) *Agenda 2000—Commission Opinion on Estonia's Application for Membership of the European Union*. DOC/97/12. Brussels. Accessed September 18, 2013: http://ec.europa.eu/enlargement/archives/pdf/dwn/opinions/estonia/es-op_en.pdf.

European Commission (1997b) *Agenda 2000—Commission Opinion on Latvia's Application for Membership of the European Union*. DOC/97/14. Brussels. Accessed September 18, 2013: http://ec.europa.eu/enlargement/archives/pdf/dwn/opinions/latvia/la-op_en.pdf.

European Commission (1997c) *Agenda 2000—Commission Opinion on Lithuania's Application for Membership of the European Union*. DOC/97/15. Brussels. Accessed September 18, 2013: http://ec.europa.eu/enlargement/archives/pdf/dwn/opinions/lithuania/li-op_en.pdf.

Evans, Geoffrey, and Christine S. Lipsmeyer (2001) "The Democratic Experience in Divided Societies: The Baltic States in Comparative Perspective," *Journal of Baltic Studies*, 32(4), pp. 379–401.

Reuters (2013) "Germany, Estonia only Eurozone Countries Cutting Debt in Q1," *Reuters*. July 22, 2013. www.reuters.com/article/2013/07/22/eurozone-debt-idUSL6N0FS0VK20130722. Accessed July 22, 2013.

Grabbe, Heather (2007) "Central and Eastern Europe and the EU," in Stephen White, Judy Batt, and Paul G. Lewis (eds.) *Developments in Central and East European Politics 4*. Durham: Duke University Press.

Habermas, Jürgen (2012) *The Crisis of the European Union: A Response*. Malden, MA: Polity Press.

Jacobi, Lena, and Jochen Kluve (2006) "Before and After the Hartz Reforms: The Performance of Active Labour Market Policy in Germany," Discussion Paper Series No. 2100, *Institute for the Study of Labor*.

Kitschelt, Herbert (1995) "Formation of Party Cleavages in Post-Communist Democracies," *Party Politics*, 1(4), pp. 447–472.

Krebs, Tom, and Martin Scheffel (2013) "Macroeconomic Evaluation of Labor Market Reform in Germany," *IMF Working Paper WP/13/42*, International Monetary Fund.

Krickus, Richard J. (1997) "Democratization in Lithuania," in Karen Dawisha and Bruce Parrot (eds.) *The Consolidation of Democracy in East-Central Europe*. New York: Cambridge University Press.

Lewis, Paul G. (2000) *Political Parties in Post-Communist Eastern Europe*. New York: Routledge.

Marshall, Monty G., Ted Robert Gurr, and Keith Jaggers (2013) *Polity IV Project: Dataset User's Manual*. Center for Systemic Peace. Accessible at: www.systemicpeace.org/inscr/p4manualv2012.pdf.

Munck, Gerardo L., and Jay Verkuilen (2002) "Conceptualizing and Measuring Democracy: Evaluating Alternative Indices," *Comparative Political Studies*, 35(1), pp. 5–34.

Plakans, Andrejs (1997) "Democratization and Political Participation in Postcommunsit Societies: The Case of Latvia," in Karen Dawisha and Bruce Parrot (eds.) *The Consolidation of Democracy in East-Central Europe*. New York: Cambridge University Press.

Raun, Toivo U. (1997) "Democratization and Political Development in Estonia, 1987–1996," in Karen Dawisha and Bruce Parrot (eds.) *The Consolidation of Democracy in East-Central Europe*. New York: Cambridge University Press.

Thorhallsson, Baldur, and Rainer Kattel (2013) "Neo-Liberal Small States and Economic Crisis: Lessons for Democratic Corporatism," *Journal of Baltic Studies*, 44(1), pp. 83–103.

Vachudova, Milada Anna (2005) *Europe Undivided: Democracy, Leverage and Integration After Communism*. New York: Oxford University Press.

10 On the *pouvoir constituent* of the European Union

Erik O. Eriksen

Introduction

Proper handling of the eurozone crisis calls for decisive action through effective and legitimate institutions.[1] Up to now this has been in short supply. The politics of the day has been crisis management and damage control. Heads of governments who lack a European mandate in these matters have agreed upon a series of financial, economic, social, and wage policies that affect the well-being of many Europeans. The Lisbon Treaty states that such issues belong to the remit of the member states.[2] According to critics, the acute eurozone crisis has been met with a "wall of words," and a fiscal compact to toughen budget rules bound to end in austerity and social misery.[3] The sovereign debt crises have been allowed to unfold for a long time; uncertainty, gridlock and paralysis prevail because of narrow-minded political leaders.[4] The whole integration project may be put at risk. Jürgen Habermas has delivered one of the most ardent and sharpest critiques of the handling of the crisis. For him the choice is now between post-democratic-executive federalism and transnational democracy. His model of the latter is one of a democratic multilevel political order in Europe—"a federation of nation states." The question is whether this model is viable. Can it provide a proper legitimacy basis for the Union?

The point of departure for Habermas' reasoning is the remarkable legal developments after World War II, whose main thrusts have been to protect human rights. Both persons and groups have become recognized as subjects of international law. There are no lawless areas left. The Westphalian condition of organized anarchy is tamed by law.[5] The very concept of sovereignty has thus changed, from denoting the state's supreme legal authority to uphold the law within a certain territory and being independent from any external authority (Morgenthau and Thompson 1993: 321), to one that subjects state power to higher-order principles. In principle, states enjoy the rights of political sovereignty and territorial integrity only as long as they are governed in a morally tolerable way. However, the duty to intervene or to help cannot fall on the international community as a whole as it does not possess agency.

The "juridification of international relations" in the wake of the establishment of the UN has paved the way for invoking democratic principles beyond the nation state. Habermas (2012a) tries to solve the integrational problems in Europe (and of world citizenship) with reference to the idea of eighteenth-century thinkers Emmanuel Sieyes and James Madison of mixed constituent power ("pouvoir constituant mixte").[6] He gives the idea a new twist: The stateless euro polity—based on two constituent subjects: the citizens and the state—represents a new stage in the process of the constitutionalization of international law without abolishing the achievements of the nation state. But can this work as the legitimation basis of an entity which is not a state but more than an international organization?

On the one hand, Habermas is right in envisaging a stateless European Union, as the euro-polity emerged as a response to the problem of nationalism and of international relations in which no higher authority exists to control the internal affairs of the nation states. A state-less entity beyond the nation state would be the answer to the claim that one should not replicate at the supranational level what went wrong at the national level, and which created the need for supranational organizations in the first place.

On the other hand, one may question Habermas' weak supranationalism. In his reconstruction the nation states are basically left unaltered. The putative lack of supremacy for European law weakens the EU's capability to act and to constrain the members. Lack of action is today part of the EU's legitimacy problems. For an order to achieve stability and legitimacy, agreement on the basic structure is required, as well as on the polity structure that corresponds to it. Systems of domination require justification with regard to the relevant characteristics of the political community to be regulated as well as with regard to the purposes and interests to be realized. In Habermas' conceptualization it not clear in what capacity Europeans are equals. The weakness of this reconstruction of a legitimate EU is that the requisite unifying component, through which the European citizens can identify themselves as equals, is lacking.

I proceed by first clarifying the cosmopolitan dimension to European integration,[7] then I outline Habermas' model of the EU based on two constitution-making subjects and why it is shaky on constitutional grounds. Thereafter, I argue that there is a political universitas in Europe based on entrenched dignity protection, and also that there is a European community of obligations as a result of the integration process. There are reasons for solidarity. Lastly, I point to the moral as well as the functional imperative of political integration. It has become a roadmap for solving the crisis.

Domesticating International Relations

The vision of a better Europe is built into the integration project: a Europe united on the principles of equality, freedom and solidarity reminiscent of the French Revolution. The turn to the formation of European nation states in its wake deprived the revolution of its cosmopolitan content.[8] Nationalism undermined the universalistic potential of the humanitarian and democratic principles during the first half of the twentieth century. Europe after 1945 (and 1989) might be able to revoke them and install them at the proper level, that is, above the warmongering international "system of states."[9] A better Europe—a post-humiliation society—should be built. Instead of the humiliating Versailles Treaty after WWI, Germany got the status enhancing Schuman plan in 1952.[10] Humiliation occurs when the integrity, the dignity, of the parties is not respected. The right to have one's dignity protected goes, as we will see, to the heart of the European integration project and is evocative of cosmopolitanism: namely, that the ultimate units of concern are persons, irrespective of borders.

Building on the idea of peace without humiliation, a new regime of European cooperation with wide-ranging effects, and one which abolished the right of individual states to take the law in their own hands was initiated. In the words of the "founding father of European integration" and the first Statesman of Interdependence, Jean Monnet:

> We are starting a process of continuous reform which can shape tomorrow's world more lastingly than the principles of revolution widespread outside the West.
>
> (Duchêne 1994: 390)

What is remarkable is that the master plan of this project was initially not spelled out—if there ever was such a plan. The European integration process has neither been driven by ideology, nor by blueprints or grand designs, but by mundane and pragmatic problem-solving, underpinned by a more or less tacit normative commitment.

Monnet relied on the "step-by-step" method and what he called "dynamic disequilibrium": "The building of Europe is a great transformation which will take a very long time [...]. Nothing would be more dangerous than to read difficulties as failures" (Jean Monnet, cited in McCormick 2012: 4). There would be setbacks, but piecemeal engineering was set in motion with a view to a hitherto unprecedented goal—a democratic supranational federation. And, in fact, in Europe states have managed to domesticate international relations among themselves and have created a union for peaceful and prosperous cooperation united under Community law. We witness the development of a political order that is neither based on a culturally homogenized people nor brought about by coercion and brute force. The EU is a voluntary, although powerful, entity that respects the identities of its constituent parties.

> The European Union is the first—by definition voluntary—federation in the history of mankind that recognizes the dissimilarity of its constituent parties. The EU is a political body which is committed to respecting the distinctive national identities of its member states and

citizens, yet at the same time subjects them in many significant areas to the jurisdiction of a common government,
(Offe and Preuss 2007: 194)

A new political order has arisen, and one which has transformed the state of affairs among European states. Classical international law guaranteed the equal status of sovereign states and the state's independence from outside intrusion. In the Westphalian order, states are sovereign with fixed territorial boundaries and are entitled to conduct their internal and external affairs autonomously, without external actors checking their protection of human rights. There is no supranational power to sanction and punish violations of international law, nor to interfere in internal affairs in case of violations of human rights. Through the integration project, the European states have sought to overcome international anarchy and aggression. By institutionalizing supranational dispute mechanisms, a peaceful settlement of conflicts is enforced. In the spring of 1945 "it was clear to most observers that a system of sovereign nation states had no built-in mechanism to prevent further disasters" (Fossum and Menéndez 2011: 78). However, how exactly was the warmongering "system of states" brought under control?

The Fusion of Constitutional Orders

It is widely held that there is in fact no constitutional unity in the EU, in the sense that there is no willingness to contemplate the European Court of Justice (ECJ) as the sole judicial master of both legal orders. Constitutional pluralism prevails (Avbelj and Komárek 2012). There is however a distinct constitutional tradition established by the EU, which, according to John Erik Fossum and Agustín José Menéndez (2011), can be seen to represent the first instance of establishing a new constitutional order out of a set of already existing state-based constitutional arrangements. The EU was initially established through a distinct and historically specific constitutional authorization in the sense that the member states' constitutions sanctioned supranational integration. The process originated with the "synthetic constitutional moment" of The European Coal and Steel community (ECSC), which brought forth the regulatory ideal of a common constitutional law.

The construction comes equipped with a conditional license from the member states: i.e., the established structure and further integrative moves must comply with human rights and democratic procedures. The legitimacy of the EU's constitutionalism hinges on this core requirement. On the one hand, the EU system must be compatible with the basic constitutional norms and principles shared by the constitutions of the member states. On the other hand, European institutions must be structured so that it is possible for the citizens to understand themselves as the authors of the laws to which they are subject. Direct popular authorization is not abolished but rather suspended so as to preserve peace and foster prosperity. In the multilevel constellation that makes up the EU there is the acceptance of a reciprocal responsibility to respect collective decisions, even though popular authorization is in short supply. That this is in itself has legitimating force (See Weiler 2001: 68), can be explained by the fact that consent may be neither necessary nor sufficient for legitimacy because of the associative political obligations which are at work. Legitimacy has to do with the obligations that stem from being member of an association that is needed (or cannot be avoided) and the readiness to accept reciprocal vulnerabilities (Dworkin 2011: 320; 2013:12).[11]

However, the further the constitutionalizing process proceeds, the greater the need for direct popular authorization and sanction. This is in line with the so-called *Solange* judgments of the German Constitutional Court, which made further integration and ceding of sovereignty conditional on democratization. *Solange 1,* from 1974, establishes that as long as European law does not protect fundamental rights equivalent to that provided by national law nor has achieved the similar level of democratic legitimacy for its law-making power, the Court would keep reviewing secondary Community law according to the standards of the national constitution.

Even though there is no formal EU constitution, and the EU treaties do not meet the democratic standard, EU law, which stems from and is embedded in the member states' democratic constitutions, grounds the presumption of acceptability. Observance of this structure ensures not only that the EU structure is seen as constitutionally sanctioned but also that the EU structure has an element of popular authorization. Compliance can be expected because:

a   The initial authorization of European integration, through the establishment of the ECSC (the European Coal and Steel Community) was voluntary.
b   The ensuing applications for membership by individual states have generally been supported by popular referenda.
c   Citizens' representatives are involved in the decision-making procedures through which EU law is made.

The EU then does not represent a constitutionalization of already constitutionalized orders—an *imperio in imperium*—but a fusion of orders.

Two Constitution-making Subjects?

In line with such a perspective, Habermas (2012a)[12] contends that the EU's basic "constitutional" order represents two major innovations in the process of pacifying the international state of nature: First, supremacy of EU law is granted in the areas in which it has competences but the binding effect of EU law is neither grounded in the monopoly of violence at the European level nor in the final decision-making authority of the EU. The

EU does not have the competence to increase its own competences ("Kompetenz-Kompetenz") and does not possess coercive means, but can nevertheless count on compliance for the reasons mentioned.

The second innovation has to do with the sharing of the constitution-making power between the citizens and the states (the European peoples). Democracy in the Union rests on two pillars.[13] The EU is a union of states and of citizens, epitomized by the role of the Council, composed of member states' representatives, and the directly elected EP—representing the states and the citizens respectively. The treaties speak of the peoples of the member states and of the citizens of the Union.[14] The co-decision procedure—formerly the Community method—has become the ordinary legislative procedure of the EU. The EP and the European Council participate on an equal footing in European law-making where EU has competence, with the exception of foreign and security policy, which still is intergovernmental.

Habermas builds on the EU's legal construction in foreseeing not a European federation based on hierarchy and the unity of law directly emanating from an empowered parliament and basic rights. Rather, his model is that of a federation of nation states founded on a shared sovereignty between "the 'citizens' and the 'peoples' as the constitution-founding subjects" (Habermas 2012a: 54). The nation state is seen as the main container of solidarity and democratic legitimation. The achievements of the nation state, with regard to rights' protection, democracy, solidarity and welfare, must not be put at risk but furthered by the integration process. In so far as there is "an element of institutionally consolidated political justice in these historical formations" there are reasons to insist on a constitutive role of the state at the supranational level (ibid.: 59). But can such a thought experiment work?[15]

The term "a federation of nation states" sits uneasily with the idea of democracy as a self-governing citizenry as well as with Habermas' own non-essentialist claim that we should not substantialize "the people" or "the nation" (Habermas 2012a: 48). Supra-individual entities, such as a people, a majority, or a state, are not self-authenticating sources of valid claims (Michelman 1997: 152). The people is a bodiless category (Lefort 1988). Hence the people cannot be the "the *unum*" but must be "the *plures*, the plurality or the singular" (See Pettitt 2006: 301). Popular sovereignty can only legitimately appear in pluralis—it demands access for persons, not groups or states, to a procedure of co-legislation.

Moreover, it is also strange to use "the concept of constituent power in the context of a supranational political entity based on international treaties" (Patberg 2013: 227). The concept of constituent power, which designates the crux of popular sovereignty, makes clear that the power to make positive law should be exclusively held by the citizens. Treaties, which are agreements reached by states, refer to state sovereignty—to *Willkür* and *Staatsraison*. State sovereignty designates the status states are granted under international law, and which regulates their external affairs.

Treaties, unlike constitutions, do not spring from the united will of the people but from states' willpower and bargaining clout.

Citizens' sovereignty cannot be divided or shared with another sovereign subject without losses. A collective subject like "a people" or a state cannot be put on par with popular sovereignty, as this would blur the distinction between popular and state sovereignty; that is, between the rights of the citizens to autonomous participation in collective opinion-formation processes, and the rights of the states conferred on them by international law and which concern the conditions for external action. In such a blurred system of constitution-making the following question arises: How to secure the autonomy of the citizens if there is also the autonomy of a collective (macro) subject—the state—to be safeguarded? Habermas' thought experiment is a construction that devalues the democratic principles of citizens' self-rule. There would be no criterion for approximating the autonomy principle—citizens should only obey laws that they also have been the co-authors of—when it is discounted and weighed against another principle, that of state sovereignty. Therefore, there can be pooling of state sovereignty but not a disaggregation of political subjecthood—of popular sovereignty—which then can be shared between two constitutional subjects.

Moreover, even though the member states *de jure* are "the Masters of the Treaties," over time intergovernmentalism has de facto been countered by the struggle for "a citizens' Europe" (as is most salient in the assignment of EU citizenship in Treaty of Maastricht and in EU's Charter of Fundamental Rights linked to the Lisbon Treaty). Two constitution-making subjects have not only been cooperating but also competing for hegemony in establishing the EU as it is. The European Communities may not initially have had much power and many competences at their disposal, but with the aim of furthering integration and closer cooperation, accompanied with the attainment of requested means, they transformed the constituent parties into committed members. The Euro polity has in the last decades undergone a marked change—from a largely economic organisation whose legitimacy was derivative of the member states—to an entity that today asserts that it represents an independent source of democratic legitimacy. The Court of Justice of the European Union (CJEU) embraced fundamental rights as a key principle of EU law and played a vital role in empowering the EP from early on. The CJEU has had a leading role in the democratization process of the European Union. It spurred the EU's constitutionalization dynamics: the more power is granted to EU bodies and the more power exercised, the more constitutional guarantees and democratic parliamentary legitimation are required (Conway 2012). A struggle for a "citizens' Europe" has been going on in the form of a struggle for an empowered EP. The ongoing reform process up to the Lisbon Treaty has consistently strengthened the power of the European citizens in the organizational structure of the Union (Eriksen and Fossum 2012).

In light of this background, one may question Habermas' model. The idea of two constitution-making subjects makes the EU foundationally shaky. For an order to achieve stability and legitimacy, agreement on the basic structure is required, as well as on the polity structure that corresponds to it. Systems of domination require justification with regard to the relevant characteristics of the political community to be regulated as well as with regard to the purposes and interests to be realized. A legitimate political order needs to provide an answer to the following question: In which specific capacity are its members equals? When the EU asks the individuals to see themselves as European and not merely national citizens—what then could be seen as a trigger of equal concern and respect? The question is what are the constitutive norms that express the distinctive relations of European citizens, and which could be the basis for solidarity among Europeans. In what does the political *universitas* of the EU consist and where does it reside (See Jackson 2000: 346)? The weakness of Habermas' reconstruction of a legitimate Euro polity is the lack of the requisite unifying component of the European political order.

The European nation states are profoundly affected by accession to the European Communities, and the integration process has constrained their willpower and has Europeanized identities (See Risse 2014). Moreover, the EU is a polity in its own right that contributes to global steering. It possesses higher-level political decision-making capabilities, but possesses neither a collective identity nor the coercive instruments of a state. We are witnessing a federation without a state; but how can such a polity be cohesive and effective without the competence to override the nation state, to constrain or enlarge national mentalities; and how can it be legitimate without a we-feeling and a sense of *finalité* that can provide the necessary foundation for collective European decision-making?

The Constituting Subject

Due to the pooled sovereignty of states and common constitutional traditions of European states, the question is not which level possesses the final decision-making authority, but rather whether the ruling complies with the law; whether the common legal norms are applied in a correct manner. It is only in the applicative sense that the EU enjoys primacy, and not when it comes to validity. Community law leaves "inconsistent national law valid but unapplied" (Von Bogdandy 2006: 14). The multilevel legal order in Europe, with national courts and the CJEU (and in some cases also the European Court of Human Rights) sharing jurisdictional power, ensures in principle the judicial monitoring of laws, the ability to handle "conflicts of law," and to reach conclusions in hard cases within a time limit. But on what basis? What is the single unifying principle?

The constituting subjects of treaties are states, and the constituting subject of constitutions is the individual. Both lines of authority have one single origin: the citizen. Only the rights of the individual, and the legal procedure and discipline that go with it, give unity and coherence to EU law in the multilevel constellation. At the foundational level, there is no competition between the member states and the European level; the basic unit for which both levels can claim legitimacy is the individual, her dignity and autonomy. There is and can only be one constituting subject even in a multilevel configuration like the EU.[16]

When there is a common legal basis and the individual is the sole source of legitimation for the EU, it is not necessary to settle once and for all who has the final decision-making authority: the EU or the member states. Who has the competence-competence need not be settled, because to be subordinate to supranational EU law is not to be dominated by an alien power. It is to be subjected to co-authored law. Joint European rule entails the capacity to co-determine the exercise of authority and not the final power of arbitration. Supremacy can be seen as a collision norm, which says that European law should prevail when there is conflict with national law.

But what could form the basis for establishing supremacy as a collision norm, if not the protection of human rights? Along these lines Armin von Bogdandy et al. (2012) suggest the *reversed Solange*, which aims at protecting the fundamental rights against EU member states' intrusion. Any member state's violation of human rights is infringing the "substance of Union citizenship." On the basis of European citizenship and on the basis of the adopted European Charter of Fundamental Rights, which applies only when the member states are implementing Union law, *reversed Solange* holds that "member states remain autonomous in fundamental rights protection as long as it can be presumed that they ensure the essence of the fundamental rights enshrined in the Article 2 TEU" (Von Bogdandy et al. 2012: 491).

Both in the legal and in the normative sense, the individual citizen must be seen to constitute the sole source of legitimation of modern constitutional orders. All modern legal orders are essentially individualistic orders as they universalize the legal principle of rights-based adjudication. They build on a procedural consensus—on the rules for inclusion, hearing, deliberation, and decision-making—which warrant the presumption of due hearing and equal concern for all. The right of the human being constitutes the foundation of modern law, which basically comes down to a right to have its dignity respected. Giovanni Pico della Mirandola (2012 [1486]) is seen to be the first to establish that dignity is inherent in each individual without exception, an insight fundamental to Kant and enshrined in the World Declaration of Human Rights.[17]

Autonomy is the basis for dignity and is, according to Kant, located in the law-making procedure. Autonomy is the basic democratic criterion and has two roots: autos (=self) and nomos (=law). Self and law is conjoined in this concept. The law must be self-given and this is the core of dignity:

> For, nothing can have a worth other than that which the law determines for it. But the law giving itself, which determines all value, must for that reason have dignity, that is, an unconditional, incomparable worth; and the word *respect* alone provides a becoming estimate of it

that a rational being must give. *Autonomy* is therefore the ground of dignity of human nature and of every rational nature.

(Kant 1996 [1785]: 85)[18]

Dignity resides in the law-making process: It places the law under the constraint of being "self-given" and co-authored. Individual autonomy is constrained by the fact that the autonomy of each must co-exist with the freedom of all. There is a right to have one's dignity respected, which can only be ensured by being granted a right to participate in law-making. Dignity is a value in itself, and is a basis for deriving rights. The right of the individual to have its dignity protected both links in with the cosmopolitan norm of equal respect for the individual and with democracy as it grants the individual right to participation in law-making. Cosmopolitanism implies the universalization of human dignity—all human beings possess it equally—but the right to have one's dignity respected requires democracy in a bounded territory (Macedo 2004). Dignity grants the human being membership in two communities, in the moral commonwealth—in the community of all human beings—and in a state.

The Political Universitas of the EU

On the one hand, the right to have one's dignity protected is a demand that can only be cashed in through membership in a particular self-governing political order—with borders. On the other hand, national democracies have incentives to take a free ride on others and impose negative externalities on third parties without compensation. A particular state can violate its own citizens' rights, and can fail to respect individuals with no membership rights and other states' legitimate interests. Integration itself and democracy among states are moral concerns, as democracy requires that the citizens—when their rights to have their dignities respected are being infringed—can bring their grievances before a superior authority. Any "people" can get it wrong, and need correctives; majority decisions can violate the rights of individuals and minorities, and national, constitutional courts may be lacking or may not be able to protect them. For a true republic to be realized it must be possible for citizens to appeal to bodies above the nation state when their rights are threatened. Thus there are reasons for institutions beyond a particular state in which individuals have obtained membership and which protect the basic rights of the citizen.

For the dignity of the world citizen—*kosmou politês*—to be respected, human rights need to be institutionalized in bodies above the nation states that actually bind individual governments and international actors. Already the principle of negative peace requires a superordinate instance to safeguard the right to non-interference (Niederberger 2009: 293). Organizations at the intermediate level—between the state level and the world organization—reduce dominance, facilitate accountability across borders, and provide the "international community" with some agency.

Dignity is firmly entrenched in the UN charter; in international conventions and treaties; in national constitutions, in particular in the German Constitution. It is also referred to several times in the German Federal Constitutional Court's ruling on the Lisbon Treaty (pars 57, 147, 188, 122). It expresses the general point in the following manner:

> The constitutional state commits itself to other states with the same foundation of values of freedom and equal rights and which, like itself, make human dignity and the principles of equal entitlement to personal freedom the focal point of their legal order.
>
> (par. 221)

Dignity figures prominently in EU Treaties; in Article 2 of the Lisbon Treaty; and the EU Charter of Fundamental Rights. The latter places dignity-protecting human rights as core legitimating principles: In Article 1 it is stated that human dignity is inviolable; It must be respected and protected. Article 2 prohibits the death penalty. Article 3 specifies the right to the integrity of the person; and Article 4 prohibits torture and inhuman or degrading treatment or punishment. The Preamble of the Charter states that:

> Conscious of its spiritual and moral heritage, the Union is founded on the indivisible, universal values of *human dignity*, freedom, equality and solidarity; it is based on the principles of democracy and the rule of law. It places the individual at the heart of its activities, by establishing the citizenship of the Union and by creating an area of freedom, security and justice.
>
> (Italics inserted)

One may thus speak of a ground norm, of having one's dignity respected in the EU. Human dignity is the real foundation of basic rights (Meyer 2003: 59).[19] It is a principle that digs deeper than the ordinary rights we live by in Europe and one that is in need of specification and institutionalization. I see dignity as a foundational "must" of European integration. It constitutes the moral-cognitive as well as the affective-value basis for peace and for rights-based democracy, and has been an important unifying principle enabling Europeans of different stripes to come to grips with their belligerent past. When contextualizing and counterpoising the principles of the French Revolution with the history of brutality and violence that first of all triggered the integration process, we may, in line with Theodore Adorno, reformulate the categorical imperative to: "think and act in such a way that the history of Auschwitz will not be repeated."[20]

This would imply that there are moral reasons for integrating European nation states into a supranational order that subjects their willpower to higher ranking law. The ultimate aim of the integration process, and to which other values like peace, justice and democracy speak, is then to end war and protect the dignity of the individual. This is a foundational norm that all, in fact, would agree to despite all other disagreements over values and interests. It could not be rejected with mutually acceptable reasons, and in fact it has vigorously been struggled for by Catholics, Protestants, and Humanists and supported by liberalists, conservatives, and socialists.

In light of this background, the reactions to the crisis management of the eurozone—the strong emotions this triggers—are easier to comprehend; as are the reasons for further integration. We can better understand the reactions to the handling of the present crisis: the outcry of betrayal and loss of mission, as well as the call for concerted European action. For many, the promise of a democratic, dignity-protecting Europe does not hold any longer. It has been broken by the inability to handle the exacting demands of debt, raising borrowing costs, unemployment, and structural imbalances between the countries through popularly authorized and democratically accountable bodies. Not co-determination but old-fashioned power politics has kicked in and people are humiliated—they suffer from exclusion, and new forms of dominance.

The Normativity of Co-legislation

Having one's dignity protected requires the abolition of dominance through participation in a co-legislative procedure. Dignity-protecting rights go to the core of modern constitutions, which set the rules for a free and equal association of self-ruling citizens. They establish the procedural arrangements of modern representative orders. Equal human rights, enfranchisement, one man one vote, freedom of expression, rules for deliberation, voting, and fair bargaining, make up the normative core of modern representative democracies, and have left a strong and lasting imprint on the European integration process.

Dignity, and the moral values that go with it, are reflected in the clauses for inclusion and for equal treatment as rights that are entrenched in present-day political arrangements as well as visible in the contestation, critique, and opposition to power structures.[21] These particular rights, which are salient standards for critique and validation, are consensual principles protecting the internal dignity and external freedom of individuals. They are moral in nature as they command the observance of all. The rules for inclusion and for equal treatment personify the principles of equal citizenship and membership in a body that continuously engages in processes of collective self-determination—in processes of opinion and will-formation. Only bodies that tie representatives into a structure of political accountability—of contestation and public deliberation—can claim to have institutionalized political equality and protected individuals' dignity.

This sheds light on the emotional reactions to the financial crisis, which has developed into a social, economic, and political crisis, and which has redistributed risk. The integration project was founded on the principle of peace and cooperation without humiliation. The manner in which the eurozone crisis has been tackled has brought humiliation back in—not merely in the form of economic and social exclusion, but in the form of executive, intergovernmental dominance—or post-democratic executive federalism as Habermas terms it. This is abnormal politics according to European standards. The lingering crisis, the many non-decisions, stop-go measures, and the austerity programs initiated by the Troika, have brought the European civilizing process, understood as the successive democratization of political order, to a standstill (See Altvater et al., 2013; Schäfer and Streeck 2013; Streeck 2013). In some respects, this process has even been reversed. The autonomy of the citizens and of insolvent states is being reduced and a new unaccountable hierarchy (the Troika) is making decisions with severe consequences (Smith 2014). Naming, shaming, and blaming take place among groups and states in Europe today, creating images of suppliers and spenders, of givers and receivers. Humiliation occurs in the wake of the economic meltdown. Exclusion from the labor market, from benefits and pensions has consequences for self-respect and self-esteem (Margalit 1996). Subjection to hegemonic forces instead of jointly made law undermines the idea of equal citizenship. In the place of co-membership and co-determination there are dictates and arbitrary interference. Hence the problem of dominance, which is rule without justification. It is an expression of injustice and illegitimate government (Pettit 1999; Shapiro 2012). The right not to be subjected to arbitrary power represents the crux of the right-to-dignity protection.

Associative Political Obligations

The economic meltdown of the eurozone effectively demonstrates the common vulnerabilities, the degree of affectedness and global interdependence that have been reached. It also makes clear that some are profiting and others are suffering under the same economic regime, which justifies the call for solidarity among winners and losers of the integration project. Arrangements with distributive outcomes are in need of justification. Those that have made the monetary union and/or gained from it have a duty to mend it. They are the addressees of the obligations generated by the integration process. In particular, they have a duty to put the integration process back on democratic tracks. The meltdown makes it clear that a monetary union without political union is futile and undemocratic and makes a country fiscally fragile. From the very start, the EMU was supposed to be accompanied by a parallel move to European political union. Lack of unity, of solidarity, of a collective we-feeling has been held as the main obstacle to further integration.

But even though states and groups have an interest in upholding the EMU and the internal market—or have a negative interest in avoiding its collapse—and even though there is a general obligation by those who created the institutions in the first place to remediate the failure, these do not "add up to an 'obligation,' a claim recognized as legitimately made by specific others and therefore as binding" (Offe 2014: 99). Rather it is a question of political obligations of solidarity. Such obligations, as mentioned, stem from being member of an association that is needed or cannot be avoided. There is a European community of obligations, created first and foremost by the monetary union and the internal market, which incur uneven losses and gains on the members; though risks have been (re)distributed along the complete integration process. There are thus reasons for solidarity. When institutional arrangements are inflicting harms there is an obligation to help the harmed ones. But it is unclear what exactly the "gainers" or free riders should do. What assistance is needed has to be specified through specific processes of political decision-making, because solidarity raises imperfect duties.[22]

In solidarity discourses, actors are called upon in their capacity as fellows—as compatriots, mates, and companions—to do more than can be expected by justice. Solidarity is so to say a question of *supererogation*, namely, of action beyond the demand of duty. This does not mean that solidarity is merely a question of altruism. The concept of solidarity contains a reciprocity dimension (Habermas 2013: 82ff.); not only in the sense that actors' extra-duty efforts may be recompensed at a later stage but also in the sense that actors who succeed in establishing a more robust political and economic regime will themselves profit from this in the long run. "What norms of solidarity apply to is the universe of members of an intended community, seen as a project under construction" (Offe 2014: 100).

But what could be the basis for European solidarity beyond the collective self-interest? Habermas maintains that "ethical expectations and appeals to solidarity refer to an interest in the integrity of a shared form of life that includes one's own well-being" (Habermas 2014a:11). If it is a question of preserving a shared form of life, then we need to know the quintessence and value of such. Why is it worth protecting and striving for? What could be the single unifying and motivating foundation of European solidarity?

Solidarity is the building block of every democratic community, as it expresses a universal norm that it is possible for all members to identify with. It makes clear that they have obligations towards one another. Hauke Brunkhorst (2005) analyses the evolution of solidarity from the Christian-Judean origin to the expressions it found in the revolutions of the eighteenth century. Solidarity developed from the classical ethical ideal of civil friendship in the antique (Aristotle), through the religious concept of the universal component of the self—we are all equal before God—to the way it was politically transformed and democratized as *fraternité*—universal brotherhood—by the French revolution. This concept of solidarity, freed from ethno-nationalistic and communal bonds, was further transformed and enlarged through the successive construction of the welfare state. The core of the modern concept of civic solidarity, while reminiscent of quasi-natural ethical orders (family, friendship), is forward-looking, reflecting the need to overcome present system interdependencies, which shatter established forms of solidarity, connect citizens in new ways, and call for extraordinary collective action (Habermas 2013: 100ff).

When looking closer to the "solidaristic" movement one is struck by the many interests, the many motives, norms, values, and aims, as well as the very different institutional forms—different welfare regimes—it gave rise to. However, what is the impulse that underlies this movement? The ethical self-understanding of modern welfare states—their professions and citizens— can be seen to contain a moral element beyond efficiency, well-being, and collective self-interest. There is, I submit, a common denominator reflecting our moral obligation to help those in need—those who cannot help themselves—our moral duty to fight poverty and misery irrespective of formal rights and responsibility for consequences; for social cohesion, political stability, or development of the citizens' democratic proficiencies. Solidarity refers to a community-feeling that arises in a network of social relations when help is needed and the actors understand themselves as committed to alleviate a moral problem, and the recipients do not believe there is a right to such help (Wildt 1998:212). Solidarity is the virtue that is needed when material resources are in short supply (Steinvorth 1998: 69). What provides normative unity to the European solidaristic movement and to the welfare state credo, is, I suggest, in line with the previous analysis, the call for a fair and non-humiliation society.

The appeal of solidarity today is not merely that of "we the comrades," or "we the nationals," but that of "us maltreated" and in need. In Europe the call is now for "us subjected" to unfair politico-economic arrangements, to go beyond established communities to (re)create a new or reformed order. The European institutions have brought about a community of obligations. Citizens can rightly claim compensation. There are thus reasons for help that stem from present interdependencies. The basis for solidarity today is not that of well-established communities or primordial values nor of discernable collective interests—they vary with nation, state, and group affiliation. Rather the reasons for solidarity stem from a foundational right to non-humiliation; to dignity protection that the technocratic handling of the eurozone crisis infringes. The new obligations formed by the European institutions create the solidaristic substrate of the emerging European republic. It is in the capacity of being subjected to the same law—that has non-negligible consequences and breaches the idea of equal citizenship—that the political universitas of Europe could be found. As Europeans are members of and affected by the same politico-economic arrangements they are equal, and have both a motive and a duty to respond to injustice. The trigger of equal concern and respect is then the endangered right to dignity protection, which can only be cashed in through establishing and upholding a democratic sovereign capable of collective action. Recall that democracy, which expresses distinctive relations between European citizens, is one of the EU's constitutive norms.

The Quest for Integration

One may question the EU's ability to handle crises and hardships, but the Euro-polity in itself is an answer to the quest for a correct institutionalizing of human rights under conditions of globalization.[23] The EU can be conceived of as a polity in its own right based on an authorized government, which depicts the political organization of society: that is, the institutional arrangement of the political unit. A non-state entity can make up a system of government in so far as it performs the functions of sanctioned jurisdictions. The EU should not be seen as a federation of nation states, but as a quasi-federation of states and citizens united under a common legal framework with a universalistic underpinning. The EU's commitment to basic human principles—protecting citizens' dignity—means that it has a communal vocation that is broader and more universal than that of a multinational federation (Eriksen 2009:155ff.).

The question is whether a fiscal union with an organized capacity to act—which requires a sovereign tax base and redistribution competence—can come into place without state-like punitive measures at the European level. In short, can there be a transfer Union without a state. Strong institutions are needed to control financial markets and tax havens and to iron out economic and social differences. Monopoly of power is widely held to be needed to levy taxes and enforce redistribution. Nobody pays voluntarily, the saying goes, and even less so when not everybody contributes to the same amount and ability. The challenge according to Majone (2014) is to resolve the contradiction of the eurozone, which requires the punitive and solidaristic resources of a state but is situated within a construction in which the members are neither sovereign states nor members of a federation. The European integration process in itself suggests that neither the penal state, nor an external foe, nor a collective identity is needed to get a fiscal union in place and operative. This is so for the following reasons:

First, solidarity, as well as European identity, has almost always been in short supply in Europe but this has not prevented the EU from growing in size and competence over time. The EU has developed into a power-wielding entity, with the treaties as a proxy for constitution and with political-representative institutions. European law is observed all over Europe. The EU is in the possession of some of the organizational, disciplining means of a state, which could be a trigger of egalitarian standards of justice.

Second, the eurozone has brought the members into a community of fate, in which all are dependent on all, and where some are profiting and some are suffering from the same economic regime. There are thus reasons for solidarity. European solidarity is not beyond the demand of duty. Mending the eurozone crisis has become a matter of fairness. Peace, democracy, and justice have accompanied European integration from the very start, and could once again be the moving factors.

Third, the financial sector in Europe is being stabilized by the slow creation of a banking union. In response to the pressure on banks revealed both by the global financial crisis and the sovereign debt crisis in the euro area, the EU has enacted new legislation. The creation of a Single Supervisory Mechanism, a new Bank Recovery and Resolution Directive, and the Single Resolution Regulation are recent examples of such legislation. Also, other initiatives are on the table to improve the resilience of banks and credit institutions; to avert or to mutualize risks.

Fourth, there are some signs of a transfer union as the European Central Bank (ECB) has increasingly stepped in as lender of last resort of sovereigns. Under its quantitative easing program, the ECB is buying eurozone members' debt, which is bearing down on the interest rates governments have to pay. The bank has also promised to buy more, focusing on countries in difficulty if some governments were to find their borrowing costs driven to unaffordable levels because of fears they might exit the eurozone.[24] The Treaty on Stability, Cooperation and Governance (the Fiscal Compact of 2012) commits, however, eurozone members to balanced budgets: the structural deficit is not to exceed 0.5 percent of GDP; public debts less than 60 percent of gross domestic product. There are automatic penalties for non-compliant states and supervision by the European Commission. These rules severely restrict the fiscal policy space of the member states, which already, by adopting the euro, have given up national control of interest rates and exchange rates. The Fiscal Compact generates recessionary pressure and should be abolished.

Fifth, a fiscal union is no longer a utopic idea as it has, in fact, turned into a strategy for solving the crisis:

> What a (currently shrinking) minority of EU enthusiasts among elites and non-elites would dream of for many years in terms of deepening the integration process, has suddenly, under the impact of the crisis, turned into a roadmap for an urgent rescue operation that makes the empowerment of fiscal and economic governing capacities at the EU level a plain imperative.
>
> (Offe 2013: 599)

Solidarity has so to say become a functional must, in the sense that it is needed to solve the eurozone crisis.[25]

The integrative imperative—that European integration is necessary—and the workings of constitutional democracy, which hitherto has lent legitimacy to steps of integration—the legal proceedings and collective decision-making procedures of the Union—also could pave the way for more integration.[26] Further integration depends now as previously on the will and capability at the member-state level to bring it about. Requisite measures require leadership, will and competence, and nothing will happen without popular mobilization. The urgency of the matter, the constitutional *misère* of the eurozone, the dire economic, social, and political conditions in many countries call for immediate action in order to establish a fiscal union on constitutional grounds. While Kant in his *Groundwork of the Metaphysics of Morals* holds "there is no war" as a "veto" of practical reason, one may currently say that the same reason dictates integration. Further integration is a categorical imperative—a must.

Conclusion

The development of constitutional law at the European level, in which the member states are given a crucial role, represents a major advance in domesticating international power relations. It equips the international community with democratically sanctioned agency. Also, according to official documents, cosmopolitanism is part of the self-identity of the EU. It places the individual at the core. Europe is a particularly relevant site for the emergence of cosmopolitanism as well as supranational democracy. The EU can thus be seen as a part of, and as a vanguard for, an emerging democratic world order.

But the cosmopolitan condition, which requires the constitutionalization of international law, cannot draw its legitimacy from the international law regime itself or from the putative validity of humanitarian norms. Human rights do not in themselves make up a meaningful social order. Rights must be grounded: culturally, legally, and politically. For an order to achieve stability and legitimacy, agreement on the basic structure is required, as well as on the polity structure that corresponds to it. Systems of domination require justification with regard to the relevant characteristics of the political community to be regulated as well as with regard to the purposes and interests to be realized. I see the capacity in which the Europeans are equals as consisting in a right to dignity protection that can only be cashed in through membership in a self-governing republic. Dignity goes to the heart of the European integration project. The single authority—the "pouvoir constituent"—which can give unity and coherence to the legal system in place is the individual in the form of a right-bearing subject. The EU can thus not be seen as a federation of nation states, as Jürgen Habermas suggests. Rather it must be seen as a quasi-federation of states and citizens united under a common legal framework with a universalistic underpinning. The EU is, as we have seen, a heavily embedded rights-based polity and one with a distinct regional reach. It is embedded in a political culture and premised on a common constitutional complex; on the values and democratic practices in Europe. This normative infrastructure lends legitimacy to the proceedings and collective decision-making of the supranational Union and constitutes a vital part of the common self-understandings of the citizenry.

But Europeans are also equals in another sense: they are being affected by EU institutions in such a way that their right to dignity is infringed and new obligations are created. The eurozone crisis in particular has turned Europe into a community that raises specific political obligations. There is a European community of obligations and hence there are reasons for solidarity.

Notes

1 Some of the issues dealt with in this chapter are further discussed in Eriksen 2014.
2 The Lisbon Treaty entered into force on December 1, 2009. Treaty of Lisbon, Official Journal of the European Union, 2007/C 306. See also the consolidated versions of the Treaty on European Union (TEU) and the Treaty on the Functioning of the European Union (TFEU), Official Journal of the European Union, 2012/C 326.
3 See also "Solidarity: For Sale?," Europe in Dialogue 2012/01, Bertelsmann Stiftung, at www.bertelsmannstiftung.de/cps/rde/xbcr/SIDFCCFDD004C93DF6F/bst/xcms_bst_dms_35357_35358_.pdf, date accessed September 6, 2013; Guérot and Hénard (2011).
4 See the call 'Founding Europe Anew!', initiated by Frank Bsirske et al. with 35 signatories (including Habermas), at www.europa-neu-begruenden.de/archiv/pdf/2012/founding_europe_anew.pdf, date accessed September 6, 2013.
5 In the Westphalian order states are sovereign with fixed territorial boundaries and are entitled to conduct their internal and external affairs autonomously, without external actors checking their protection of human rights.
6 The term "constituent power" ("pouvoir constituent") designates the citizens' uninhibited freedom in making and amending the constitution.
7 While in line with the cosmopolitan credo Habermas prefers,

> to focus on the more specific and demanding perspective of a constitutionalization of international law. The concept of "cosmopolitanism" tempts us to continue an older train of thought, rooted in Stoicism, that bypasses the major problem of how to tame, channel and civilize political power in legal terms even beyond the empire or the modern nation state.
>
> (Habermas 2014a: 5)

8 This gave 60 million people a state of their own leaving about 25 million as minorities within their "own" territories.
9 Thucydides already pointed out that in international relations the stronger do what they want, while the weak endure what they must.
10 According to the President of the European Parliament, Martin Schulz, it was a "Schuman plan instead of a Treaty of Versailles," see "Our Mothers, Our Fathers: Next-Generation WWII Atonement," Romain Leick, *Spiegel Online International*, March 28, 2013. See also Schultz 2013.
11 People may object to a law but still find it legitimate, and orders can be unjust but still legitimate (Rawls 1995: 175).
12 He draws on the works of Von Bogdandy 2006, Von Bogdandy and Bast 2006, and Franzius 2010.
13 See Articles 9 to 12 and 19(2), Treaty on European Union.
14 See also Meyer (2003: 24ff.) for the wording on "Federation of Nation States" and "European people" in the EU's Charter of Fundamental Rights.
15 Habermas suggests that we should regard the Union *as though* from the very beginning, two different subjects were involved in the constitution-building process (2012a :38), see also Habermas 2014b; 2014c.
16 My critique is, in fact, inspired by Habermas' own procedural conception of popular sovereignty (Habermas 1996, See also Eriksen and Weigård 2003: 129ff.) as well as of his insight that, "The EU constitution, like all modern legal systems … rests *in the final analysis* on the subjective rights of the citizens" (2012a: 35).

17 "Whereas recognition of the inherent dignity and of equal and inalienable rights of all members of the human family is the foundation of freedom, justice and peace in the world."
18 See also Rosen (2012: 62) and Habermas (2012b), who sees human dignity as constituting the moral source of human rights. See Joas (2011).
19 The moral standard of having one's dignity respected is a higher-ranking principle that does not have the same sort of validity as the constitutional principles we live by; it is constitutive for the concept of basic individual human rights and for political equality.
20 Adorno (1980: 358, author's translation). In German: *"Denken und handeln so einzurichten, das Auschwitz nicht sich wiederhole, nichts Ähnliches gesehe."*
21 Not least have these been visible in the protests and vociferous criticism of austerity measures and the Troika's dictats in Greece—the protesters' allegation of humiliation of the Greek population.
22 The problem is not merely a matter of justice, as it is not clear who is causally responsible for which effects. Justice is formal and categorical, as it raises obligatory duties. Solidarity is substantial and relative, as it creates imperfect duties.

> Imperfect duties are, accordingly, only duties of virtue. Fulfillment of them is merit (meritum = +a), but failure to fulfill them is not in itself culpability (demeritum = –a) but rather mere deficiency in moral worth (= 0), unless the subject should make it his principle not to comply with such duties.
> (Kant 1991 [1797]: 194)

23 "The EU offers unprecedented possibilities to respond to the challenges of interdependence in a deterritorialized world" (Innerarity 2014: 14).
24 See also the "blueprint" paper of the Commission and the Presidency of the Council for the actual causes of the crisis and a reform proposal: COM/2012/777/FINAL/2: "A Blueprint for a Deep and Genuine Economic and Monetary Union: Launching a European Debate."
25 If all stood for one, all would be better off. For example, the borrowing costs of debt-ridden countries decrease when the ECB declares its liability.
26 But see Joerges and Glinski (2014) for the damaging effects of the European crisis on the democratic chain of rule.

References

Adorno, T. W. (1980) *Negative Dialektik: Jargon der Eigentlichkeit*. Gesammelte Schriften Bd. 6. Frankfurt: Suhrkamp.

Altvater, E., Ulrich Beck, Peter Bofinger, Hauke Brunkhorst, Joschka Fischer, Ulrike Guérot, Jürgen Habermas, Rudolf Hickel, Paul Krugman, Isabell Lorel, Oskar Negt, Claus Offe, Ulrick K. Preuss, Wolfgang Streeck, and Hans-Jürgen Urban. (2013) *Demokratie oder Kapitalismus? Europa in der Krise*. Berlin: Blätter für deutsche und internationale Politik.

Avbelj, M., and J. Komárek (eds.) (2012) *Constitutional Pluralism in the European Union and Beyond*. Oxford: Hart Publishers.

Brunkhorst, H. (2005) *Solidarity From Civic Friendship to a Global Legal Community*. Jeffrey Flynn (trans.) MIT Press: Cambridge.

Conway, G. (2012) *The Limits of Legal Reasoning and the European Court of Justice*. Cambridge: Cambridge University Press.

Duchêne, F. (1994) *Jean Monnet: The First Statesman of Interdependence*. New York: W. W. Norton & Co.

Dworkin, R. (2011) *Justice for Hedgehogs*. Cambridge, Mass: Harvard University Press.

Dworkin, R. (2013) "A New Philosophy of International Law," *Philosophy and Public Affairs*, 41(1), pp. 2–30.
Eriksen, E. O. (2009) *The Unfinished Democratization of Europe*. Oxford: Oxford University Press.
Eriksen, E. O. (2014) *Die Normativität der Europäishen Union*. Freiburg: Verlag Karl Alber. (In English, *The Normativity of the European Union*. Houndsmills: Palgrave Macmillan).
Eriksen, E. O., and J. Weigård (2003) *Understanding Habermas*. London: Continuum.
Eriksen, E. O., and J. E. Fossum (eds.) (2012) *Rethinking Democracy and the European Union*. London: Routledge.
Fossum, J. E., and A. J. Menéndez (2011) *The Constitution's Gift: A Constitutional Theory for a Democratic European Union*. London: Rowman and Littlefield.
Franzius, C. (2010) *Europaishe Verfassungsrechtsdenken*. Tübingen: Mohr Siebeck.
Habermas, J. (1996) *Between Facts and Norms: Contributions to a Discourse Theory of Law*. Cambridge, MA: MIT Press.
Habermas, J. (2012a) "The Crisis of the European Union in Light of a Constitutionalization of International Law—An Essay on the Constitution for Europe," in J. Habermas *The Crisis of the European Union: A Response*. Cambridge, MA: Polity Press.
Habermas, J. (2012b) "The Concept of Human Dignity and the Realistic Utopia of Human Rights," in J. Habermas *The Crisis of the European Union: A Response*. Cambridge, MA: Polity Press.
Habermas, J. (2013) *Im Sog der Technokratie*. Berlin: Suhrkamp.
Habermas, J. (2014a) "A Plea for the Constitutionalization of International Law," *Philosophy and Social Criticism*, 40(1), pp. 5–12.
Habermas, J. (2014b) *Democracy in Europe: Why the Development of the European Union into a Transnational Democracy is Necessary and How it is Possible*. ARENA Working Paper 13/2014, Oslo: ARENA Center for European Studies.
Habermas, J. (2014c) "Zur Prinzipienkonkurrenz von Bürgergleichheit und Staatengleichheit im supranationalen Gemeinwesen. Eine Notiz aus Anlass der Frage nach der Legitimität der ungleichen Repräsentation der Bürger im Europäischen Parlament," *Der Staat*, 53(2), pp. 167–192.
Innerarity D. (2014) "What Kind of Deficit?: Problems of Legitimacy in the European Union," *European Journal of Social Theory*, pp. 1–19.
Jackson, R. H. (2000) *The Global Covenant: Human Conduct in a World of States*. Oxford: Oxford University Press.
Joas, H. (2011) *Die Sakralität der Person. Eine neue Genealogie der Menschenrechte*. Berlin: Suhrkamp.
Joerges, C., and C. Glinski (eds.) (2014) *The European Crisis and the Transformation of Transnational Governance*. Oxford: Hart Publishing.
Kant, I. (1991 [1797]) *The Metaphysics of Morals* (Trans. M. Gregor). Cambridge, UK: Cambridge University Press.
Kant, I. (1996 [1785]) "Groundwork of the Metaphysics of Morals," in M. Gregor (ed.) *Practical Philosophy*. Cambridge: Cambridge University Press.
Lefort, C. (1988) *Democracy and Political Theory*. Cambridge: Polity Press.
Macedo, S. (2004) "What Self-governing Peoples Owe to One Another: Universalism, Diversity, and the Law of the Peoples," *Fordham Law Review*, 72(5), pp. 1721–1738.

Majone, G. (2014) "The General Crisis of the European Union: A Genetic Approach," in J. E. Fossum and A. J. Menèndez (eds.) *The European Union in Crises or the European Union as Crises?* ARENA Report No. 2 2/14, Oslo: ARENA Centre for European Studies.

Margalit, A. (1996) *The Decent Society.* Cambridge, MA: Harvard University Press.

McCormick, J. (2012) *Crisis and the Future of Europe.* Cicero Foundation Great Debate Paper No. 12/06. Paris/Maastricht: The Cicero Foundation.

Meyer, J. (2003) *Kommentar zur Charta der Grundrechte der Europäischen Union.* Baden-Baden: Nomos.

Michelman, F. I. (1997) "How Can the People Ever Make the Laws? A Critique of Deliberative Democracy," in J. Bohman and W. Regh (eds.) *Deliberative Democracy: Essays on Reason and Politics.* Cambridge: MIT Press.

Morgenthau, H. J., and K. W. Thompson (1993) *Politics Among Nations: The Struggle for Power and Peace.* New York, NY: McGraw-Hill.

Niederberger, A. (2009) *Demokratie unter Bedingungen der Weltgesellschaft.* Berlin: Walter de Gruyter.

Offe, C. (2013) "Europe Entrapped: Does the EU Have the Political Capacity to Overcome its Current Crisis?" *European Law Journal*, 19(5), pp. 595–611.

Offe, C. (2014) *Europe Entrapped.* London: Polity Press.

Offe, C., and U. K. Preuss (2007) "The Problem of Legitimacy in the European Polity: Is Democratization the Answer?" in C. Crouch and W. Streek (eds.) *The Diversity of Democracy: Corporatism, Social Order and Political Conflict.* Cheltenham: Edward Elgar.

Patberg, M. (2013) "Constituent Power beyond the State: An Emerging Debate in International Political Theory," *Millennium: Journal of International Studies*, 42(1), pp. 224–238.

Pettit, P. (1999) *Republicanism: Theory of Freedom and Government.* Oxford: University Press.

Pettit, P. (2006) "Democracy, National and International," *The Monist*, 89(2), pp. 301–302.

Pico della Mirandola, G. (2012) *Oration on the Dignity of Man: A New Translation and Commentary*, Francesco Borghesi, Michael Papio, Massimo Riva (eds.). Cambridge: Cambridge University Press.

Rawls, J. (1995) "Reply to Habermas," *The Journal of Philosophy*, 92(3), pp. 132–180.

Risse, T. (2014) "No Demos? Identities and Public Spheres in the Euro Crisis," *Journal of Common Market Studies*, 52(6), pp. 1207–1215.

Rosen, M. (2012) *Dignity: Its History and Meaning.* Cambridge, MA: Harvard University Press.

Schäfer, A., and W. Streeck (eds.) (2013) *Politics in the Age of Austerity.* Cambridge: Polity Press.

Schulz M. (2013) *Der gefesselte Riese: Europas letzte Chance.* Berlin: Von Rowohlt.

Shapiro, I. (2012) "On Non-Domination," *University of Toronto Law Journal*, 62(3), pp. 293–336.

Smith, D. (2014) "When the Peloton Hit the Mud: Displacement Struggles and the EU Crisis," in J. E. Fossum and A. J. Menèndez (eds.) *The European Union in Crises or the European Union as Crises?* ARENA Report No 2/14, Oslo: ARENA Senter for Europaforskning.

Steinvorth, U. (1998) "Kann Solidarität erzwingbar sein?" in K. Bayertz (ed.) *Solidarität—Begriff und Problem*. Frankfurt am Main: Suhrkamp.

Streeck, W. (2013) *Gekaufte Zeit: Die vertagte Krisedes demokratischen Kapitalismus*. Berlin: Suhrkamp.

Von Bogdandy, A. (2006) "Constitutional Principles," in A. von Bogdandy and J. Bast (eds.) *Principles of European Constitutional Law*. Oxford: Hart Publishing.

Von Bogdandy, A., and J. Bast (eds.) (2006) *Principles of European Constitutional Law*. Oxford: Hart Publishing.

Von Bogdandy, A., M. Kottmann, C. Antpöhler, J. Dickschen, S. Hentrei, and M. Smrkolj (2012) "Reverse Solange—Protecting the Essence of Fundamental Rights against EU Member States," *Common Market Law Review*, 49(2), pp. 489–520.

Weiler, J. H. H. (2001) "Federalism without Constitutionalism: Europe's Sonderweg," in K. Nicolaïdis, and R. Howse (eds.) *The Federal Vision*. Oxford: Oxford University Press.

Wildt, A. (1998) "Solidarität: Begriffsgeschichte und Definition [Solidarity: Conceptual History and Definition]," in K. Bayertz (ed.) *Solidarität—Begriff und Problem*. Frankfurt am Main: Suhrkamp.

Conclusion
European Identity, Crises, and Integration

Gaspare M. Genna and Ian W. Wilson

This volume examined the complex relationship between European identity, solidarity, and cooperation among integrating states, which is at the heart of much of Habermas' writings. Our findings demonstrate that Habermas' ideas in *The Crisis of the European Union* (2012) are difficult to apply due to the complex realties present in Europe. When examining the underlying values associated with cosmopolitanism, we see evidence that such values are associated with European integration. However, the association tends to dissipate when difficult times are present—such as those of this writing in November 2015, with a large-scale refugee crisis and increasing fears of terrorism in the wake of the attacks in Paris on November 13, 2015 resulting in increased intra-European border security and an upspring of national sentiment. We suggest conceptual tools that governmental and societal leaders may find useful in grounding common solutions into the cosmopolitanist framework. Last, we reviewed cases to see if we can find evidence of cosmopolitanism's application and what impact it would have in the policy and institutional arenas. All of these essays emphasizing events prior to 2015 bear striking relevance to debates now dominating both the European Parliament and European national parliaments.

Habermas' (2012) views the application of cosmopolitism as imperative because of two innovations. First is the subordination of the sovereign member states to EU law. The second is the shared sovereignty between the member states. For these two innovations to produce viable policies and solutions that benefit the continent, citizens need to trust each other to produce policies that have mutually beneficial goals. These goals need to keep in mind the need for human dignity, which is embedded in basic human rights. We also pointed out that he has deep concerns over the current approach to solving the European economic crisis, because the EU is not taking the cosmopolitan path.

By way of foundation, we began by looking at some of Habermas' ideas in context. Bailey noted that Habermas advises Europeans to adopt a cosmopolitan democracy. Such a democracy needs supranational institutions and other continental forums. As Bailey demonstrates, however, such venues do not necessarily promote a pro-integration consensus since anti-integration views also have access. At best, they are places to battle ideas.

As he notes, national ideas and priorities are not forgotten when individuals enter these institutions. In the case of rights for minorities, some countries may have differing views or do not prioritize such rights. It is possible that institutions without cosmopolitan values will not produce the outcomes Habermas seeks.

Fredette points out the diverse interpretations of Habermas' view of human dignity. Human dignity, of course, is an important reason for adopting a cosmopolitan world view according to Habermas. If human dignity cannot be seen as an "an indivisible whole," then explaining cosmopolitanism and its potential to aid in resolving European Union crises may be in jeopardy. As she notes, the cry for human dignity may also limit individual freedoms because one's view of dignified expression may reduce the ability of others to express their identity. Therefore, the concept of human dignity must be true to the ethos of inclusion and not simply an artifact of individuals protesting the humiliation of others.

Our foundation section does not negate the ability of cosmopolitan identity to aid in developing solutions for European crises. Instead, it uncovers the complexity that often occurs when ideas are put into action. European institutions in and of themselves are not solutions. They are venues where individuals can cooperate to solve common problems. Values guide the problem-solving process. However, what if the values are overbearing and limit the freedoms they espouse to protect?

Genna's chapter seeks to clarify how cosmopolitanism works in promoting the solidarity among the European peoples via the role of trust. Individual trust in the European nationalities improves the likelihood of supporting regional integration. The integration process produces the institutions, and, in turn, the laws and policies that produce common solutions. If support for integration is not based on European solidarity, then we would be hard-pressed to see evidence that cosmopolitanism is in play. His chapter does evidence that solidarity with the lesser economically developed southern and eastern countries does in fact explain why individuals would support integration.

Westfall's findings partially concur. She notes that the abstract belief in cosmopolitan values aids in explaining support for European unification. However, when challenged with the application of those values, we see less explanatory power. This was particularly the case when she measured cosmopolitanism in terms of discriminatory preferences in immigration policy. In this case, the connection between cosmopolitan values and support for integration disappears. She suggests that policy that embraces a cosmopolitan view of integration needs to do so at the theoretical or idealist level because when reality becomes uncomfortable, the capability of cosmopolitanism to be the driving force for unification will dramatically diminish. She concludes that we may be currently witnessing this in the economic crisis.

In building our foundation, we saw that Habermas' ideas are not clear cut. When underlying cosmopolitan values are in place, they can help explain support for the integration process, which is necessary for the production of common solutions to the economic crisis. When the harsh reality is present, individuals will lose sight of these values. If leaders choose to emphasize and foster cosmopolitan values, what tools are available?

To answer the question, Skidmore examines how Habermas' notation of cosmopolitanism gives legitimacy to the European Union. Cosmopolitism is the way minorities can be saved from being outvoted or otherwise obstructed by the majority will. By applying a universal concept of morality into the law, human dignity can be preserved. What would be universally accepted comes out of the historical evolution of rational thought present in European culture. By comparing the legitimacy behind the appeal to human dignity with that of Pope Benedict XVI (aka Joseph A. Ratzinger), he concludes that both Habermas and Pope Benedict agree that the common European history leads us to the same point of legitimacy. However, Habermas and Benedict would disagree as to the source guiding Europeans to the point of legitimacy (secular vs. religious views).

Wilson's conclusions provide us with additional tools through his analysis of the spiritual twins in the novel *Austerlitz*. He finds that the Jewish protagonist and the gentile author, although outwardly different, are spiritually twinned. He emphasizes that the novel includes mediating spaces across four European countries and the use of three languages to mediate a story of the interactions of diverse Europeans. The characters focus on their sameness rather than on their differences because of their need to move past a common crisis. The outcome of the novel gives us an important cultural element in developing a cosmopolitan Europe.

Our tools section, therefore, provides two important, and perhaps overlapping, aspects regarding cosmopolitanism. Cosmopolitanism comes out of a historical struggle among the European peoples. The diversity within a relative small geographic space that, in large part, led to millennia of conflict, disguises the commonalities among Europeans. When Europeans seek to reconcile their past, commonalities come into the light. The second aspect is the logic of rationality. By applying rationality, Europeans can see that divisions marked by identity will likely produce suboptimal outcomes for many, while promoting continued divisions that cycle through more conflict. By legitimating cosmopolitanism using these tools, we can foster a sense of human dignity that does not limit individual freedoms while it provides a binding ideal for European institutions and keeps values in place when harsh realities hit. In that light, the final question we sought to answer was how well the EU is applying Habermas' vision of cosmopolitanism.

Haakenson mapped out the explicit factors influencing higher educational reform in the EU while also taking into account non-cosmopolitan factors, namely the implicit and explicit economic challenges posed by China and the US. The latter, he concludes, are outpacing the desire to produce cosmopolitan citizenship. The economic imperative of outcomes undermines the educational process. In other words, the economic rivalry with China and the US fosters an urgency to produce competitive workers and products while undermining the Habermas vision.

Myers examined the expansion of public-private partnerships in Germany and the UK. The EU standards regarding such partnerships, which aim to reduce government economic involvement, require that the public good is maintained and not sacrificed for purely private gain. She finds that both countries do adhere to these standards. However, the application of oversight to safeguard these standards are more rigorously applied in Germany than in the UK. Germany's greater oversight is due to the federal arrangement giving local entities greater say. Germany also has a neo-corporatist system, which gives societal interest greater say. The neo-corporatist arrangement requires greater collaboration among economic interests and a formation of a common identity. That is, the public good and the private good are not mutually exclusive. This arrangement is, in part, a feature of cosmopolitanism.

Rossbach argued that the formal EU accession process helped to create a "cosmopolitan political space" for newer members. The better the member states did in adopting this type of political space, the better prepared they were in implementing the economic reforms needed to resolve the financial crisis. He supports this hypothesis using the experiences of the Baltic States. He credits the EU accession process for applying Habermas' "building blocks" for a democratic society, and the strong EU insistence on Baltic States applying these democratic reforms. The experience of the Baltic States shows that the building blocks were needed to successfully implement the economic reforms.

Eriksen examines the current EU institutional arrangement and concludes that the EU is a heavily embedded rights-based polity. It finds itself inside a political culture based on a common constitutional arrangement that values European democratic practices. There is a sense of common obligations and therefore reasons to apply solidarity. Solidarity is based on the notion of equality and the protection of dignity. Dignity, is in fact, at the "heart of the European integration project."

The institutions section's findings tell us that when Habermas' cosmopolitan ideas are in place, Europe can come together to solve its common problems. Since underlying values inform the policy outcome, respect for human dignity is possible. The question left unanswered by this section, and the book as a whole, is to what extent cosmopolitanism is currently in place and whether the EU has the capacity to use cosmopolitanism, and its associated notion of solidarity, to cope with its current and developing problems.

The last question is very pertinent currently. When we started our project, the crisis at hand was economic in nature. Europe was dealing with hard decisions regarding potential banking defaults and mounting and unsustainable sovereign debt. One can argue that these problems were of their own making: political decisions both at the supranational and national levels produced the crisis environment. Therefore, it would be up to the Europeans to enact the solidarity needed to overcome financial ruin.

The current refugee problem is a product of the massive political instability across North Africa, the Middle East, and Central Asia. Peoples as near as Libya to as far as Afghanistan are running away from death and destruction in their homelands. While EU and national foreign policies may, in some part, be responsible for the economic decay found in these countries, they are not responsible for the Islamist ideology that has taken advantage of the state failures. Nonetheless, the problem is before them as hundreds of thousands of refugees seek safe haven in relatively more stable and prosperous European countries. The forces of the Islamist ideology have also brought their destructive power to European capitals, which is generating fear and impacting on the chances of refugees settling in European countries. The yet to be answered questions will be: Can Europe expand the concept of cosmopolitanism to include the refugees? Can they act in solidarity to help? Lastly, can they develop a coherent foreign policy, using cosmopolitan principles, in their fight against extremism?

This crisis is constantly developing. Since we began writing this conclusion, the refugee crisis in Europe in the fall of 2015 has contributed to major changes to the enforcement of borders within the Schengen zone. While Germany's openness to Syrian refugees led one country after another to increase border controls (first Hungary, then Germany itself, followed by Austria, Slovenia, and Croatia), we also saw a shift in debates about cosmopolitan ideals after the Paris attacks of November 13, 2015; these attacks led to a declaration of emergency powers in France for only the second time since World War II and the restoration of document checks at all of its borders. The European project faces renewed redefinition. In the wake of such developments, Habermas' cosmopolitanism takes on even more urgency.

In two pieces originally published in *Le Monde* in French translation—one short essay that appeared as the refugee crisis began to come to a head and an interview following the November 13 attacks—Habermas maintains the emphasis we describe in this volume. He argues that the refugee crisis highlights the limitations of the current structure of the EU, driven as it is not by a parliament and a common government but by compromises made by its constituent national member states (Habermas 2015a). Habermas called for Germany and France to take the lead and to call for the euro nations to develop common solutions to the crisis (ibid.). His hope lay with an appeal to France's own political tradition, which he hoped would pressure Germany to formalize its commitment to accept refugees (ibid.).

However, after the Paris attacks, such optimism must be tempered. Indeed, French Prime Minister Manuel Valls said in an interview with the German newspaper *Die Suddeutsche Zeitung* on 25 November, "We cannot accommodate any more refugees in Europe, that's not possible," seeing in the restoration of controlled immigration a determinant of the fate of the EU (Nienaber 2015). Valls expressed admiration for Germany's moral stance in working to accept Syrian refugees, but said ultimately, "It was not France that said: Come!" (ibid.). Habermas' late-summer optimism about French political traditions seems untenable during the state's current crisis mode.

Habermas himself strikes a cautious note in briefly weighing in on Europe after the Paris attacks. He refers to the French nation as "deeply wounded" and continues:

> Both, the terror and the refugee crisis, are—perhaps for the last time— dramatic challenges for a much closer sense of cooperation and solidarity than anything European nations, even those tied up to one another in the currency union, have so far managed to achieve.
> (Habermas 2015b)

We interpret this comment as ominous but not dismissively pessimistic. Following Habermas, challenges to European solidarity are central to its growth and adaptation. Should such challenges lead to greater commitment to European cooperation within its population, the crises could move Europe further down its cosmopolitan path. While we expect further complicating developments in the European project, we continue to believe in the usefulness of Habermas' lens for viewing those changes.

References

Habermas, Jürgen (2015a) "La France et l'Allemagne doivent prendre l'initiative," *Le Monde*, September 9, 2015. www.lemonde.fr/idees/article/2015/09/09/la-france-et-l-allemagne-doivent-prendre-l-initiative_4750233_3232.html (last accessed: March 2, 2016).

Habermas, Jürgen (2015b) "The Paris Attack and Its Aftermath," *Social Europe*, November 26, 2015: www.socialeurope.eu/2015/11/habermas-paris-attack/ (last accessed: March 2, 2016).

Nienaber, Michael (2015) "French PM Says Europe Can't Take in More Refugees: *Sueddeutsche Zeitung*," *Reuters*, November 25, 2015: www.reuters.com/article/us-europe-migrants-france-germany-idUSKBN0TE0NP20151125 (Last accessed: March 2, 2016).

Index

abortion 48
accession process 181, 218
active and passive leverage 181
active leverage 181
austerity 6, 9, 49, 57, 70–1, 73, 105, 158, 175, 178–80, 184, 186–9, 192, 204, 213
autonomy 14, 46–8, 51, 145, 151, 198, 200–1, 204
Aviation Security Act of 2005 40

Baltic States 9, 175–7, 179–91, 218
Benedict XVI 7, 108, 114–15, 119, 217; *see also* Ratzinger, Joseph
Berlin 146
Berlin, Isaiah 42, 51
budget 2, 18–19, 78, 161, 178, 185–7, 189, 192
burqa 46–7, 51; *see also* niqab

China 142, 148–51, 153–6, 217–18
civic solidarity 3, 5, 9, 22, 78, 85, 124, 177, 179, 205
civil society 14, 16–17, 22–7, 31–4, 36, 110, 123, 182, 184
constituent subjects 193
cooperation 6, 9, 37–8, 42–3, 58, 61–2, 77, 149, 155, 194, 198, 203, 208, 215, 220
Copenhagen Criteria 180–3
corporate incomes 158
cosmopolitan 2, 4–9, 13, 15, 17, 30–1, 37–8, 42, 50, 57, 70, 77–84, 86–91, 93–6, 98, 100, 121–6, 130, 133–6, 141, 143, 145, 175–6, 179, 182, 187–8, 193–4, 209–10, 215–20; *see also* cosmopolitanism; cultural cosmopolitanism
cosmopolitanism 4, 6–9, 37, 40, 52, 57, 59, 61, 63, 65, 67, 69–73, 75, 77–83, 85, 87–8, 91–5, 99–100, 121–2, 124, 126, 129, 134, 136, 141, 153, 179, 187–8, 194, 209–10, 215–19; *see also* cosmopolitan; cultural cosmopolitanism
cultural cosmopolitanism 122, 134; *see also* cosmopolitan; cosmopolitanism
culture 4–5, 14, 23, 28, 50–1, 63, 73, 83, 88, 112–17, 120–5, 134–5, 142–3, 149–50, 155, 160, 165, 184, 209, 217–18
currency 1, 105, 110, 141, 184–5, 187, 220

debt 1–2, 4, 21–2, 58, 70, 78, 91, 105, 118, 120, 132, 141, 152, 167–8, 175, 178, 190, 192, 203, 208, 211, 218
democracy 4, 6, 9–10, 13, 15–17, 19–25, 27, 29, 31–5, 63, 65, 68, 73, 75, 77, 80, 101, 107, 109, 111, 116–17, 120, 124, 136, 143, 173–4, 176, 180, 182–3, 189–92, 197, 201–2, 206, 208–9, 212–13, 215; *see also* democratic deficit; democratic satisfaction
democratic deficit 9, 16, 22, 36, 65, 154, 157, 177, 188; *see also* democracy
democratic satisfaction 65; *see also* democracy
deregulation 29, 159, 170–1, 178
diffuse support 59
dignity 2, 4–6, 8–9, 37–53, 107, 111–12, 114, 117–19, 193–4, 200–4, 206–7, 209, 211–13, 215–18
discrimination 45–6, 88, 90–1, 93, 96, 98–100
distribution 19, 83, 158–9, 162, 172–3

economic crisis 1–2, 4, 9, 35, 52, 70–1, 77–8, 146, 178–9, 189, 191, 215, 217
empathy 44, 130

Index

equal worth 38, 40, 46
ERM II 185; *see also* Exchange Rate Mechanism II
Estonia 175, 180–91
ethnicity 85–6, 88, 91, 99–100, 117, 122, 183
euro 1–2, 4, 9–10, 16, 18, 20–1, 30, 33, 40, 51, 66, 78, 80, 84, 94, 100, 105, 110, 120, 134, 141–2, 148, 172, 175–9, 181, 183–5, 187, 189, 191, 193–4, 198–9, 207–8, 212–13, 219; *see also* eurocrisis; Eurozone
eurocrisis 16, 22, 179; *see also* euro; Eurozone
European Central Bank 20, 105, 188
European Commission 1, 13, 16, 18, 24–6, 29, 33, 65, 68, 105, 146–7, 155, 169, 182–3, 186, 188–90
European constitution 6, 24–5, 31, 35
European Council 13, 16, 18–20, 147, 180, 197
European identity 1, 8–9, 14, 28, 60, 62, 65, 83, 106, 110, 116, 144–5, 207, 215
European integration 1, 6–9, 13–15, 17, 23–4, 28, 31–2, 34, 57–9, 61, 63–5, 67, 69–76, 79, 87–8, 92–3, 99–101, 110, 116, 118, 157, 159, 161, 163, 165, 167, 169, 171, 173, 182, 194, 196, 202–3, 207–9, 215, 218
European Parliament 3, 6, 13–14, 17, 19, 31, 34–5, 68, 117, 119, 210
European Social Survey 79–80, 82–3, 85–6, 88, 100
European solidarity 6, 38, 78, 93, 205, 207, 216, 220
Europeanization 33, 81, 95
Euroskepticism 38, 57, 75, 118; *see also* Euroskeptics
Euroskeptics 2; *see also* Euroskepticism
Eurozone 1, 5, 49, 52, 70, 78, 105, 117, 175–6, 178, 184, 187, 189–90, 192, 203–4, 206–9
Exchange Rate Mechanism II 185; *see also* ERM II
exile 132, 134
extremism 109, 219

faith 7, 105, 107, 109–11, 113–17, 119
federation 169, 177, 192, 194, 197, 199, 207, 209–10
fiscal compact 189, 192, 208
flexible labor 160, 163, 171
Frankfurt School 108, 142

Fraternité 205
freedom 4, 20–1, 47, 49, 51, 68, 107, 112, 125, 145, 170, 176–7, 193, 201–3, 210–11, 213
friendship 126, 128, 131, 134–5, 205, 211

Germany 2, 5–7, 9, 14–16, 18, 20–9, 32–4, 36, 48, 51, 70–3, 77–87, 89, 93–5, 99, 105–6, 108–9, 118, 120, 123, 125, 127–8, 132, 134–6, 147–8, 155, 165–7, 169–71, 173–5, 178–80, 187, 189–91, 194, 218–20
globalization 5, 8–9, 27, 154, 157–8, 171–4, 207
Great Separation, The 116

Habermas, Jürgen 10, 52, 101, 119–20, 136, 155, 173, 191, 220
Hartz Reforms 178–9, 188, 191
healthcare 159, 165–70, 172
history 1, 6, 17, 31, 33–5, 52, 107, 110–12, 117, 119, 136–7, 149, 155–6, 182, 184, 189, 194, 202, 213–14, 217
Holocaust 121–2, 126–7, 129–30, 132–4, 136–7; *see also* Shoah
human dignity 4–6, 9, 37–53, 107, 111–12, 114, 117–19, 201–2, 211–12, 215–18
human rights 4–6, 37–47, 49–53, 77, 80, 83, 110–12, 124, 143, 192, 195, 199–203, 207, 210–12, 215
humiliation 44, 47, 49, 194, 203–4, 206, 211, 216

identity 1, 7–9, 14, 17, 28, 35, 49, 60–5, 73, 75–6, 83, 88–9, 92–3, 99–100, 105–6, 108, 110–11, 114, 116–17, 123–5, 132, 141, 144–5, 171, 184, 190, 199, 207, 209, 215–18
immigrant 83, 85–6, 88, 93, 97, 99–100
immigration 79, 83–6, 88–94, 96–101, 117, 119, 123, 125, 216, 219
immigration policy 84–5, 88, 91, 94, 96, 216
inequality 85, 162, 174
injustice 4–5, 37, 204, 206
integration 1–2, 5–9, 13–15, 17, 19, 23–4, 27–8, 31–2, 34, 37–8, 45, 57–61, 63–7, 69–77, 79–80, 83, 87–8, 92–4, 96, 99–101, 110, 116, 118, 126, 141–2, 149, 153–4, 157–9,

161–3, 165, 167, 169–71, 173, 177, 182, 184, 191–9, 201–5, 207–9, 215–18
intergroup trust 57
International Monetary Fund 20, 105, 173, 175, 188
interpersonal trust 58
Islam 52, 115–16, 120

John Paul II 107, 114, 120

Kant, Immanuel 38–41, 43–4, 50, 52, 111, 125, 141, 143, 153–4, 156, 200–1, 209, 211–12
Kindertransport 126, 130, 132

language 34, 40, 50, 109–11, 114, 121, 125, 133, 143–4
Latvia 9, 175, 180–3, 185–7, 189–91
legal integration 45
legitimacy 2, 9, 18, 22, 32, 60, 65, 73, 75, 107–8, 118, 173, 176–7, 188, 193, 196, 198–200, 208–9, 212–13, 217
literature 8, 79, 88–9, 92–3, 121, 125–6, 137
Lithuania 175, 180–7, 189–91

Maastricht Criteria 178
media 6, 14, 17, 27–31, 33, 35, 135–6
MEP 19, 20–2; *see also* Member of the European Parliament
morality 4, 37, 39–40, 42, 50, 52, 110–12, 144, 217

narration 130–1
narrative structure 128
narrator 8, 126, 128, 130–4, 136–7
National Health Service 165
nationalism 1, 4, 65, 73–4, 76, 88, 92, 110, 118, 194
niqab 46–7; *see also* burqa

obligations 25, 71, 122, 165, 180, 193, 196, 204–6, 209–10, 218
outrage 44, 46–7, 49, 115

Parex Bank 185
passive leverage 181
personality rights 48
photography 136–7
political cohesion 58–61, 66, 72
political community 2–3, 5, 7, 57–8, 60, 63, 74, 123, 193, 199, 209
political culture 4–5, 23, 73, 123, 184, 218

political parties 6, 14, 19–20, 22, 24, 32, 101, 191
popular 14–15, 21–2, 28, 31, 100, 195–8, 208, 210
postnational 3, 5, 10, 22, 116–17, 124, 134, 136
privately funded initiatives 160, 170
privatization 9, 157, 159–60, 162–3, 165–6, 170–1, 174
profits 158–61, 167, 174, 185
public goods 157, 159–60, 162, 165, 170, 173
public opinion 5, 7, 64, 73–5, 87–8, 99, 123, 186
public sphere 4–6, 8, 28, 30, 32, 34–5, 109, 111–12, 114, 123, 125, 141, 144, 160, 165

race 43, 83–6, 88, 91, 100, 122
ranking status 39–40, 50
Ratzinger, Joseph 7–8, 108, 112–16, 119–20, 217; *see also* Benedict XVI
reason 7, 30, 39, 43, 71, 78, 105, 107, 109–20, 143, 155, 200, 209, 213, 216
referenda 15, 106, 196
referendum 2, 15, 24, 36, 101, 105
refugees 105, 117, 125, 219–20
religion 7–8, 52, 107, 109–10, 113, 115–16, 119–20, 122, 164
right to privacy 47
Russian minorities 182

Schengen zone 219; *see also* Schengen
secularism 8, 107, 117
Shoah 128; *see also* Holocaust
social contract 157, 164–5
social identity theory 7, 61, 64, 76
social policy 16, 161
solidarity 1–3, 5–7, 9–10, 17, 22, 38, 59, 70, 77–9, 83, 85, 93–5, 101, 107, 109–11, 114, 118, 124–5, 176–7, 179, 193, 197, 199, 202, 204–8, 210–11, 214–16, 218–20
South London Trust 167–8
sovereign debt 1, 4, 118, 192, 208, 218
sovereignty 2–3, 15, 17, 77, 116, 176–7, 192, 196–9, 210, 215
subordination 3, 215
supererogation 205
supranational 2–3, 17, 21, 63, 176–7, 193, 195, 197, 200, 202, 209, 215, 218
supremacy 3, 175, 193, 196, 200

Terezín 128–9, 131; *see also* Theresienstadt 127, 129
terrorism 52
Theresienstadt 127, 129; *see also* Terezín
transnational 4, 6–7, 9–10, 13–16, 19–24, 28–31, 33, 37–8, 60, 123, 142, 160, 173, 176, 192, 212
Treaty Establishing a Constitution for Europe 2, 15

trust 1, 3–4, 7, 9, 21, 40, 57–9, 61, 63–75, 101, 167–9, 172–3, 182, 215–16
twins 126, 131, 217

utilitarian support 58–9

Van Gend en Loos case 3
voter turnout 16, 18, 34

xenophobia 125